BUILDING LENIN'S RUSSIA

BUILDING
LENIN'S RUSSIA

BY SIMON LIBERMAN

UNIVERSITY OF CHICAGO PRESS
CHICAGO · ILLINOIS

ACKNOWLEDGMENT

I wish to express my appreciation of Dr. Albert Parry's aid in bringing this book to the attention of the English-reading public. I am deeply grateful to him for the enthusiastic way in which he has stood by me in the reorganization of my narrative. The views expressed in this book are, of course, only my own.

I also want to thank the many fellow-workers of my revolutionary youth, without whose persistent encouragement and friendship this book might not have been written.

Simon Liberman

Jacket design by Alexander Liberman

University of Chicago Press · Chicago 37
Agent: Cambridge University Press · London

CONTENTS

v

(1)

THE KREMLIN CALLING

THE TELEPHONE RANG. THE TIRED VOICE OF A WOMAN-SECRETARY SPOKE: "COMRADE Lenin wants to see you. Come to the Kremlin tomorrow at three."

The summons was in response to the suggestion of my friend, Leonid Krassin. The time was hungry, cruel, heroic November, 1918. The Soviet government, one year old, was fighting for its existence. I was not a Communist; but, ardently desiring the survival and welfare of my native Russia, I was working with the Soviets in my old occupation, the timber industry. It was a hard job. Chaos prevailed everywhere, and many Communists were only adding to it by their grandiose but impractical decrees and regulations.

Lenin realized this, on some occasions more clearly than on others. "Blunderheads" was the term he applied to his overzealous Communist administrators—but they went on with their fantasies just the same. Krassin, an old friend of Lenin's and, unlike me, a Communist, tried to help Lenin. To the new Red cause Krassin gave his considerable experience as an engineer and a businessman, gained in the years he had spent in the capitalist enterprises of the old regime. At this point, in the winter of 1918, he was in charge of the Red Army's supplies.

Krassin had quite a row to hoe in his field, and he appreciated my problems readily. Lenin, in turn, valued Krassin's efforts and advice. And so, on that memorable day, from his room in Moscow's Hotel Metropole, Krassin had telephoned his suggestion to Lenin:

"Liberman, of whom you have heard, is here in my room now. He has brought me important information on what's going on in the timber industry. You should see him, I think."

My evil genius was a certain Michael Larin, a brilliant but erratic man. One of the top Communist leaders of that era, he believed—and inspired many others to believe—that a socialist revolution and one hundred per cent Communism could be achieved within a few months, despite the chaos of the time.

That November the Germans were withdrawing from the Ukraine and the Crimea after several months of ruling and plundering in those rich provinces.

They were leaving because they had been defeated in western Europe by the American, British, French, and other Allied troops. Peace was dawning in Europe, but not in Russia. Civil war continued to rage in my country, and many provinces were cut off from Moscow.

Battling on many fronts against the Whites and their French, English, and other foreign friends and assistants, the Soviets felt besieged. Throughout Soviet Russia swept waves of arrests, and the death penalty for civilians, as well as for the military, was an everyday occurrence. The economic collapse was aggravated by hit-and-miss nationalizations and disorderly expropriations. Disintegration everywhere reached catastrophic proportions.

In the timber industry it was the same story. Requisitions, confiscations, sequestrations, were the order of the day. Red officials could not cope with the hundreds and thousands of sawmills and lumberyards the owners of which had fled or been liquidated and which were now supposedly under these officials' control.

And yet the immense forests of Russia were of paramount importance to the Soviets in this tragic hour. Wood was fuel, above all. The White armies barred the Soviets from the coal of the Donets Basin and from the oil of the Caucasus. As early as the summer of 1918, train service was being disrupted all over Lenin's Russia for lack of fuel.

But Michael Larin and his friends had impatient solutions for everything. On August 27, 1918, on Larin's initiative, Lenin appointed a so-called "dicta-torial triumvirate" to run the entire timber industry of Soviet Russia. Neither property rights nor production norms nor, for that matter, any other legal or economic considerations were to hinder these three men in their conduct of the industry.

All three were Communists. Two of the "Timber Trio" were statisticians, of no experience either with wood in any of its forms or with fuel in general. They knew nothing of any business. The third man was a forester from a distant province, who, it turned out, had scant executive ability even though he might have known wood. While the two statisticians were old party members, the forester had joined the party during the revolution, declaring that his had always been a Communist heart under the uniform of His Majesty's Forester Corps.

Frightful results marked the work of the Timber Trio. Michael Larin was these men's god and boss, and it was his spirit and decrees that guided them. Stock piles of wood dwindled to nothing. Black-market methods flourished. Private speculators, not the state, benefited. Among others, some former merchants of timber were rather happy over this turn of events; they had previously signed contracts to deliver firewood to large mills, receiving sizable advance payments. Now that all stock piles of firewood had been declared national property, these men were being removed from their old places of business; they neither intended nor were able to refund the advances to the mills, which had, in the meantime, also been nationalized. It was even said that some of the merchants themselves, through their employees, abetted nationalization on a local scale. They could not or would not deliver the firewood, and nationalization was an easy way out for them.

When I came to Krassin with this tale of woe, I found that his room at the Metropole was in the same hall as Larin's suite, but at the opposite end. There was something symbolic in this. At one end of the corridor, in Larin's domain, fantastic plans were being prepared, decrees feverishly manufactured, and all kinds of utopians and ne'er-do-well inventors stewed in a state of constant excitement. At the other end sat sober and practical men of Krassin's stamp, business-like economists and cool-headed experts willing to work with the Soviets for Russia's good—and, it must be admitted, also a fair number of figures out of the old regime, people who still hoped somehow to halt the irresistible rush of events and regain their former positions of wealth and power. Krassin dominated and helped them all, for Russia's sake far more than for their own. It was in this spirit that Krassin made it possible for me to see Lenin.

I had seen and heard Lenin before November, 1918, but from afar. And long before the revolution of 1917, I had known about Lenin and had often discussed him with my friends.

Before the revolution, when we talked about Lenin we pictured him as a fanatical plotter, who, in the interests of his beloved party, was ever ready to sacrifice everything and everybody. I was a Menshevik, which meant that I belonged to that wing of Russian Marxism which preached a "bourgeois revolution." This meant that the overthrow of tsarism was to be followed by the establishment of a bourgeois and strictly democratic republic. The consequent growth of capitalism in Russia, we thought, would be accompanied by the workers' struggle for socialism. Therefore, although the Russian revolution was to be of a moderate or bourgeois nature, a dominant role in the upheaval was to be played by the Russian workers.

But Lenin had insisted all along on his own vision of the shape of things to come. Long before 1917 he said that a real people's revolution, to be carried out by the workers in an alliance with the peasants, should call for ruthless Jacobin methods. Not only hostile social groups and their property would have to be sacrificed, but—if the revolution demanded it—millions of workers and peasants would have to suffer the same fate. So said the master. He was the first Russian revolutionary to cast doubts on some of the more humanitarian principles of the French Revolution. Unlike so many of us, he considered Russia and the rest of the world ripe for a socialist revolution.

"From a democratic revolution," said Lenin once, "we shall at once shift over to a social revolution. We shall do so within the possibilities of our strength—the strength of the class-conscious and well-organized proletariat. We are for an uninterrupted revolution. We shall not halt halfway."

It was naturally impossible for me not to feel some enmity toward this man.

3

I had first seen Lenin in early April, 1917, when he returned to Russia after long years of exile abroad. I was present at his first public oration in Petrograd on April 4. "All power to the Soviets!" was the slogan he proclaimed on that occasion. At the same meeting, I remember, Lenin was opposed by spokesmen of other socialist parties and by some of his former comrades in the Bolshevik group. They charged him with anarchist tendencies, with an aspiration to bring back the teachings of Michael Bakunin, that nineteenth-century apostle of anarchism, who had said: "To be a revolutionary is to be in a minority and to impose forcibly one's will, the will of the minority, upon the majority"; also: "If you are your people's friend, lead them in the face of gunfire, for the people themselves do not know what is good and what is bad for them"; and again: "For a revolutionary, the present is nothing, the future is all." Lenin, the Bolshevik, seemed to have brought these same doctrines to the Soviet of Workers' Deputies in Petrograd in 1917.

During that summer of 1917, while the Provisional Government of Alexander Kerensky tried to rule Russia, I often saw and heard Lenin as he delivered fiery speeches from the balcony of the requisitioned villa of Kshesinskaya, the ballet dancer who at one time had been a mistress of the last tsar. Later, in the days of the October-November revolution organized by the Bolsheviks against Kerensky, I saw Lenin in the Smolny Institute, formerly a school for nobles' daughters but now serving the Bolsheviks as their headquarters. A short time before his party's successful bid for power, Lenin had been hiding in Finland, his appearance changed to avoid detection: his beard and mustache had been shaved off, and he had worn dark glasses, which were discarded once the uprising had brought about victory.

Throughout that period of 1917 my attitude toward Lenin and his party remained negative. But, at the same time, I was aware of the revolution's implacable forward surge; an upheaval was inevitable; there was no turning back for Russia and her people. Good or bad, this was my country, and I could not leave it. Gradually, too, I began to realize the vast difference between Lenin and most of his companions-in-arms. Lenin was the solid firm core around whom the others rallied, closing their ranks. Lenin had a deep, unshakable faith in the Russian revolution. His faith was contagious—at times.

Late in 1917, after seizing power, the Bolsheviks of Lenin took their initial steps as a government amid strange and contradictory surroundings. The new government called itself a dictatorship, and it was one in fact; but this did not prevent it from hastening the elections for a constituent assembly on the basis of an ultra-democratic law introduced by the late-lamented Kerensky government. The Soviet government also began by abrogating the death penalty at the front (behind the lines it had been abolished *de facto* even before the November revolution). Opposition newspapers of sundry political hues continued to be published, criticizing Lenin's government, day in, day out. The opposition parties existed and functioned pretty much as before. When, two months after the November revolution, the Cheka or Soviet secret police office

4

(later known as the O.G.P.U.) was first established, it was empowered to investigate, but not to punish, political crimes. It was a strange time; the dictatorship had not yet found its proper stride!

The Cheka's main task was to fight sabotage. Its very name was made up of the initials of the Cheka's full name: the All-Russian Extraordinary Commission for the Struggle against Counterrevolution, Sabotage, and Profiteering. But the sabotage of those early Soviet days was not quite of the kind that came later. No one wrecked machines, set fire to warehouses, or destroyed stock piles of vital supplies. The phenomenon which the Bolsheviks then branded as sabotage was in actuality a gigantic boycott of the new government by the state's old-time employees.

Refusal to work with or for the "usurping" Bolsheviks and their new government was the idea and practice of the intelligentsia and, above all, of the enormous body of state employees, a body that by late 1917 had grown disproportionately as a result of the first three years of World War I. Their refusal to work led to a stoppage of all routine in governmental offices. It was a strong weapon, but in the long run it proved to be a boomerang, hitting those who tried to use it as much as the Soviets against whom it was taken up. This boycott or, as the Soviet leaders then called it, "sabotage" was actually the first harbinger of the civil war which was destined to flare up in full force a few months later, in the summer of 1918.

But personally I was not only a Menshevik opposing the Bolsheviks; I was also a businessman with much experience in the timber industry between the two revolutions—the abortive one of 1905 and the successful one of 1917. With the overthrow of tsarism in March, 1917, I had returned from private business to the affairs of my Menshevik party. Now, after November, 1917, and the Bolshevik triumph, I was one of a small group of non-Bolshevik intellectuals who disapproved of the boycott. We were business experts, and as such we felt that this boycott was harmful to the country, and we considered such tactics doomed to defeat anyway.

What unified our group was not a program but a common mood, which was both anti-Communist and antiboycott. Among us were Vladimir Groman, an outstanding economist, later persecuted by the Soviet government; Vladimir Sher, a prominent Menshevik, who had held an important military post under Kerensky; Nicholas Kutler and Alexander Khrushchev, minister and vice-minister of finances, respectively, prior to the revolution; Vasily Meshkov, a well-known shipowner; and Nicholas von Meck, president of the Kazan Railroad (and of the family celebrated for the financial support which one of its women, Catherine von Meck, had years earlier given Peter Tschaikowsky, the composer).

Presently I accepted a responsible post in my field—I was a Soviet specialist, or *spets,* as it was called for short, working with the Communists. I did this on the advice of those of my friends and acquaintances who were members of the new government, and with the approval of Y. O. Martov, the leader of the

Menshevik party. My new job was in the railroad fuel-supply bureau; I was to see that Russia's locomotives had firewood. In the spring of 1918 I followed the Soviet government in its removal from Petrograd to Moscow.

And yet, although I served the Soviet regime as a non-Communist business expert, I continued to be a political opponent of the new government. And in time the employees of the Central Timber Committee were to elect me as their delegate to the Moscow Soviet of Workers' Deputies. My Communist rival in the election was George Lomov, chairman and director of the government office of which I was business manager. Nor was I the only Menshevik in the Moscow Soviet—at the time we were two- or threescore strong. Alas! our group did not last. We were soon unseated as deputies, and many of our number were arrested by the Cheka. But at the moment, at the very dawn of the new regime, we still had the illusion that collaboration with the Bolsheviks was possible.

"Comrade Lenin wants to see you." The phrase ran through my mind again and again on that November day in 1918 as I was preparing myself for the meeting at three o'clock.

I shaped and weighed my words carefully hours beforehand. How, indeed, was I to present my ideas to Lenin? The Red terror was already rampant; people were easily "expendable" for what they had done and for what they might have done. I was doubly handicapped: a *spets,* I also belonged to the Menshevik party. And here I was, about to see the head of the state in order to criticize harshly one sector of his economic system—this at the time when thousands of armed men were fighting for and against this system. How to speak to Lenin convincingly enough about the most practical ways of stock-piling Russia's fuel—to Lenin who believed that even the impossible and the impractical were possible and practical for the workers? To Lenin who had said again and again that he had proved many times and would prove repeatedly in the future that "the working class could successfully storm heaven itself!"

A few minutes before three o'clock I stood at the guarding booth near the Kremlin gates. The booth looked freshly nailed together of raw, unplaned boards. The heavy ancient buildings all around seemed to emphasize the hurry and clumsiness of this new construction. Inside the booth a tall, energetic man, a young Lett, awaited me. He was in charge of the Kremlin's guard. Handing me my first pass of admission to Lenin, he detailed one of the soldiers on guard to escort me to the building where Lenin had his office, a distance of some 250 or 300 yards from the gate.

The court around the structure housing the Soviet Russian government was deserted, and we met hardly a soul once we had entered the building. On a staircase landing sat a guard with a studied air of indifference to passers-by. His furred hat with ear-flaps and his greatcoat with brass buttons and a fur collar reminded me of old Russia. The stairs in the dimly lit hall had a gray

6

and almost dirty appearance. I slowly climbed to the third floor and found myself in front of a door which was still two steps higher.

On opening the door I beheld a small chamber, one which certainly lacked the grandeur we usually associate with the site of governmental deliberations. It was a nearly square room, with three doors and a low ceiling, beneath which I saw three very low windows hung with heavy draperies of faded reddish color. Between the doors, office tables were arranged in a T, with notebooks and pencils neatly placed in obvious readiness for the next session.

The room was dim, despite the sunny day, its light struggling through the heavy draperies. A number of armchairs stood along the walls. The furniture was ill assorted, apparently gathered from various places. A worn, faded carpet covered the floor. The whole scene reminded me of the reception room of a provincial lawyer. Later I had frequent occasion to visit this room; for this was where the sessions of the Council of Labor and Defense were held; an adjoining and much larger chamber served for the sittings of the Council of People's Commissars.

I was met by a small, thin, hunchbacked woman with sad blue eyes. Her pince-nez was too large for her little face, and it hung too near the end of her nose, making her face seem even sterner than it actually was. And she looked even smaller than her true size because of a warm knitted shawl in which she was wrapped. There was something icon-like in her stilted gestures, in the entire gaunt appearance of this small walking corpse. Yet her voice sounded soft as she asked me to sit down, adding: "Vladimir Ilyich will be with you in a minute."

She had hardly finished her sentence when I heard rapid steps outside. A door from an adjoining room opened, and Lenin came in, ascending a step leading to the door. He looked at me with close scrutiny but shook my hand with vigorous encouragement. "Glad to see you," he said. "Krassin and Ryckov spoke to me about you." He burred his *r*'s slightly. His air, as he sat down in one of the armchairs, was one of hurry: "Let's talk, I'm listening."

(2)

LENIN

AS I SPOKE, LENIN FOLLOWED ME ATTENTIVELY, AS IF TRYING TO SHOW THAT MY words interested him very much indeed. I soon began to feel at ease and gradually passed from the specialized subject of lumber and firewood to Michael Larin's half-baked decrees in general. Lenin interrupted me:

"Of course, we make mistakes. There cannot be a revolution without errors. But we are learning from our errors and are glad when we can correct them. Now about these decrees [he spoke of the Timber Trio's latest lawmaking], don't forget that we are in the midst of a revolution. Our government may not last long, but these decrees will be part of history. Future revolutionaries will learn from them—perhaps from these very decrees of Larin's which now seem so absurd to you. We ourselves keep the decrees of the Paris Commune before our eyes as a model."

As I argued back, he continued to listen to me with the same close attention and, at the same time, looked into my eyes as if concentrating hard. All through the conversation I felt this sharp look on me.

Later, while Lenin and I were still talking, Krassin came in, with his usual smile. He was followed by my immediate chief in the Supreme Council of Economy, Alexis Ryckov, who did not seem surprised at finding me with Lenin—apparently he had been told beforehand of my visit. As these two joined us, it became clear to me that Lenin had wanted to hear me first alone and then to come to conclusions together with his two aides. Bidding me goodbye, he said:

"Our mistakes should be corrected not by experts but by us ourselves. The correction should come from above only. Therefore, whenever you have ideas on this subject, telephone directly to me, and I will make the necessary changes myself."

I left with the impression that my visit had not been particularly successful. But the next day Larin asked me to come to see him. True, he did not reveal by so much as a single word that Lenin had instructed him to listen to me and take my proposals into consideration; nevertheless he did listen to me carefully from then on.

This visit began a long series of meetings between Lenin and me. Soon it became known in the Communist party, as well as among the experts, that Lenin was always willing to receive me.

These meetings gave me an opportunity to observe Lenin at close quarters. As I discussed practical problems with him, an awareness grew within me that he was not only a revolutionary but a profoundly educated man, too— that he possessed all the qualities necessary for a man to rule a great country.

One remarkable gift you noticed in Lenin at once: he could quickly draw people to himself, even when they were outsiders—nay, even when they looked on his policies with a fishy eye or downright hostility. In this respect he was different indeed from other top-ranking Communists! Each time I happened to converse with one of the latter, I knew that, in spite of the trust or at least the attention and politeness he displayed toward me, there were some ulterior thoughts in his mind. Plainly, these others stopped short of accepting me completely. When they talked with me, they did not say everything they meant. Moreover, as I talked, I had a feeling that some of my words might become known to the Cheka within an hour or two.

None of this feeling plagued me when I talked with Lenin. He could indeed be all attention, all charm, apparently putting all his cards on the table. As he tackled a stranger, he first of all endeavored to convert him. That is why Lenin was always so soft spoken, almost wheedling, seemingly so good-natured, artless, even simple.

He also appeared to be totally devoid of selfishness. Whoever chanced to see him soon said to himself, "Here is the chief of a great state who wants absolutely nothing for his own self!" It is possible, however, that Lenin's amiability was mainly his practical attempt to hold onto people he considered useful. To quote a classic phrase from Nicholas Gogol's *Inspector General,* "Give me this little string—when one is traveling even a piece of string will come in handy."

The magnetism was in Lenin's face, especially in his eyes. And yet his face was in no wise akin to those noble, inspired faces worshipped by the Russian intelligentsia—the faces of Leo Tolstoy, Alexander Herzen, or Nicholas Chernyshevsky.

Lenin's little beard did not really fit his face. It looked too much like the neat wisp of Napoleon III's beard. I could more easily imagine Lenin with no beard at all or with one that grew more tumultuously—a bush of a beard. Lenin kept his little beard and mustache well trimmed, thus revealing his fondness for order—this despite a certain carelessness and even sloppiness in his manners. In this detail the great paradox of Lenin was reflected: his firmness in final action, nothwithstanding his gentleness in preliminaries; his concreteness and practicality, in spite of his constant theorizing and dogmatism.

When I knew him, Lenin always wore the same dark-colored suit, with pipelike trousers that seemed a trifle too short for his legs, with a similarly abbreviated, single-breasted coat, a soft white collar, and an old tie. The necktie, in my opinion, was for years the same: black, with little white flowers, one particular spot showing wear. When, sitting at his desk, he received visitors, one could notice that the heels of his shoes were somewhat higher than the ordinary size. In one hand he always held a pencil, while the fingers of his other hand were inserted between the pages of a book lying open before him, as if he were comparing one page with another and yet another. When he worked or talked, he also wrote notes or messages, scribbling on each page of his notebook from top to bottom and tearing them off one by one.

This is how he spent his time presiding over the Council of People's Commissars and the Council of Labor and Defense. Usually he appeared from an adjoining room, swiftly seated himself at the conference table, and, opening the session, ran it as smoothly as a good conductor directs his orchestra. All the parts had been learned beforehand; for, ahead of each session, Lenin would come to an agreement with representatives of the various commissariats involved in the proceedings. Once the deliberations began, he dispatched brief messages to the different members of the council, inquiring as to their opinion or suggesting that they take the floor for or against this or that proposal. Suddenly, brusquely, he would move to close discussion and would at once begin to dictate the council's decisions.

During the deliberations his sly smile might tell you that he was preparing

9

a new move, but never just what it was going to be. Even those who were used to his methods did not know until the very last minute in precisely what ways he would engineer a clash between opponents, exactly how he would direct the general argument and play the game, and what final decisions would be reached. He alone knew his mind and plans.

Nevertheless, my early caution and even distrust of him soon disappeared. Regardless of my political views, I gradually developed a warm feeling for Lenin personally; I was entirely willing to work with him. As, in later months and years, I met and conversed with him, I outlined those new projects and ideas which came to me in the course of my work, and I shared with him impressions gathered during my trips throughout Russia and abroad. Some of my proposals thus communicated to him were subsequently accepted and put into effect—the conversion of governmental enterprises into trusts among them.

Both before and after the Russian revolution, at home and in foreign lands, I had occasion to meet many prominent people. I grew to know some of them well, in their personal lives no less than in their occupations, and almost invariably I became somewhat disappointed. There is an ancient saying that the closer you are to a mountain, the bigger it seems; the closer you are to a man, the smaller he is. Lenin was one of the very rare exceptions to this rule. Not that he was perfect—by no means. He had a number of unpleasant traits. And many people found it both possible and natural to disagree violently with both the general principles of his policy and the particular course of action this policy called for. His public speeches, with their endless hammering of one and the same iron-stark idea, with elementary phrases repeated again and again, seemed to me monotonous and at times dull. His articles and books were, for the most part, an oversimplified discourse on the laws of man's social development.

The more often I visited him, however, the better I knew him and the bigger he loomed in my eyes. He was a great man, by far surpassing his aides and fellow-fighters (among whom, of course, there were many striking personalities). In sum, he had those singular and extremely rare qualities which are given to but a few and which make a man a true leader. With time, much in this complex being became clear to me—clear and logical. Gradually, the repellant features of his actions as a political leader in prerevolutionary Russian life receded from my consciousness.

Lenin had a deep faith in the "goodness" of the revolution. I have already noted that in this respect he resembled Michael Bakunin, the nineteenth-century anarchist. Lenin actually regarded himself as a Russian Jacobin, but of the Marxist order. That is to say, he believed in the supreme liberating mission of the working class. But he also maintained that in its everyday struggle for existence the working class was incapable of rising above its immediate economic needs. According to Lenin, that is where the leaders of the proletariat came in. He said that the task of such leaders was to "push" the

10

workers. If these leaders were real revolutionaries, they would guide the proletariat along the path of class-consciousness, of revolutionary struggle. Most of these leaders were enlightened persons hailing from a class hostile to workers. Karl Marx and Friedrich Engels did not come from the working class, Lenin would recall. They sacrificed their wealth, position, comfort. The working class, too, might have to make sacrifices in the course of its revolutionary fight. It might even have to sacrifice an entire generation of its own; yet, in compensation, future generations would lead a happier life.

With these ideas Lenin wanted to reach the workers first of all. That is perhaps why his writings and speeches were so elementary and monotonous —he wished to hammer these thoughts into the workers' minds.

But outside his writings and speeches Lenin was neither primitive nor dull. In my face-to-face meetings and man-to-man talks with him I beheld a genuine leader and an active revolutionary, but also a deep thinker and a highly cultured man. I saw a human being endowed by nature with all that was needed to lead the masses. He knew the masses. He knew their needs. He also knew how to induce them to go forth to sacrifices and even death. He was inflexible in his principles, yet flexible and full of compromises in practice—in handling people. That is why, when he did not consider a person his political opponent, Lenin was governed by his own humaneness and even gentleness.

In the end I was not shocked when I read that Anatole Lunacharsky, Lenin's commissar of education and the arts, once compared Lenin's head, particularly his forehead, to that of Socrates.

My second visit with Lenin came of his own initiative. A month after our first talk he sent for me. By then it was quite plain that the Timber Trio had failed completely. Far from being useful, the Trio only kept on aggravating the chaos in our industry. It was therefore essential to return to methods of economy of a more reasonable and traditional character.

Again Krassin and Ryckov were present. Lenin discussed with us a project creating a Central Timber Committee to replace the Trio. The committee was to consist of five members, one of whom—I—was to be the business manager; another—a leading Communist—the chairman. The others were to include a delegate of the Forestry Department of the Commissariat of Agriculture and two representatives of the Central Wood Workers' Union.

This plan obviously mirrored Lenin's new impatience with the experimenting of the Trio and his growing confidence in me. Of special interest was the fact that the need for once more utilizing prerevolutionary timber-merchants was recognized. In this direction I was to be given wide powers. As we were about to rise and go, Krassin addressed Lenin: "Very well, Vladimir Ilyich, but who is to be the Communist chairman of the committee? You know that our blunderheads need a typical Soviet icon."

Strange coincidences do happen sometimes. No sooner had Krassin asked his question than the door, through which Lenin had earlier entered, slowly

11

opened once again. A man stepped in. He was of medium stature, broad-shouldered, his face swarthy, his mustache long and black. He looked about forty. He was dressed and shod in leather from head to foot: a leather cap, a leather jacket buttoned up to his throat, leather breeches, and high boots of extra-heavy leather. With slow heavy steps, saying not a word and without removing his cap, he crossed the room. His entire appearance somehow made me think of Cromwell.

The man was Josef Stalin.

"Why not make him chairman of our committee?" Krassin wondered aloud. Ryckov protested weakly, saying that Stalin was not suitable for this work; he was overruled by Lenin and Krassin.

But it was not my destiny to work with Stalin: five days later he left Moscow and my committee for the southern front. Another Communist, George Lomov (whom I have already mentioned), took his place on the committee.

From that winter on, until his death in January, 1924, I visited Lenin fairly regularly—about twice a month, except for the time when he was very ill, especially toward the end of his life. I came mostly for the sessions of the Council of Labor and Defense, but Lenin often wished to see me alone, before the council gathered. He talked to me in his office, and I never had to wait for him more than two or three minutes.

For me these conversations were so pleasant, they calmed and encouraged me to such an extent, that I soon looked forward to them almost with impatience. They were bright spots in my difficult work, and they spurred me on.

In December, 1918, at the close of our second meeting, Lenin said to me as I was leaving: "Remember, you don't have to use intermediaries when you want to see me. Call Fotieva directly [that was his secretary], and if there is anything of importance bothering you, I'll see you."

At the sessions of the council which I thereafter attended, the representatives of the various government departments usually made their little speeches. They were Communists, of course. We specialists were then asked to comment, each by the people's commissar in charge of the specialist's department. Discarding this method in my case, Lenin would address me directly: "And now, Comrade Liberman, what would you say about this?" This occurred so many times that, outside the council, when I broached a subject to Krassin or Ryckov, they often said: "Better talk it over with Ilyich [that is, with Lenin], he listens to you."

Sometimes during my visits to Lenin, the door in the back of the room opened, and a heavy-set woman slowly walked in. This was Nadezhda Krupskaya, Lenin's wife and lifelong companion. Quietly she would cross the room, glancing at Lenin with her large and somewhat protuberant eyes but seldom uttering a word. Later, when Lenin was recovering from the first attack of his illness, I used to see her passing through the room with a seemingly unconcerned look, but actually thinking of neither God nor man, neither Russia nor the revolution, but only of her Vladimir Ilyich.

(3)

BLOOD ON THE RAINBOW

A PECULIAR ATMOSPHERE PREVAILED AT THE CONFERENCES OF THE HIGHEST AD-
ministrative councils of Soviet Russia, presided over by Lenin. Despite all the
efforts of an officious secretary to impart to each session the solemn character
of a cabinet meeting, we could not help feeling that here we were, attending
another sitting of an underground revolutionary committee! For years we had
belonged to various underground organizations. All of this seemed so familiar.
Many of the commissars remained seated in their topcoats or greatcoats; most
of them wore the forbidding leather jackets. In wintertime some wore felt
boots and thick sweaters. They remained thus clothed throughout the meetings.

One of the commissars, Alexander Tsuriupa, was nearly always ill; he
attended these sessions in a semireclining position, his feet stretched out on a
near-by chair. A number of Lenin's aides would not take their seats at the
conference table but shoved their chairs around helter-skelter all over the
room. Lenin alone invariably took his seat at the table as the presiding officer
of the occasion. He did so in a neat, almost decorous way. Fotieva, as his
personal secretary, sat beside him.

At that time all the top-nochers of the Communist party were undoubtedly
one close-knit family. Lenin was not merely a chairman but a recognized chief
to whom everyone brought his thorny problems. The commissars quarreled
among themselves in their daily work, but here Lenin had the last word; and
all alike left these meetings reassured, as though their quarrels had been
those of children now pacified by a wise parent.

Here I never heard arguments over matters of principle; the discussion
always revolved around the problem of finding the best possible methods of
carrying out a given measure. Matters of principle were decided elsewhere—
in the Political Bureau of the Communist party. The Bureau in that period
consisted of Lenin, Trotsky, Zinoviev, Kamenev, and Sverdlov, with Dzerzhinsky and Ryckov as alternates. The two highest organs of the government
which I knew—the Council of People's Commissars and the Council of Labor
and Defense—discussed practical ways to effect measures already decided upon
by this inner sanctum of the party—its Political Bureau.

Occasionally the political situation of the time threw a gloomy light on some
problem of special interest to me. Once I attended a meeting of the Council
of Labor and Defense to discuss ways and means of increasing the production
of timber in those forests which had been state property even under the tsars.
I was shocked and shaken by what happened at that meeting.

Good management on the part of a large corps of foresters trained in special
Forest Institutes had distinguished those state forests. Each man was in charge
of an entire district, and the number of such districts and their managers ran

13

into tens of thousands. Each district had its own workers, cattle, and equipment. Everywhere the foresters had long enjoyed well-established economic relations with the peasantry.

At first the new Soviet government had an idea that it would be enough to issue orders, and, presto, these long-time state employees would fetch timber and firewood to the docks, railroad stations, and cities. But the general economic collapse affected this branch of Russian economy, too. A complete stoppage stagnated work in these state forests, as well as elsewhere.

A Soviet decree was then made public, obliging every peasant living near a government forest to prepare and transport a dozen cords of wood. But this raised the question of what to do with the foresters—what to demand of them. In the eyes of the Soviet authorities, these foresters were part and parcel of that sabotaging intelligentsia to whom the new government gave short shrift.

The meeting of the Council of Labor and Defense, discussing this particular problem, was attended by Felix Dzerzhinsky, among other commissars. He was the ruthless head of the dreaded Cheka. After listening a while, he said: "In the interests of justice and equality I move: That the foresters be made personally responsible for the fulfilment of the peasants' quota. That, in addition, each forester is himself to fulfil the same quota—a dozen cords of wood."

A few members of the council objected. They pointed out that foresters were intellectuals not used to heavy manual labor. Dzerzhinsky replied that it was high time to liquidate the age-old inequality between the peasants and the foresters.

"Moreover," the Cheka head declared in conclusion, "should the peasants fail to deliver their quota of wood, the foresters responsible for them are to be shot. When a dozen or two of them are shot, the rest will tackle the job in earnest."

It was generally known that the majority of these foresters were anti-Communist. Still, one could feel an embarrassed hush in the room. Suddenly I heard a brusque voice: "Who's against this motion?"

This was Lenin, closing the discussion in his inimitable way. Naturally, no one dared to vote against Lenin and Dzerzhinsky. As an afterthought, Lenin suggested that the point about shooting the foresters, although adopted, be omitted from the official minutes of the session. This, too, was done as he willed.

I felt ill during the meeting. For more than a year, of course, I had known that executions were decimating Russia—but here I myself was present while a five-minute discussion doomed scores of totally innocent men. I was shaken to my innermost being. A cough was choking me, but it was more than the cough of one of my winter colds.

It was plain to me that, when within a week or two the executions of those foresters took place, their deaths would not have moved things forward one single iota. I knew that this terrible decision stemmed from a feeling of resentment and revenge on the part of those who invoked such senseless

14

measures. I recalled earlier conversations with some of the participants in this meeting, in this decision; they had privately assured me that the Russian revolution would not repeat the tragic errors of the French Jacobins, that innocent blood would not be shed, that the Russian revolution was one hundred and fifty years younger than the French Revolution, that it was a revolution of workers who had themselves suffered from injustices and so would not permit any new atrocities. Alas, each revolution had its own logic and its own laws!

As, in my depressed state, I was leaving the meeting, I was approached by a man whom I recognized as Lenin's chauffeur. "Are you Comrade Liberman?" he said. "Vladimir Ilyich told me to take you home because you aren't well." Lenin must have noticed my cough during the meeting.

As I was getting into a Kremlin automobile I thought bitterly: here is a cruel contrast, indeed—while he was deciding to shoot scores of innocent people, Lenin had also remarked to himself that I was suffering from a bad cold and must be fetched home in his car.

Later I found out that such important decisions, practically changing the policy previously declared by the Bolsheviks, were always discussed and adopted by the Political Bureau of the Communist party and afterward became mandatory on all members of the party, *including Lenin* and all the commissars. Thus the discussion of such matters within the Council of People's Commissars was a mere formality.

Another example was Tikhvinsky's case, which occurred at about the same time. Tikhvinsky had been an old Bolshevik, and in prerevolutionary times had belonged to Lenin's underground group. Lenin and Krassin had been his intimate friends. As a young man he had been in charge of a chemical laboratory in which explosives were manufactured for the fighting unit with which Stalin and Krassin had been associated. But, sometime before World War I and the Russian revolution, Tikhvinsky had left the Bolsheviks and had become absorbed in peaceful chemistry.

After the November revolution of 1917 all the "former" Bolsheviks occupied a privileged position. They were in personal contact with the "top" of the party and the new government. Although they did not participate in the "new construction," they were "our own people." The new rulers, with slightly sarcastic smiles, would ask these prodigal sons when they intended to return to the party's bosom. Most outstanding among such temporary absentees were Maxim Gorky and Leonid Krassin, both of whom did soon stage spectacular comebacks to the party's faith and works.

Others continued to stay away, feeling both sympathetic and critical toward their old party. Indignant over the experiments of their former friends now in power, these men never missed an opportunity to point out that the startling practices of the Bolsheviks were a far cry from their own erstwhile ideas and dreams. Still, they considered themselves apart from Lenin's enemies; they were more on Lenin's side of the barricade than not in the fight at all. For that reason they often felt free—and were effective in doing so—to act as intermediaries and defenders of all those persecuted by the new Soviet government. To a degree they were a link between the new authority and those who refused or hesitated to recognize it as authority.

Now one of these privileged go-betweens, Tikhvinsky, was himself arrested! The arrest happened in Petrograd. The news came as a thunderbolt to the former Bolsheviks. "An accident," they tried to reassure one another. Russia, they reminded themselves, would not follow in the footsteps of eighteenth-century France where the revolution became a monster devouring its own children.

Maxim Gorky, then residing in Petrograd, rushed to Gregory Zinoviev, Lenin's "viceroy" in that city. Immediately afterward he journeyed to Moscow to see Lenin.

It was a dark winter morning, and I dropped in to see Krassin. For the first time in my life I found him pale and shaken. He said, "Gorky was here a minute ago....." Then he exclaimed:

"They've killed Tikhvinsky! Despite Lenin's promise! But it's impossible! But perhaps Lenin knew all the time that Tikhvinsky was to be killed. And does our revolution have its own implacable laws? In that case, where will all this get us? Lenin loved Tikhvinsky very much, he was on such close terms with him!" Krassin's face grew longer and greyer, as though he had aged suddenly.

All the telephones in his offce were ringing, and he soon heard and relayed to me the Cheka's explanation of Tikhvinsky's execution: Lenin's counter-manding order had come too late, they said. This was, of course, a lame excuse. Actually, such executions were never carried out without the final approval of the highest organ of the party, the Political Bureau, headed by Lenin himself. Then I remembered George Plekhanov's remark that "Lenin is baked of the same dough as Robespierre," to which Lenin replied, taunting his fellow-founder of Russian social democracy: "Yes, a Jacobin joined with the working class is the only true revolutionary."

Not long after this, Trotsky gave orders to arrest Admiral Shchasny, commander of the Soviet Navy, and have him tried by the Revolutionary Tribunal. Until the very last no one thought that the admiral would be executed, even if he were found guilty as charged. But Trotsky insisted on the death sentence—as a revolutionary warning to others. Trotsky loved "the pathos of distance," by which he meant a division of humanity into the rulers and the ruled. By shooting the admiral he wanted to intimidate the tens of thousands of tsarist officers whom he had brought into the ranks of the Red Army and the Red Navy. At the same time, there was a rumor that the admiral fell victim to the machinations of old reactionary officers who wanted to take revenge upon him for having become the head of the Soviet Navy.

It was in April, 1918, that I had moved from Petrograd to Moscow to be at the center of government. On arriving, I appeared at one of the luxurious private houses on Povarskaya Street, which had been converted into the headquarters of the Wood Workers' Union. The two upper stories were occupied by the offices of the union, while the lower two were given over to those new government agencies which were to administer Russia's timber industry.

In the union offices I discovered changes typical of the times: the old Menshevik leaders had been removed, and Bolsheviks (since March calling themselves "Communists") were running everything. At that moment the new bosses were trying to find new forms of organization for the Russian timber industry. They had no experience in this field, and the task before them was not an easy one: they had to set in working order an enormous economic machine. I was asked to look into the problem.

The chairman of the union, a certain Zholnarovich, a sprightly fellow, announced to me: "Although you are a bourgeois, you may consider yourself as one of us. We know your past activities, and we hope for good things from you. Comrade Larin says you're the only man who can figure out the right setup for the timber industry."

Thus began my association with Zholnarovich. At that time he was at the head of the entire timber industry in Russia. He proved to be perhaps the most interesting personality among those wood-turners, who, by the will of fate, had become directors of Russia's great enterprises.

A worker and an old Bolshevik, he viewed all moral principles as so much twaddle of rank bourgeois invention. Since his own party had confidence in him, it was he who received the assignment to purge all the Mensheviks from his union, replacing them with Bolsheviks.

In the beginning he seemed to have mixed feelings toward me. He listened to me and generally treated me with respect, realizing that his immediate superiors—Ryckov, Lomov, and Larin—had a good opinion of me. Yet our relations remained strictly on the official side, and during that particular period it was rather a strain to work on an impersonal basis. One day there was a knock on my apartment door. When I opened the door, there stood Zholnarovich. "We've been working together for several months now," he declared, "but still there is no real contact between the two of us. Let's get organized."

Setting a gallon bottle of vodka and a jar of pickled cucumbers on my table, he began to organize. It was about five o'clock on a summer afternoon. One hour earlier my wife, with our son and her sister, had arrived from Petrograd. We adults closed the door on the four-year-old boy and started to consume the vodka and the pickles. Soon our spirits rose considerably. We drank first to the world of the future, then to the world that had vanished. Tears welled in our eyes. In a little while we were busily reproaching ourselves and had presently expanded our soul-scratching into a general *Weltschmerz*.

17

The Soviet government, on the whole, trusted me, especially after that December of 1918 when Lenin's confidence in me became known. I needed this confidence, perhaps more than any other Soviet official. The reason for this need was that, in the era of the rapid nationalization of all Russian economy, my department proved to be a strange exception—an oasis in which capitalist and semicapitalist principles still prevailed, with Lenin's own approval.

In Russia, which has 60 per cent of all the forest land of Europe and Asia, the timber industry has always played an important role, and during the first years of Soviet rule it acquired an extraordinary significance. For this was the time when wood was the basic fuel of the land, in the absence of coal and oil cut off from Moscow by the civil war and foreign intervention. Even after the Germans had withdrawn from the Ukraine and the Whites had been defeated, the situation remained relatively unchanged because chaos continued to reign in the coal and oil regions, depressing the output of fuel catastrophically. This explains why the Soviet government was compelled to devote so much attention to the problem of getting wood for the needs of its industries, transport, and population.

In contrast with other industries, large or small, the production of firewood depended on peasants'—not workers'—labor. The custom was to hire peasants to chop wood in the forests nearest to their villages. Some of these forests, as I have said, had been state property even in tsarist times. Others had been but recently expropriated from private owners, becoming Soviet state property after the revolution. Dependence on peasants' labor made this industry a completely separate branch of Russian economy. Lenin realized, far more clearly than any of his aides could, that methods used in wood production had, of necessity, to be different from those applied in other industries.

Those were the times of the so-called "food quotas"—the first and most primitive method employed by the new government to obtain grains and other raw foodstuffs from the villages. The peasants were ordered to hand over to the state all their alleged surpluses. The theory was that the peasants had more food and other produce than they needed for their own survival. In reality, the villagers themselves lacked bread, meat, and other provisions. Not surpluses, but the foods needed by the hungry people themselves, were exacted from the countryside by strong, at times armed, pressure from the cities. It was true that the cities of Russia were starving—but the villages were likewise far from well off.

Such were the circumstances amid which I found that my department was forced to gather firewood in the forests with the peasants' labor as my only man-power. It would have been futile to pay the peasant-lumberjacks with thousands or millions of devaluated rubles; they could not buy anything with the money. We were thus compelled to make two extremely "radical" decisions.

First, we drew upon private initiative. We called upon individuals who wanted to profit through old capitalistic methods. These were mostly timber-merchants of the prerevolutionary times who had somehow managed to remain alive and were by then lying low or occupied in other pursuits. We made them capitalists once more, signing contracts with them, by virtue of which they obligated themselves to produce definite quantities of firewood in definite localities.

Second, we had to provide these capitalists with credit. This was not merely money, which was of no more value to them than to the peasants, but much more precious food. With that food the entrepreneurs were to pay the peasants for lumberjacking in the state forests.

These men were unique "capitalists" indeed. They had by this time either lost their former capital or hidden its remnants, some as caches of gold, others as currency in foreign banks. None would think of risking whatever they had salvaged by investing it in these new operations with the Soviet government. Thus we had no choice. From the scant reserves of the People's Commissariat of Food supplies, we began to issue to these "capitalists" the staples needed most by the peasants: salt, sugar, broadcloth, and, above all, those felt boots without which work in the wintry forests would have been impossible. It sometimes happened that the peasants received the very same products which had only a short time before been requisitioned from them as their "surpluses." Such was, for instance, the case with some oats we were issued by the commissariat.

But we resorted to the aid of these private entrepreneurs as only one of our methods. From 1920 on, when the Soviet state began to export its lumber to foreign lands, the peasants were ordered to deal directly with the government, eschewing in many cases the intermediary stage of contracting. They were ordered to do this as a sort of labor service expected of them by the government. Every peasant was obliged to cut down so many cords of wood in designated forests. Every horse-owning peasant had to transport a certain quantity of wood. All this wood had to be delivered by the peasants to river jetties, cities, and other terminal points.

Thus the activities of our department were based on two different principles: private initiative and voluntary contracts, on the one hand, and forced labor as a set duty to the state, on the other.

There was trouble from the outset. The contractors, on obtaining large quantities of precious products as advance payments or operating capital, naturally tried to keep a substantial part for their own use or resale—as a kind of illegal excess profit. The state paid them millions of rubles as their legal profit, but this money meant much less to them than the portion of foodstuffs and other produce which they might be able to hold out for themselves. And on occasion they succeeded in withholding as much as one-fourth of these products—most of which was sold on black markets for monstrous sums.

Another weakness of the arrangement had to do with that percentage of loss which the timber industry had for years allowed in rafting its logs down Russia's rivers. The number of logs finally delivered by rafting is always somewhat smaller than the number originally cut in the forests. A checkup of the true extent of this loss is absolutely impossible. Our contractors took advantage of the natural loss. They exaggerated it by telling us that they had prepared certain quantities of wood (for which they had allegedly issued foodstuffs to the peasant-lumberjacks) and by delivering to us much smaller quantities. We knew that they were thus concealing for themselves much of the food and other provisions which they were supposed to give to their crews.

We had to struggle ceaselessly against this dishonesty. Some former timber-merchants helped us in this fight, for they considered that such cheating jeopardized the fate of their entire group, defeated and scattered as it was but still hoping for the return of private enterprise and prosperity. But others persisted in their chicanery and opposed my countermeasures.

I wanted to separate the two operations: I wanted these new contractors to work with their lumberjacks up to the point of rafting but not beyond, the rafting itself to be done by other men and means as an entirely separate business. In this way we could demand from the contractors a full performance, not recognizing any losses of wood on the waterways.

My proposal naturally aroused great resistance among many of the timber entrepreneurs. They preferred the old system, and for obvious reasons. In their fight against me they often used exceedingly dubious methods and were not above intriguing against me with various Soviet officials and even denouncing me to the Cheka!

As a result, my relations with the Cheka were extremely complicated and not very pleasant, as we shall see later.

⟨4⟩

CHIEF MAGICIAN

THE EARLY PHASE OF MY WORK IN THE SOVIET TIMBER ADMINISTRATION WAS dominated not by Zholnarovich and his forthright methods of "organizing," but by the far more dynamic personality of Michael Larin.

Born Michael Lurie in 1882, he adopted Larin as his revolutionary pseudonym sometime after 1901, the year he joined the Social Democratic party in the Crimea. In 1918, when I met him for the second time after a long interval, he was a very tall man, with regular features, large black eyes, and a little pointed beard. He had been crippled by infantile paralysis, now had difficulty in moving his legs and left arm, and his chest was sunken in and his shoulders protruded sharply forward; I could feel great tension in every step he took. As he talked, he often grew overexcited and would burst out laughing, his mouth becoming distorted and his whole face transformed into a horrible human mask. It was strange to see by the side of this cripple a stately, beautiful

20

woman—his wife, who was his companion in all his wanderings the world over.

From 1918 to 1920 this Communist was famous in Russia as her "magician of economics." Indeed, for better or for worse, Soviet Russia did owe to him her first great economic upheavals, including the socialization of her industries and the establishment of the initial central economic agencies. I often visited the Hotel Metropole, where Larin lived and worked, and so had a chance to see some of his activities at a close range. At one time I tried to influence the organization of the timber industry and give it a more rational basis by making use of my old acquaintance with Larin.

I had known Larin especially well back in 1906, in Kiev, during the elections to the Second Duma, that short-lived and otherwise curtailed parliament of the last phase of tsarism. In that period Larin, a Menshevik, attempted to become a member of the electoral college as a peasant representative of the Ukrainian organization known as the "Spilka." He managed to steer clear of a number of political shoals and reefs and was nominated under an assumed name, when all of a sudden his secret was out. The tsar's government learned that this was Larin, an underground Social Democrat, and he had to flee from Kiev. I helped him by getting him a passport.

I next heard of him in 1915, when, residing in neutral Stockholm and using German data, he became a regular contributor to the Moscow daily newspaper, *Russkiya Vedomosti*, in which his brilliant articles on the Reich's economy caused considerable comment. In those years of World War I, Germany was making her first experiments with organized war economy, considerably restricting the rights of private industrialists and businessmen, and, with every month, extending governmental control over all of economic life. As a socialist, Larin saw in this development the first practical effort to build a collective economy. The logical sequence of these German trends, to his mind, was a centralized and all-embracing state apparatus. His articles, some of which appeared also in solid scholarly monthlies, aroused great interest and much discussion among the intellectuals of Russia. At that time one of the reasons for the success of these articles was the contrast they seemed to offer between the efficiency and skill of Germany's leaders, on the one hand, and the slovenliness and blunders of the tsarist government, on the other.

Through all this, Larin continued to be a Menshevik. When in 1917 the revolution broke out, however, and Larin among other exiles returned to Russia, he quit the Mensheviks and went over to the Bolsheviks. It was a natural step for him. At that point the Mensheviks would not even listen to plans for a rapid liquidation of capitalism, a socialization of industries, and the like. And these were Larin's dreams exactly. He buzzed around with grandiose schemes which were to revolutionize man's entire economy by turning the capitalist chaos into a harmonious system of socialism.

When the Bolsheviks seized power, a wide field was at once opened for Larin's utopias and fantasies. He became the inspirer and the founder of a whole range of industrial "Tops" and "Centers," which for a time were greatly publicized. This meant that he organized central administrations and leading committees for all the industries in sight. It was he who originated the Soviets' monopoly of Russia's foreign trade. It was he who laid bases for the Gosplan, or State Planning Commission, and for the Supreme Council of People's Economy. And from him, too, came the idea of abolishing the old division of Russia into purely administrative provinces and counties and replacing them by new regions of economic significance.

Lenin greatly respected statistics and all kinds of figures in general. That is why Larin, who always juggled statistical data, impressed the new government at its very inception. Larin succeeded in gathering around himself a sizable group of well-educated and exceptionally talented non-Communist economists. They found it easy to work with him because they had known him in "pre-Bolshevik times." As for Larin, appreciating their experience and knowledge, he treated them with friendly confidence, which was, nonetheless, somewhat tempered by caution.

Larin flourished in 1918 and 1919, during the era of passionate enthusiasm for a complete overhauling of Russian economy on entirely new lines. His two-room apartment at the Metropole was also his office. Each room had as its master-feature a huge table piled high with papers and well-sharpened pencils. And this is how Larin worked: He would listen to the recital of a project in one room; then, while his visitors debated among themselves, he would step into the other room to get busy with another scheme. He wrote his conclusions in pencil. In the process he had to lift his left hand with his right one and place it on the table to hold the paper on which he wrote. At times he looked like the Russian version of a figure that had stepped out of an El Greco painting.

At Larin's, one met people from all over, from many and sundry branches of the new government: military, supply, transport, whatnot. All of them were trying to pull Larin over to their side in the constant arguments between departments—arguments as to which departments had what rights. And of friction between the new departments there was no end. Also at this period Larin took upon himself the writing of a multitude of decrees and resolutions, especially for a young chairman of the Northwestern Council of People's Economy, who frankly said that he did not know much about economics. The young chairman's name was Vyacheslav Molotov. He traveled far in time, without Larin's help.

Dzerzhinsky, the chief of the Cheka, was sometimes called "the Saint-Just of the Russian revolution." Larin, who performed radical operations on economic bodies, might have been called the Saint-Just of Russian economics.

But Larin's star did not shine for long. The contrast between his fantasies and life's reality was working against him. The opposition to his measures grew bolder with every day. He was forced out of one governmental agency after another. Ryckov was the first daring soul to demand Larin's resignation—

from the Supreme Economic Council. Lenin granted the demand. This was followed by similar requests on the part of other leaders in other agencies.

Larin was still liked by the leaders, but they became less and less in awe of him. Presently they sneered at his projects and reforms. At one meeting (I do not recall whether it was in the Council of Labor and Defense or the Council of People's Commissars), while some statistical data were being discussed, one of the commissars expressed his disapproval of the whole thing by exclaiming: "Oh, that's one of those inventions by Larin!" At this Lenin smiled patronizingly, and with him everyone else smiled, even the youngest and most respectful persons present.

Larin receded into the shadows. Within three years of the November revolution his role had come to an end. In February, 1921, Lenin wrote in a private letter to one of his more trusted planners:

"The Central Committee [of the Communist party] has decided to let Larin stay [in the State Planning Commission] *for the time being*. He is a great menace because this man disrupts all work, since by his very nature he *usurps power*. He demotes all the chairmen, *drives the experts away,* speaks in the name of the Party without a shadow of right to do so, and so on. It will be your *difficult* task to subordinate, discipline, and moderate Larin. Remember: the minute he 'begins' to transgress limits, rush over to me (or send me a letter). Otherwise Larin will send crashing the *entire* Planning Commission."

A few months later, on May 27, at a conference of the Communist party, Lenin mercilessly attacked Larin in public:

"His talent properly belongs not in any sphere of practical work, but in parliamentary opposition or journalism. He is indefatigable in manufacturing all sorts of projects. He has told you that in January, 1920, he offered us a good project. But were we to gather all the projects of Comrade Larin, and were we to select the good ones, these would prove to be a tiny fraction of the whole. When a certain resolution was adopted, Larin told me: 'You gave us a little finger, well, we'll take the whole hand.' That made me think—although I had known this before: 'Now we'll know how to bargain with Larin. When he asks for a million rubles, we should give him one-half of one ruble.' "

After this it was impossible to find use for Larin's unusual but rather peculiar talents. For a number of years, in the 1920's, individual Communists at the top would still ask for Larin's advice when important projects had to be prepared. But they did this either out of respect for his past or out of sheer pity for the man.

Larin died in 1932.

But in 1918 Lenin still viewed Larin's "legislative" decrees as a model which future generations would follow in making their socialist revolutions. The fact that I had known and aided Larin in our Kiev days of 1906 enabled me now to drop in on him at the Metropole whenever I liked and to have frank talks with the magician of economics. Sometimes Larin regarded me as a "servant of the bourgeoisie" and stubbornly defended his views against mine. That he counted himself among the topmost creators of the revolution was clear from every phrase of his.

Indeed, Larin's name is historically associated with the very first stages of the nationalization of industry in Russia. History textbooks fix the start of this development at June 18, 1918, the day when Lenin's decree for such nationalization was published. But actually this decree was not so decisive, and its true significance was quite different.

The seizure of factories and plants, begun toward the end of 1917, went on spontaneously, with elemental and unguided force, all those months prior to the publication of the decree. Both before and after the decree, the process of nationalization dragged on for more than one year. The central power was weak. Local organizations—such as regional and city Soviets, workers' committees, and so forth—considered themselves "autonomous," and they nationalized or merely expropriated private enterprises on their own initiative.

Nevertheless, the history of the June 18 decree is interesting, and both Larin and I had something to do with it. The Treaty of Brest Litovsk of the preceding March, as well as later agreements between the triumphant Germans of Kaiser Wilhelm II and the defeated Russians of Lenin, intrusted the protection of German property rights in Russia to the German embassy in Moscow. According to the treaty and the subsequent agreements, the embassy was to present the German claims to the Soviet government within a stated period, also to list the Russian enterprises in which German capital had been invested. The Soviet government was compelled to honor such claims and lists, and German interests and capital enjoyed a sort of immunity.

This gave certain Russian industrialists all kinds of hopes and ideas. They began to scheme the sale, real or fictitious, of shares or even of entire banks, plants, and other properties to the Germans. In this way they planned to safeguard their interests; later, with a political change, they might recover their lost property from the Germans. It must be said that at that time everyone, including the highest Soviet officials, considered the survival of the Soviet government most unlikely and a return to an approximation of the old system inevitable. On April 20, 1918, following the conclusion of the Treaty of Brest Litovsk, there arrived in Moscow the first German ambassador to the Soviets, Count Mirbach. Almost immediately a fair number of as-yet-unliquidated Russian businessmen, bankers, and industrialists made a point of getting in touch with him.

On the other hand, even to many non-Bolsheviks it seemed that such an excess of trust in the Germans spelled danger and was most unpatriotic. Giving Germany the lion's share of Russian industries would make the German bosses of Russia for an indefinite, and certainly a very long, period of time. The plans and efforts of those Russian industrialists and bankers who wanted to save their property by an agreement with German concerns clearly represented a great menace to Russia's national interests.

And so two schools of thought and action came to the fore among the Russian industrialists. One group was ready to make a deal with the Germans, while the other was patriotically dead-set against it. The second group was quite numerous, too. It included men like Alexis Meshchersky, one of the mainstays of prerevolutionary Russian capital, who up to 1918 headed the gigantic Sormovo-Kolomna metalworks. He now declared to me and to others that it was imperative to draw Lenin's attention to the threatened enslavement of Russian industry by the Germans.

Meanwhile, rumors of deals between Russian and German capitalists multiplied. Prompted by several of my friends—economists and engineers working for the Soviets—I decided to broach the matter to Ryckov, my old friend and now Lenin's trusted aide in the Supreme Economic Council. (This was several months before I first met Lenin and gained his confidence; in the summer of 1918 I needed intermediaries.)

"You are constantly raving against Russian industrialists for their lack of patriotism," I told Ryckov. "You hold that the workers with their revolution will do more for Russia's defense than any other class. And yet such bourgeois leaders as Meshchersky and others have expressed fear that one-half of Russian industry will soon be in German hands. They want the Soviet government to take steps to halt this pernicious development. And, after all, how will you Communists build socialism in your factories when side by side with you the Germans will continue their business as usual on those old capitalist principles of theirs?"

The very next day George Lomov, one of the chief party economists, telephoned me to say that Lenin had just ordered the formation of a three-man committee to compile a list of all large industrial enterprises which were to be nationalized at once. The list was to be prepared within forty-eight hours. The committee would exist and function in secret. Three prominent Communists would comprise it, and Larin and Lomov were two of them. In addition, three non-Communist specialists were to be attached to it, and I was to be one of these experts.

I suggested that some of the old and experienced industrial leaders be asked to collaborate, but Lomov replied that this would be "inconvenient." However, I was delegated to see them after the committee was through with its work, to show them the list drawn up by us and to explain that the main aim of the sweeping nationalization of all those industries was to protect them from falling into German hands.

A curious detail was encountered in the course of our work. During our deliberations on the committee, the question arose of what to do about that property of Russian firms which happened to be abroad. Should we nationalize it as well? We finally decided to limit our nationalization to domestic capital and equipment. Kutler, the former tsarist minister of finance, speaking to me privately, approved of this decision, saying: "Including Russian property abroad would only have aroused opposition on all sides and a lot of unnecessary friction in general."

Thus was born the famous decree of June 28, 1918. Larin was its chief author, of course. Here he was in his element, with the vast and breath-taking plans, on a true revolutionary scale, for nationalizing all Russian industries.

At last there remained but one problem: what role to assign to the former owners after their plants were nationalized. This brought forth much debate. Larin's radicalism in particular, and the era's maximism in general, demanded that the old bourgeois be removed from industry entirely. But we, the experts, realized clearly that without its former leaders Russian industry would be doomed to a long crisis and eventually a total collapse. Hence, as a supplement to the June 28 decree, we proposed governmental instructions that all the owners and managers of industrial establishments remain at their posts and continue their work.

At midnight of June 17 I went to see Larin at the Metropole. I tried to convince him that our proposed supplement to the next day's decree would benefit Russian economy and that to some extent it would lessen the shock of the nationalization news when it reached the West and affected Western public opinion.

Larin balked. He accused me of "Menshevik eructations." He had been a Menshevik himself and now secretly feared that his new friends, the Communists, might accuse him of excessive moderation, of erring on the side of caution, of willingness to compromise with capitalism. He was now one of the most irreconcilable of the Communists.

In the end, however, he gave in to my arguments. High approval of this amendment to the June 28 decree—Lenin's own approval, I believe—was secured by telephone. I had wanted quick action, and I got it: our group considered it desirable to publish the decree and the supplement simultaneously.

It helped but little, though. By this time the revolutionary passion was so high, the distrust of former owners and managers so deep, that hardly any heed was paid to our supplement on the spot, wherever the nationalization was actually being carried out. Larin really won his argument, even if he did not know this on that night in June, 1918.

In those years of 1918–20 Larin's apartment at the Metropole, as I have said, was constantly crowded with little Larins, so to speak, obscure enthusiasts from all over Russia who came to him with all sorts of weird schemes.

Thousands of people, intoxicated by the revolutionary storm, felt immense strength within them. They sincerely believed that by one lightning stroke they could solve Russia's and humanity's most complex problems. Through Larin they submitted to the Soviet government extraordinary discoveries and astonishing inventions. At Larin's and elsewhere in Moscow I had frequent occasion to meet these schemers and inventors.

Most of them were young peasants and workers. They lacked education but were overflowing with Red ardor, with devotion to the Communist cause. Many had distinguished themselves at the front in Russia's civil war. Now they were agitated by ideas which seemed to them of planetary significance. Each of them was convinced that his invention could produce immediate miracles. With unshakable faith and courage they stormed the most dangerous sectors of the economic front. Toward non-Communist officials of the Soviet regime their attitude was one of distrust and suspicion.

My own department naturally attracted inventors of all kinds of improvements for the timber industry, especially those which might make it possible to economize on food and fodder. Almost daily I had to receive these "scientists" and other "geniuses" who came to me with letters of introduction from various people's commissars. On bringing his project to me, each visitor tried to impress me with the fact that it was "a state secret." He would preface his factual exposition with an eloquent little speech, something like this:

"Revolutionary Russia has her sons at the fronts, fighting and dying for her. But she also has her geniuses capable of producing great new things which will help to defeat the counter-revolution."

Only then would he launch into the explanation of his invention, which only too often had no practical value whatever. But if I tried to tell him so, I ran tremendous risks to life and limb.

(5)

THE GENIUSES

ONE DAY DZERZHINSKY, HEAD OF THE CHEKA, TELEPHONED ME. THIS WAS LATE in 1919 when my department was struggling with the difficult problem of fuel —of stock-piling and transporting firewood in the hungry and cold Russia of that period. By then the Cheka had become a stern institution with both judicial and executive powers, and one which sent thousands of people to face its firing squads. Each telephone call from Dzerzhinsky ran shivers down our spines. But this time Dzerzhinsky sounded amiable. He said:

"I have here a young comrade who has just arrived from the front. He can facilitate your work of getting fuel. I want you to receive him. Listen to him carefully, and report to me tomorrow. He is a talented young comrade. At the front he has won a fine reputation as a Communist and a fighter."

My department was only three blocks away from the Cheka. In a few minutes an extremely well-built young man appeared in my office. His military uniform was all leather, from cap to boots. There was fire in his eyes as he turned the key in my door behind him and stepped toward my desk. He stared at me, then asked: "Are you a member of the party?"

Upon hearing from me that I was not a Communist, he threw the key upon my desk before him, drew a revolver out of his pocket, and put it down beside the key. He then pulled out a thick oilskin-bound notebook. This, too, he placed on the desk.

"At the front," he said, "things are now going well for us. This is because we know how to die for the new order. But behind the lines everything goes badly. This is because many strangers, even traitors, have wormed their way into the rear. We Communists must not only fight—we must also create. And so I, on many sleepless nights, thought of this fuel problem. If we don't get fuel, General Denikin and his Whites will take and throttle us with their bare hands. You will find the solution of this problem in my notebook. You must at once put it into effect."

I was silent. He added threateningly: "My invention is a secret of much importance. There are traitors in your department. If they get hold of my notebook, the secret will fall into the hands of the Whites, and that will be a terrible calamity."

Cautiously I peeked into the notebook. To my dismay I saw scores of pages filled with logarithmic and other mathematical calculations. Gently I asked the inventor to explain to me the essence of his great idea. This is what he told me:

He had invented a small motor which was to be attached to every lumberjack's neck or back. The motor would accumulate the energy of the fall of each tree as it was chopped down. Such progressively stored energy would allow the lumberjack to expend less and less effort as he went on cutting trees. As a result, the lumberjacks would need much less food to sustain them.

It was clear to me that this invention was one of the legion known in history as *perpetuum mobile*. I had no doubt as to its fantastic futility. But there was that revolver on the desk.

Gingerly, sparring for time, I said that the proposal was most interesting and that by all means it should be tested. Meanwhile, to guard it against traitors, the notebook should be locked up. I offered my safe for this purpose, suggesting that he take along with him the key to the safe after locking up his wonderful notebook. The next day (I promised) I would discuss the proposal with my experts—in his presence, of course.

He hesitated, then used my telephone to ring up Dzerzhinsky. He asked the Cheka chief whether he could trust me with his notebook until the next morning. The reply was affirmative. He left the notebook with me, and departed.

When he was gone I telephoned Dzerzhinsky. To my frank appraisal of the invention, Dzerzhinsky responded, with a note of disappointment in his voice: "That's strange. Our technical committee has examined this proposal and has found it worth while."

I knew what this meant. I might be arrested and charged with sabotage. Therefore I immediately called up Ryckov and requested that the project be ent over to the Scientific Committee for its decision. I was passing the buck, to be sure, but somehow I had to take this awful responsibility off my shoulders.

Ryckov listened to my tale with the greatest satisfaction. The people's commissars were always delighted to hear such comical stories involving their friends and colleagues. Besides, there was an antagonism of long standing between Dzerzhinsky's secret police and Ryckov's Supreme Economic Council. I could imagine with what pleasure Ryckov would recount the episode to Lenin, remarking to the chief: "You can see for yourself what Dzerzhinsky's Cheka is doing!"

I was rid of the young "genius" and his motor quickly enough, but another case was a far more difficult one. This second inventor's project ascended the highest steps of Soviet hierarchy. Somewhere in the Soviet archives it can be found in folders entitled *Glavshishka,* or the "Chief Pine Cone Administration." It caused much debate and trouble in its time.

One morning the chairman of the Central Timber Committee, George Lomov, telephoned to ask me to receive a certain Comrade Ravikovich and hear what he had to say. Presently the man, in his middle thirties and with a very assured air, arrived in my office and delivered this speech:

"I am an old Bolshevik, a dentist by profession. These days I am serving at the front. I know that the fate of the revolution depends on our fuel supplies, and this is what I think should be done.

"I come from Korostyshev in the Volyn province. We have beautiful pine forests out there. During my furlough at home not so long ago I was lying in a hammock when a pine cone struck my forehead. That gave me my first interest in pine cones. I began to study the problem of pine cones. I learned that each pine tree yields so many cones annually. [He named a figure.] I also ascertained that these cones burn remarkably well. I came to the conclusion that Russia, with her nine hundred million acres of woods, can obtain from these pine cones twice as much fuel as she will ever need. And so, here is my project:

"All pine cones are to be declared national property. The entire population, but mainly children up to twelve years of age, and old folks from sixty to seventy, should be mobilized to bring in pine cones from forests. Special baskets are to be issued to them. Storehouses for pine cones must be erected near railroad stations. Each mobilized person is to have his quota of pine cones to be brought to such storehouses. This shall be his labor duty to the state.

"The cone crop is to be taken to specially built plants for processing. You see, the cones will have to be pressed before they can be used as fuel for stoves, ovens, boilers, or locomotives. There are many mills in Russia which used to press sunflower seed for oil. They are idle now for lack of raw material. These are the mills which can and should be used to press the pine cones. Thus the entire problem of Russia's fuel will be solved!"

The visitor looked at me triumphantly. He went on to declare that all this was no daydream, that his idea was already being put into effect by the Central

29

Fuel Committee, for Lenin himself was interested in the plan. The project, the inventor said, had been approved in principle, and two million rubles had been allocated for initial experimentation in the forests. Why did he come to me, then? Because the project was about to be tried out on a national scale. My help was needed at this stage. Lenin said so.

"Vladimir Ilyich not only approves of the idea, he applies it himself," the visitor added proudly. "A carload of pine cones has been delivered to the Kremlin to stoke Comrade Lenin's own office stove."

Still I was skeptical. But I worried less than in the case of the young warrior and his perpetual-motion machine. This was not an exalted soldier but a mere dentist. I was not afraid. Calmly I explained my doubts to the visitor, saying, nevertheless, that I would refer his project to our Scientific Committee.

I felt that the dentist saw in me a non-Communist expert whose attitude toward revolutionary talents was naturally one of skepticism. As he left my office he openly announced that he did not trust me. He informed me that the project would be pushed along regardless of what my Scientific Committee might say about it.

Soon after this interview I had to go abroad for some five months. I had forgotten all about the dentist and his pine cones until, on the very day of my return to Moscow, I was summoned before the Council of Labor and Defense. This was a special session called to discuss the newly created Chief Pine Cone Administration! The agenda of the session, shown to me, bore these ominous words: "Comrade Liberman's explanations."

It was a cold Moscow day. When I came into Lenin's office, I noticed a little iron stove behind his chair. The stove was apparently stoked with the dentist's fuel, for near by lay a small pile of pressed pine cones. The room was very warm. At Lenin's side sat Ksandrov, chairman of the Central Fuel Committee; in addition, there were a representative of the Cheka whose special task was to combat lawbreaking in the fuel industries and delegates from various other Soviet departments. Last but not least, there was the dentist-inventor, Comrade Ravikovich.

All of them looked at me significantly, expectantly. Lenin's glance at me had a sly, almost cunning expression. All those present were dressed in the usual manner: felt boots, sheepskins, leather jackets. But I, having just returned from abroad, still wore a western European suit, with a collar, necktie, and shoes. This difference in attire somehow separated me from the others. I felt isolated, a stranger.

When the session finally opened, it began with energetic complaints against me. The gist of the complaints was this: five months ago a solution had been found for this cursed fuel problem. It had been put into my hands, and what had I done? Nothing, absolutely nothing. I was a bottleneck. The current fuel crisis was a result of my negligence, perchance even of my dishonesty. I must be held responsible. The Cheka man squinted gleefully at the glowing tove, then at me. Lenin raised his head from his book: "Comrade Liberman, how do you explain your carelessness and negligence?"

I began to outline my skeptical attitude toward the dentist's obsession. Were the use of pine cones for fuel at all possible, I said, many other countries—especially those suffering from a lack of coal—would have solved their fuel problem very easily. Take Sweden, I suggested, the country from which I had just returned. Sweden had no coal but many pine forests. Sweden could get fuel from her own pine cones, if our dentist was right. Yet the Swedes, a smart people, had to import coal from England; and Moscow's proposal of creating a combined Swedish-Russian syndicate to sell Soviet timber abroad could not be realized because Sweden depended upon England for her coal and did not want to displease the British by doing business with us. "If I had suggested pine cones as a source of fuel to the Swedes," I concluded, "they would probably have put me in an insane asylum."

My arguments, I felt, did not make much of a dent. My concluding words even seemed to create an atmosphere of outright hostility toward me. I did not know at the time that Lenin himself was supporting the Central Fuel Committee in this matter of pine cones. Thus my words, unbeknown to me, appeared to be directed against him personally.

I have read that in every tragedy there is always a grain of comedy as well. I might add that in a comic incident there is often a tragic note. So in this comedy of the pine cone. No sooner had I finished my general explanations than the Cheka man rose. The tragic aspect began.

The Chekist opened a large file and began to recite an indictment of me, from time to time staring at me fixedly. It turned out that the dentist, since his visit to me, had managed to secure a few more million rubles for his experiments; that, to prove his idea thoroughly practical, he had on his own initiative moved one of the idle oil mills from the Vitebsk region, lock, stock, and barrel, to a point on the Volga-Moscow Railroad and had undertaken to ship trainloads of pine cones to be pressed at that mill. The pressed cones were to be sent to Moscow, to members of the Soviet government for their personal use and experiment. However, to the dentist's acute disappointment, not a single trainload of cones had yet arrived at the mill.

The reason was simple: the locomotive consumed all the cones on its way to the mill; the cars arrived empty because of the locomotive's natural appetite for fuel. The dentist and the Cheka would not, however, accept this plain explanation given to them by the train's crew. They decided it was sabotage. The Cheka started an investigation, and now the stern young Chekist turned to me with this question: "Whose ill-will is it that has caused this situation—that not a single trainload of pine cones has so far reached the mill?"

The chairman of the Fuel Committee, Ksandrov, interposed a sneering remark that I should not try to defend myself with the example of such a bourgeois country as Sweden. "Sweden is no model for us," he said.

Lenin again lifted his head from his book to demand what he called "sub-

stantial" explanations from me. I responded by pointing out that most Rus
sian pine forests were to be found in the north of European Russia and ir
Siberia, while our oil mills were in the treeless steppes of the Ukraine anc
other southern regions. This meant that trainloads of pine cones would have
to cross enormous distances to reach the oil mills. These hauls would consume
from three to ten times as much fuel as could be gotten from the very same pine
cones carried such long distances. Moreover, the building of storehouses for
cones, the manufacture of baskets for cone-gatherers, and other features of the
dentist's program would require much effort and expense—much more than
the effort and money involved in ordinary lumberjacking.

These arguments impressed Lenin, who was always receptive to common
sense. Although busily reading that book of his all through this discussion
he had heard everything that had been said, had grasped all the pros and cons
had weighed and digested them in his mind. He was ready for action. There
was a hint of a grin in the corners of his lips, and from the expression of hi
eyes I realized that his suspicion of my motives had been dispelled. This did
not prevent him from dictating the following resolution for the Council'
minutes:

"Firstly, to reprimand Comrade Liberman for his negligent approach to
matter which deserved serious study and implementation.

"Secondly, to refer the entire matter to a special scientific board, which i
also to be given all the arguments presented by Comrade Liberman."

This resolution pained me deeply, not because of its contents, but because c
the effect it would have among the various governmental departments, espe
cially the Cheka, in their attitude toward me. On this first day after my return
from abroad I was particularly sensitive to native approval or disapproval o
my work. I reached my apartment in a very depressed mood. An hour late
the telephone rang. I was surprised to hear that the Kremlin was on the wire
that Lenin wished to speak to me.

"Comrade Liberman," said the voice, burring its r's, "I noticed that th
Council's resolution made you sad. Ah, but you are a soft-skinned intellectual
The government is always right. Go on with your work as before!"

And this was the end, for me, of the Chief Pine Cone Administration. Soo
it was gone not for me alone—the project itself was abolished.

Inventors of the visionary category are common to all lands. In wester
Europe, however, they are rarely given a hearing, and many end up as starvin
and embittered men. But in Soviet Russia in 1918–20, they could and did reac
not only numerous important officials but the head of the state himself. Leni
received them, insisted that the various commissariats give them an oppor
tunity to explain their ideas, and even demanded trials for those officials wh
were guilty of red tape in dealing with such inventors and their blueprints.

When a plow invented by a certain Professor Fauler was held up in
commission, Lenin, overruling the Supreme Economic Council and the Peo

ple's Commissariat of Justice, called for a public trial of the members of the commission who, in his opinion, were responsible for "tying up" the invention. "Not so much in order to punish them severely," he explained, "as to reprimand them publicly and so disprove the general idea that the guilty go unpunished."

Moreover, all these inventors—good and bad—had access to the public treasury. Money was freely spent on them; and, when tests showed that a given invention was not practical, its blueprint was filed away with neither criticism nor regret for the funds expended. In the archives of the Soviet commissariats future historians will doubtless unearth a veritable graveyard of wild projects. The hopes they once kindled!

And yet, there were men who truly glimpsed the future among these inventors scurrying from office to office with their dog-eared portfolios bulging with enticing blueprints and dreary luncheon sandwiches.

Once, in a group of down-at-the-heel enthusiasts, I beheld a man named Bazhanov. He was one of the throng that brought their projects to the reception rooms of the commissariats, which sometimes were nothing more than cold, empty stores, serving as makeshift Soviet offices, with packing-boxes in lieu of desks and chairs. Bazhanov was young and stately, but his cheeks were sunken and his eyes feverish. He wore the uniform cap of his prerevolutionary profession, that of a mining engineer. Coal mining was his passion as well as his profession. With much ardor, for hours, he would argue that in western Siberia the Kuznets Basin had fabulous riches which must be opened up forthwith. He went everywhere with his statistics and diagrams. I met him in the company of Larin, that other lover of figures abounding in zeroes.

Later I saw Bazhanov in Lenin's office. Lenin received the young engineer upon the latter's return from the Kuznets Basin, whither he had finally been sent at his own insistence. Outstanding experts snickered at the man. And, I must admit, when I heard him in those days, I, too, regarded his words as so much utopian prattle.

At that time we kept our eyes riveted on the Donets Basin in the Ukraine, which then seemed the only promising zone of coal production. The war and the revolution with their ravages had decreased the yield of the Donets Basin mines to 40 per cent of the 1913 level. But even the seemingly high output of the prerevolutionary years could have been increased tenfold had better methods been used, and they were indeed introduced later, improving the Donets Basin production enormously.

In those starving, bloody years of 1918–20, when the Donets Basin mines stood idle because the miners had gone away in search of bread or to fight in the Red Army's ranks, it seemed insane to begin digging coal in the faraway Siberian wilderness. If we had had any miners available, we would have employed them in the near-by Donets Basin. And why should the Siberian coal be dug? To satisfy the Ural industries alone! Besides, there were no metalworks in western Siberia at the time, and the nearest Ural works were some thirteen hundred miles away from the Kuznets Basin.

Still, Bazhanov went on hammering everywhere that the coke from the Kuznets Basin produced more calories of heat than even the highly valued English coke. In the end Lenin agreed and made the young man responsible for developing that region.

Today many people say, and rightly, that the creation of the Ural-Kuznets industrial region was a master-stroke which saved Russia in the present war after she had lost her Donets Basin to the Nazis. But I remember those three years when Bazhanov came to Soviet sessions with requests for funds and food for his workers, and the commissars jeered at him, "Here is Bazhanov again! When are you going to make us snug and warm with your Kuznets coal, eh?"

And I recall another fiery Russian of that era, a chemical engineer who held a minor post in one of the small craft enterprises. Everywhere he went he would pull out of his briefcase a batch of books to prove that in western Europe, especially in Germany, many essential by-products were extracted in the process of charcoal burning. He reminded us that the Ural mining industry was using charcoal, but that all the by-products—such as methyl alcohol, sugar, etc.—were being wasted. And he had his scholarly papers on the subject, all prepared and ready to be delivered to any official or before any audience, to show what riches Russia was thus squandering.

His papers and charts at last reached Lenin—the man who repeatedly said, "We must capture the minds, the imaginations, of the great mass of workers and peasants with a stupendous program of reconstruction which would take ten to twenty years to realize." In the chemist's papers and charts Lenin saw definite possibilities for his program. This was how certain agencies and plants were established, and the by-products finally saved and utilized. A special commission of experts was sent abroad to investigate foreign methods of doing this work. And now, in the war industries of the Soviet Union, these products do, in fact, play a tremendous part. But when the process was first considered, many prominent experts in Russia thought that it would be much simpler and cheaper not to bother with any domestic production of these items but to import them from abroad instead.

Similar examples are almost countless, and, seen in today's perspective, they are in many ways inspiring. Take, for instance, a group of young enthusiasts from the northern provinces who arrived in Moscow with a brand-new idea. They pointed out that in the Arkhangelsk and other northern regions more than 30 per cent of wood shavings were needlessly lost. This loss, they said, increased the cost of lumber production. Why not decrease it by building big cellulose plants close to the sawmills? Whatever cellulose could not be utilized in Russia might be exported. Although it was known that in Europe and Canada cellulose was overproduced and that the export prices we would get would not cover our production costs, the project was tried out, for the Soviet government needed foreign exchange. Today these cellulose plants occupy a high place in the industrial system of the Soviet Union.

Out of the past, likewise, looms the picturesque figure of Reikunov, a Communist who served as vice-chairman of the Central Timber Committee. Later, in the course of nationalizing Russia's textile industries, he earned the reputation of a Soviet Simon Legree. Eventually he was removed from office for drunkenness but, in view of his earlier production record, was given one more chance. He was sent to Turkestan to develop irrigation for the Soviet cotton fields in the central Asiatic region. At the time, I remember, people used to jest that "Reikunov will irrigate, not cotton with water, but himself with alcohol." As a matter of fact, he did quite a job. Today this region supplies all Russia with much-needed cotton.

Then there was a delegation from Belorussia. Reinforced with two experts, they came to Moscow to convince us that it was not worthy of Russia to tolerate those swamps near Minsk. They proposed forming labor battalions expressly to drain their native marshes. The drainage of the Zuyder Zee in Holland was their inspiration. They said to us that if Holland—small, reactionary, capitalist Holland—could succeed, why, Russia could do *anything*. Just such eager souls in time developed the marshes near Moscow into a remarkable peat industry, despite all the sober statistical and commercial calculations of the hostile experts in that field to the contrary. Elsewhere in Russia, similar optimists won out in the matter of developing clay-slate works out of wasted space and materials. Sad to say that we, the experts, the "generals of industry," often laughed at such fantastic projects in their initial stages. We thought, for instance, that Petrograd (when it had not yet become Leningrad) would always depend on imported raw materials and that all these elaborate plans to find such materials near by were a loss of time and energy. But visionaries proved otherwise to us.

There was hardly a field without its ardent reformer. At one of the innumerable sessions of the Council of Labor and Defense devoted to the problem of stock-piling firewood, a tall fellow spoke up. His little flaxen beard was neatly trimmed; his high boots shone like a mirror; he looked folksy yet well-groomed. He began to tell us that the chief trouble with the Russian peasant, whether he tilled his acres or tried lumberjacking and wood-carting, was his pitifully weak horse. The man pointed to Canada's example: "That's where they know how to improve the breed of their horses. We must learn from the Canadians." To our astonishment he poured forth statistics, diagrams, budget proposals, and the like. It all ended in commissioning some experts to go abroad in order to purchase pedigreed stallions and mares.

Some such projects were the result of much reading of books; others were brought from foreign lands by returning exiles. Old Russia was going through the throes of rebirth, rebuilding, reshaping. Many Russians, and not alone foes of the new regime, regarded with alarm all this enthusiastic experimenting.

Lenin himself thoughtfully asked: "What is socialism?" And gave his own answer: "It's industrialization plus electrification." The whole plan of Russia's electrification, which Lenin had so much at heart, was eventually a success mainly because Russia was remolded from her old provincial division into a system of logically delineated economic regions.

In this connection I recall that once, while riding in Krassin's parlor-car, in the company of Maxim Gorky and Karl Radek, I heard our host speak mockingly of some of the so-called "builders" of new Russia. Gorky did not agree with all of Krassin's doubt or malice. "The Russian peasant has grown clumsy and uncouth," Gorky said. "He is like a sturdy but crooked tree. We must run him through a cruel machine, breaking his bones, then we will reset those bones right. And that will make Russia what she should be—great."

Everyone agreed. And yet, to men and women past their youth, such a surgical operation seemed too much of a torture. They could not accept it wholeheartedly. But these were apparently the sort of people of whom the Bible speaks:

"Among these there was not a man of them whom Moses and Aaron the priest numbered, when they numbered the children of Israel in the wilderness of Sinai. For the Lord had said of them, They shall surely die in the wilderness. .... Surely there shall not one of these men of this generation see that good land."

(6)

THE CHEKA AND I

IN THE SUMMER OF 1919, RUSSIA'S CIVIL WAR RAGED ITS FIERCEST FOR THE REDS, and fortune smiled on the Whites. Moscow was living through anxious days. General Denikin's White soldiers were approaching Tula, close to Lenin's capital, the last strong point before Moscow. The mighty of the Kremlin frowned and were talking of evacuation. The plan was to move the Soviet government to Perm in the Urals. The plan was kept a secret from the general population, but all sorts of rumors about this impending flight were bruited around Moscow. The evacuation of certain government offices was regarded as a practically decided matter.

Preparing for this step, Communist officials drew up for the various departments lists of the managing personnel who were to leave Moscow with the government. Most of the persons thus selected were Communists, but in certain and rather rare cases non-Communists were added.

Whenever Communist bosses needed certain non-Communist experts for the future Soviet base in the Urals but were not quite sure of the experts' loyalty, the top-notch Communists sounded out the candidates in cautious, prolonged conversations. At that time there were as yet many government employees and members of the intelligentsia who pinned their hopes upon Denikin and wanted to remain in Moscow—to greet the White general.

It was taken for granted that I, being loyal to the idea of rebuilding Russia, would leave Moscow with the Soviets. However, among the men I knew and worked with, there were those—particularly the former capitalists—who meant to stay behind. One of them came to me "to talk things over." He was a former lumber magnate now employed by the Soviet government. Apparently feeling that he owed me a debt of gratitude for certain recent favors, my visitor declared:

"We had a talk in our circle [at first I did not realize what he meant by 'our circle'] and I was delegated to assure you that your family will be safe. As you are to be evacuated with the Soviet government, we want you to tell us your wishes as to what we are to do about your child when the new government comes."

He even expressed his willingness to take my son into his family for a while. He only wished me to instruct my family beforehand to trust him when the time came to save them.

Indeed, in the confidential list of several hundred people needed and trusted by the Communists for their retreat, I presently found my name. It was bracketed with the names of some old Bolsheviks. Later I was told that Lenin himself put me there.

But the list was never used. The danger passed in the late fall, with the sudden and utter defeat of General Denikin's forces by the young Red Army. My former capitalist visitor did not, after all, have to rescue my family. His own fate read like a cruel jest. He was soon an émigré in Berlin, then he moved to Latvia, and finally returned to Russia, where he eventually perished.

The fact that I had been selected by Lenin for evacuation and at the same time was assured by Lenin's enemies that my family would not suffer was symbolic of my entire career in Soviet Russia. It was characteristic that Lenin trusted me while the Cheka did not.

The stern Cheka watched my department and all my actions with the greatest possible suspicion. From the viewpoint of the secret police there was plenty of evidence against me. In that period of "integral socialization," any encouragement of capitalistic activity, even though sanctioned by the Soviet government, led to confusion and indignation among the Chekists. And I was guilty of such sanctioned encouragement. Moreover, I was not a Communist, but only a *spets* with a Menshevik and capitalist past.

Every denunciation of me, every evil rumor about my work, was carefully recorded and filed away. Gradually a dossier accumulated, and the very existence of the dossier was in time a dangerous matter for me—a source of struggle and conflicts aimed at me and my activity.

The Cheka had strange allies in this fight against me. As I have said, certain unscrupulous former capitalists of the timber industry, angry at me for reasons of their own, did not hesitate to work against me with Dzerzhinsky's agents.

Yes, these private wood-contractors did seek and find paths leading to Dzerzhinsky's office. One of them, for instance, had a brother who held a prominent post as an investigator in the Economic Division of the Cheka. Doubtless he received certain "reports" about me. There were also, both in the provincial and in the Moscow offices of the Cheka, numerous agents who had formerly been employees of various lumber firms. Some of them had preserved contacts with their former bosses. Through such and other channels the Cheka received sundry information, in part incorrect and sometimes full of downright and deliberate distortions of facts. This was the way many lumber-merchants, for the most part violent opponents of the Soviet government, managed to establish a center of influence in the Economic Division of the Cheka, finally succeeding in some of their intrigues against me and my orders.

The leading Chekists felt that, since the orders from above were to tolerate all this semicapitalist activity in the timber industry, the state, in the course of such toleration, could at least "get results" from my department. This meant that all private lumber-merchants must, without fail, deliver exactly the quantity of wood they contracted to deliver. Otherwise this Soviet retreat from revolutionary principles, and especially the expenditures of the precious products belonging to the Commissariat of Food Supply, could only help the capitalists whom Liberman allegedly headed and protected in order to perpetrate a gigantic fraud against the Soviets. And so, to improve its control over my department, the Cheka created a special three-man committee or, to use the term of the time, another *Troika* or Trio. This particular trio consisted of F. Eyduk, Jacob Peters, and Varlam Avanesov.

Eyduk, an old Lettish Bolshevik, was in charge of the Soviet end of the repatriation of Russian and German prisoners of war after the Brest-Litovsk Treaty of March, 1918. Later, during the liquidation of the anarchists in Moscow, he commanded a battalion of Lettish rifles which did most of the mopping up for the Bolsheviks in that bloody episode. In 1920 he was in Archangel, where he unleashed the Cheka terror against the Whites, following the failure of the British and American intervention in northern Russia. Now, back in Moscow from these exploits, he was the chairman of the Trio appointed by the Cheka to control my department and a member of the presidium of the Cheka.

His friend Peters was then in his middle thirties. Also a Lett by origin, the son of a farmhand and himself a farmhand in his prerevolutionary youth, he had been a Latvian socialist ever since 1904, a factory worker until 1912, and a Communist and one of the earliest Chekists in the Soviet era. Like Eyduk, Peters owed his sinister reputation, from 1918 on, to the terrible executions he instituted wherever he went in Russia.

The third member, Varlam Avanesov, was a tubercular Armenian with an underground revolutionary record which went back to the late 1890's, when he had been a member of the Dashnags, or Armenian nationalists. By the early 1900's he had embraced the tenets of socialism and later joined the Bolsheviks. His illness brought him first to Davos, Switzerland, then to the balmy isle of Capri, off Italy. It was in Capri that Maxim Gorky, also a consumptive, lived, wrote, and held a miniature court of his Bolshevik friends, who came to visit him from all over their western European exile. Avanesov became close to Gorky and his Bolshevik associates. Returning to Russia, Avanesov kept very much to himself, chiefly because of his affliction. A tubercular patient of Moscow doctors to the end, he was, nevertheless, a willing work horse in the new Soviet government. During the period of my work with Lenin, Avanesov was Stalin's deputy in the People's Commissariat of Government Control, a job calling for much devotion and close attention to routine tasks.

Such were the three men who now summoned me to appear before them. I was not the only one. Several employees from certain timber organizations were told to present themselves, and there were also men from other departments. When my turn came, I was asked to explain some of the steps I had taken in my work at the time of Denikin's threat to Moscow.

At the end of the session Eyduk announced, slowly but loudly: "By order of this committee I have drawn up a list of persons whose activity is under suspicion. Liberman's name heads the list."

He held a pencil that was blue at one end and red at the other, and from where I sat I could see that he scribbled something against my name with the red end of the pencil. He went on: "If three months from now the railroads stop because of lack of fuel, there will be a further mark against this name, there will be a red cross against it—and I will liquidate this man. No arguments or excuses will be of any avail."

It is easy to imagine what impression this threat made on all those present. When the meeting closed, many of my subordinates were afraid to come close to me. They furtively hurried past this candidate for the firing squad and soon were gone, scattering in all directions like mortally frightened mice.

Eyduk's Trio then readied a series of measures aimed at improving my performance. Some of these were especially characteristic of the time we lived in. New employees appeared in various offices of my department—they were the eyes of the Cheka. Next, the Council of Labor and Defense was urged by the Cheka to separate the rafting work of my department from its supply operations and place each part under different supervision.

It was this latter proposal to the council that unexpectedly proved to be my temporary salvation. It was precisely the action I had proposed long before the Cheka thought to embarrass and trap me with it.

Long before the meeting at which Eyduk threatened to shoot me, I had seen the signs of trouble; I had known that dangerous clouds were gathering over my head. I had explained the situation not only to Ryckov and Krassin but to Lenin himself. Foreseeing the turn events might take, I had on one occasion handed Ryckov a sealed letter, requesting him to open it only in case my position became truly dangerous. In this letter I had frankly and fully described the impossible situation which had come to prevail in the timber industry and had suggested several remedies. As luck would have it, among my suggestions was the very one now advanced by the Cheka—that of separating the two major operations of my department.

The moment to act seemed to have come after Eyduk's threat to liquidate me. Accordingly, I asked Ryckov to open and read my letter at that session of the Council of Labor and Defense where the Cheka's proposals were to be heard. But Ryckov, instead, handed the letter to Lenin. The next day Lenin's secretary, Fotieva, telephoned me: "Vladimir Ilyich is informed of everything that has taken place in this case. He requests that you continue your work calmly while waiting for further instructions."

Another day passed, and my chief, George Lomov, came to me with an excerpt from the minutes of the Council of Labor and Defense. It ran more or less as follows:

"Having acquainted itself with all the explanations presented, the Council of Labor and Defense reprimands Comrade Eyduk for his behavior in this matter, which behavior is incompatible with the dignity of a Communist and a responsible official. We suggest that he call on Liberman with his apologies. We instruct Lomov, in his capacity as head of the Central Timber Committee, to gather together all the employees and to confirm to them our confidence in Comrade Liberman's work."

A telegram signed by Lenin was sent to all the party and governmental offices, once more voicing his confidence in me and my work. Thus triumph! But for a brief spell only.

True, Eyduk and other men of Dzerzhinsky's dreaded agency now refrained from attacking me openly. But they continued to shadow me. More Chekists were sent to act as my employees, actually to spy on me. Soon I was surrounded by persons who, I did not doubt, reported to the Cheka all my conversations, telephone calls, the contents of my correspondence, instructions to my subordinates, and everything else. There was a ceaseless watch over all my movements. And when, beginning with the summer of 1920, I had to assume numerous duties in the foreign-trade field and thus, of necessity, began to have contacts with the capitalist world outside Soviet Russia, the suspicion and shadowing on the part of the Cheka increased a hundred fold. Finally my position became unbearable. I decided that I must have a man-to-man talk with Dzerzhinsky himself. But how to reach the forbidding Chekist chief? Through Lenin, of course.

This was toward the end of 1920. At one of my meetings with Lenin I once more, but now in stronger terms than ever, told him of the difficult conditions under which I had to work. I said that the Cheka must change its attitude toward me if I was to continue my service to the state. I said that I could convince Dzerzhinsky of my honesty and loyalty to the Soviets if only I could have a heart-to-heart talk with him.

Lenin at once telephoned Dzerzhinsky and asked him to see me. Dzerzhinsky complied. The appointment was for seven o'clock of the next evening, not in the Cheka office, but in his private apartment. The Torquemada of the Soviets apparently wished to please Lenin; he would allow me to unburden myself in a place away from the oppressive atmosphere of his agency.

At the appointed hour I appeared at the address given me by Lenin. Dzerzhinsky's flat turned out to be a few modest rooms. The room in which I had to wait was small and most unprepossessing, with dark-red draperies of a rather poor appearance. The furniture, as in so many Soviet offices and apartments of the time, seemed middle class but ill assorted, collected, as it had been, in a haphazard manner from a number of requisitioned houses.

While I waited, a woman of about forty entered the room. The lines of her face were severe; her raven-black hair was done in an old-fashioned way— parted in the middle, combed smoothly on both sides, and brought into a knot at the nape of her neck. Such faces can sometimes be seen in old engravings of the early and middle nineteenth century. As if in keeping with her face and hair, her dress was black and long, and she had a scarf over her shoulders. She was very erect and had the air of the mistress of this house. Indeed, she was Dzerzhinsky's wife. She asked me to wait, then walked out, and soon from another room I heard the sounds of a piano. The wintry room was cold; I was freezing.

But I did not have to wait long, as Dzerzhinsky came in a few minutes later. His long scrawny figure in a private's greatcoat and boots seemed lankier than ever in this small room. His face with its high forehead and a little narrow beard reminded me of another old print.

My host was extremely polite. He begged my pardon for being late, and then lowered himself into an armchair without removing his greatcoat. In a moment his wife appeared with a glass of tea for him—none for me. The tea seemed strong and was the same dark-red color as the draperies all around us. Dzerzhinsky introduced his wife to me and then, in a business-like manner, told me to go ahead with what was on my mind.

I spoke for twenty minutes. Not once did he interrupt me with either any remark or any question of his own. I tried to explain to him why, in my opinion, it was necessary to use certain principles of private enterprise in the socialized industry, why my entire policy was approved by Lenin, and so on. As I spoke, I realized that my tone was becoming increasingly strong and sure. At last I concluded:

"I can fulfil my duties only if I enjoy your trust, just as I enjoy that of Vladimir Ilyich. I don't mind if anyone representing you is placed by my side. But I can't work if I am made to feel constantly that I am being shadowed and watched by men who are hostile to me and ignorant of my work. If you find it impossible to free me of such surveillance, then I will have to ask my chiefs to relieve me of my duties altogether. I don't think I am indispensable, and I am ready to continue my work as a subordinate in the same office or in

41

some other Soviet organization. But if I must hold the responsible job I have now, I must have your support."

"Concretely, what do you want of me?" he asked.

I suggested that he send to all the provincial committees of the Communist party and to the Cheka organs in charge of timber work telegrams instructing them to help my department. I also suggested that he tell his own main office in Moscow that the activities of my department were based not on my, Liberman's, personal views and policies but on the policies of the Soviet government itself.

Dzerzhinsky was silent for a moment, then said: "All right. Write me a text of the necessary telegram, and I'll think it over."

I composed a telegram. It was sent out unchanged the very next day over the signatures of Ryckov, the chairman of the Supreme Council of Economy, and Dzerzhinsky, the chief of the Cheka.

In time to come I saw Dzerzhinsky privately only once more, a little while before his death, amid tragic circumstances. But his influence was omnipresent, and I must add here that once while discussing my difficulties with the Cheka, Lenin said to me: "Now you see for yourself that you wouldn't have had all these troubles if you were a member of our party."

It was with an effort that I managed to be polite, yet firm, in my reply: "Vladimir Ilyich, Bolsheviks, like singers, are born, not made. I simply wasn't born to be a Bolshevik. You yourself would lose respect for me were I to join your party merely to escape all these troubles. My whole life has been such that I cannot be a Communist." Lenin must have agreed, for he did not argue with me.

(7)

NO BOLSHEVIK

IT IS EASY TO SHOW EXACTLY WHAT I MEANT WHEN I TOLD LENIN THAT I HAD NOT been born to be a Bolshevik. I was born in a Jewish family, in a small village in the Ukraine. My father was engaged in farming, and he hoped that his only son would follow him in this work. But life decreed otherwise, just as it decreed that I should never be a Bolshevik.

My family was exceptional in the sense that, though it consisted of third-generation farmers, they zealously preserved their tradition of Judaism. My maternal grandfather divided his time between working the soil and reading his ancient Hebrew tomes. His brother, singularly enough, was my father, who had married the old man's daughter—his own niece. My father was far more of a farmer than my grandfather. Black loam meant much more to him than any wisdom of books.

Thus it was my father who really headed the farming enterprise of the family. The land was not ours; we leased it, an estate of some four thousand

42

acres, from a Polish magnate. A fishpond and a flour-mill were part of the estate. Four times a year a grand spell of fishing was undertaken in the pond with the help of the villagers, each peasant receiving as his payment a certain share of the netted fish.

The mill functioned mainly for the needs of the muzhiks. Generally there was a close bond between our family and the villagers, and we knew all their joys and sorrows. In want or sickness they came to our family for help, which was always readily forthcoming.

I never saw the owner of the estate, the Polish nobleman. There was a rumor that, having had a share in the Polish insurrection against the tsar in 1863, he had been exiled to Siberia. I did not know for sure. His house on a hill beyond the village was inhabited by his two sisters—spinsters. The original unwritten agreement of the lease, concluded between my great-grandfather and the nobleman, specified that our family was to take care of all the needs of the nobleman's sisters. We occupied a house below the mansion of the two old ladies, with a garden common to both dwellings. The garden was overgrown with berry bushes, fruit trees, poplars, and weeping willows along the banks of a zigzagging stream. We met the two old ladies mostly in that garden. We treated them almost with veneration. I would kiss their hands, and they would kiss me on the head. With their black shawls upon their hunched shoulders they looked forbidding, but actually they were all kindness. They used to take me into their house to treat me to their raspberry jam. Their tenderness to us Jews perhaps had its roots in their hatred for the Russians of the tsar who had put down that Polish revolt of 1863 and who had had as little liking for Jews as for Poles.

The two hundred inhabitants of the village alternated their work between their own modest allotments of land and the sugar-beet fields of the nobleman, leased by our family. We hired these men as farmhands, and my father was always with them. He preceded them at planting time, solemnly and almost religiously throwing the first seed into the pungent black loam out of the seed-bag slung across his shoulder. Astride a horse, he headed these peasant men and women at other seasons of work, too, as, singing or playing their musical instruments, they made their way into the fields.

My grandfather, on the other hand, would come riding into the fields only after he had had his fill of sacred study among his old folios. I was the only male grandson in the clan, and my grandfather wanted me to be a Hebrew scholar rather than a farmer. But my father loved nature, the earth, the smell of manure. He was happy when he saw me in the company of village boys, atop the bare backs of our horses. Father was fond of horses, too. He loved to ride them, and when he harnessed them to his favorite buggies, he always selected the friskiest animals possible.

No greater contrast could be imagined than that between the physical appearance of the two brothers—my grandfather and my father. My grandfather was a tall, lanky man with a long beard, his eyes red from too much peering over the small ancient type of his books, his clothes old fashioned—the traditional clothes of a Hebrew scholar. He looked the very picture of Don Quixote when he mounted his horse, particularly on windy days. My father, on the contrary, was of middle stature, broad-shouldered, and stocky. His beard was red and round; his hair was parted in the center. He seemed strikingly like a solid, prosperous peasant of the Russian steppes—which he actually was.

When, on Hebrew holidays and other high occasions, my grandfather would begin his long mystical discourses with his visiting cronies, my father, forced to be present, often fell asleep. In his turn, father would become animated in the circle of his peasant friends, discussing fertilization, crops, the current market for the beets and grain. My mother was mortally ashamed of such uncouthness on the part of her husband. She bitterly lamented her fate—the sacrifice she had had to make, for the sake of her family's material welfare, in marrying her simple nonintellectual uncle. Her dearest dream was to see me, her only son, grow up a great Hebrew savant, a deeply religious man like her father.

At the age of seven I was sent to a neighboring Jewish hamlet, there to live and study as befitted the future Hebrew sage. I was miserable. Coming home infrequently, I felt torn bodily away from the village, the fields, the horses, the Ukrainian peasants I loved so much. The study foisted upon me was too dry in its scholastic forms, despite its romantic and mystic substance, which, in years to come, was to have its good influence on my personality and life.

The peasants were sorry for me. Knowing my loneliness, they would visit me on their market-day trips to my hamlet. At times, in secret, they took me back to their homes in the village. Learning of this, my father smiled indulgently; I think he was actually pleased. But my mother was terribly upset; she did not want anything to interfere with my studies.

This early feeling between me and the peasants was an important factor in my development. It was destined to prevail upon and conquer my grandfather's plan for raising a traditional Hebrew scholar. My love for the people made me in time a revolutionary, even if not a Bolshevik.

A logical sequel to this early kinship with the plain people of the countryside was the influence of Russian literature, of all the tremendous liberty-loving drives so characteristic of the Russian intelligentsia of the end of the last century and the beginning of this.

I learned to read Russian. The local priest and the local teacher began to give me books. The priest's two sons, prominent Russian officials both, would come from St. Petersburg to their father's house for brief visits. Their very dress and manners made me daydream of traveling to faraway cultured lands —or at least to St. Petersburg. I wanted more knowledge. I wished to be a part, not of this narrow life and arid Hebrew study, but of the great, wide, modern world. I was in my teens and eager to be an adult.

I decided to run away from home. The teacher and the priest encouraged me. And so, at the age of sixteen, with my scant belongings packed in a small parcel, my entire capital consisting of five rubles, I left for the nearest big town—Zhitomir.

This was a great blow to my grandfather. He wept over his parchments and books as he thought of his only grandson's defection to "the enemy"—to the crass world of disbelievers. My mother, too, was heartsick. Only my father was rather cheerful about it all. I think he understood that my motive in leaving home was not really the search for worldly goods. He knew, I believe, that I wanted knowledge and freedom rather than any materialistic gain despised by my grandfather.

In Zhitomir I settled in the house of a distant cousin, who was both a rabbi and a physician. As a doctor, he was a graduate of the Military Medical Academy in St. Petersburg. He was an idealist, a reformer, who sought a more enlightened life for the Jewry of Russia. He and his friends strove to make the young of their people aware of more up-to-date ideas than orthodox Judaism could give them. The Jews must participate in the main stream of Russian and western European culture!

Among other youths flocking to Zhitomir from the ghettos of other small towns and hamlets, I lived the life so desired for us by my cousin and his friends. We studied in the local library; we tutored one another; we found teachers in the most surprising strata of that town's society. We had no money, and we often starved; but we studied hard, preparing to take our examinations for the entire course of the tsarist high school, so as to be able to enter one of the few universities of the nation.

Having usually spoken either Yiddish or Ukrainian, I found that my main need was of good instruction in the Russian language. A new teacher had just come to Zhitomir, and I took lessons from him. He was a fine teacher— and an efficient revolutionist, a propagandist par excellence. At the end of each lesson he would silently hand me antitsarist publications printed by various revolutionary organizations in the underground. He was a Marxist. Thus came my first systematic acquaintance with Marxism.

I began to consider myself a regular Social Democrat after I had read George Plekhanov's book *On the Monistic View of History*. A living influence in the same direction was Nicholas Berdyayev, then a Marxist exiled in Zhitomir by the tsarist government. Later he was to become a Christian philosopher. (Despite our subsequent difference in political and social views, we remained friends for years to come; now and then my spiritual doubts and seekings were to bring me to visit him, for long and fruitful talks.)

My real baptism as a revolutionary occurred during the period of my study in Zhitomir. A pogrom of the Jews took place in that town, and I fought back as a member of a self-defense unit. The tsar's police and Cossacks helped the pogrom bandits by attacking our unit. A saber's slash cut me near the collar-bone and nearly blinded me in the right eye. I lost consciousness and came to

45

only in the evening of that fateful day, on a hospital cot. Some of my comrades were near by, also wounded; others had been killed. My wound healed rapidly, but the memory of the first battle with the tsar's henchmen remained forever. Soon afterward, on leaving the hospital, I was subjected to police searches and other tsarist persecution. I felt I was indeed a full-fledged revolutionary.

I was a Menshevik from the very beginning of my Marxism. In this I was decided by the idea of the people's right to self-government, to true democracy, the principal characteristic of Menshevism. For even in those early years Bolshevism, on the contrary, was based on the premise that a revolutionary minority could and should lead the majority of the people, despite the latter's wishes, if need be. And that idea was eventually to bring a dictatorship to Russia, in the name of "the people's interests."

It must be noted, however, that in my spiritual development and early revolutionary work I was guided not by Marxism as a theory, not by any dry economic formulas of the Social Democratic movement. The basic and decisive factor was in my moral searches, my general idealistic strivings. What I day-dreamed of was a kingdom of freedom, equality, and social justice; for, mark you, I had come out of that Jewish milieu where the old traditions of romantic mysticism were still alive, where the word "miracle" was a true clarion call that woke men's hearts. This feeling fitted in perfectly with the sermons of certain Russian moralists and sociologists, who addressed themselves, not to man's mind alone, but to his conscience and emotions, too.

When I had passed my high-school examinations, I resolved to go to college. A university education would have practical consequences of much importance to me: the diploma would give me the right to move all over Russia as I pleased, a right denied to Jews unless they were within a privileged category; a university course, when completed, would put a Jew in this category. And I wanted to move freely about the nation—to live, if I wished, in its largest cities, where political life was throbbing, where I could come closer to the very sources of the Russian working-class and socialist movement.

But since the doors of Russian universities were not open to me, a poor underprivileged Jew, I decided to break the vicious circle by going abroad, there to gain my higher schooling. And so I left for Vienna and its university, earning my way through college by tutoring. Celebrated philosophers, econo-mists, and historians were among my professors. Young Austrian and German socialists were among my fellow-students, some of whom lived to become famous as the leaders of Europe's political and intellectual life.

I remember my introduction to the first of May as a workers' holiday. I was greatly impressed by the sight of the gay, yet determined, multitude, parading with flags and music in the name of socialism and international solidarity. Fiery speeches by Victor Adler and other Austrian Marxists were to me soul-lifting and inspiring, a strange and unforgettable experience.

The events of 1905 in Russia brought me back to the homeland. I plunged

46

at once into the widening, rising revolutionary movement. Odessa was my destination—for the heroic tale of the uprising of the crew of the battleship "Potemkin" had suggested great possibilities in that seaport.

I came with a letter of recommendation from Plekhanov himself, whom I had met by then. This gave me entree into the underground Social Democratic organization of Odessa, then uniting both the Mensheviks and the Bolsheviks. I also participated in the local labor-union activities, then mostly illegal from the viewpoint of the tsar's gendarmes.

Thus passed the years of 1905–7, years of much tumult, high hopes, and bleak disappointment. Among my friends and fellow-undergrounders were many persons who were to distinguish themselves ten and more years later in the revolution of 1917. In 1905–7 I worked with them in the Odessa organization, for I was soon a member of the local committee of the Social Democratic party. We met at secret assemblies; we also got together at rare intervals of rest and leisure. When the tsar's police were too close for these men's comfort, I helped my new comrades. I myself was often only a step ahead of the pursuing gendarmes, but my star seemed to be lucky. Often I managed to get out of the tightest possible corners untouched. And again, as on so many occasions in my childhood, it was simple men and women of the people who came to my aid amid those dangers. My feeling of sympathy and respect for the masses was ever and again refreshed and strengthened.

Those who assisted me were Jews as well as Gentiles. Well do I remember the time when, at the very doorway of a house where a clandestine meeting of our Social Democratic committee was to take place, I spotted some suspicious characters. Detectives, I decided. It was too late to turn away. Boldly I kept on walking, but, instead of entering the doorway, I used the near-by gate leading into the courtyard of the same house. This was to suggest to the detectives that I lived in the house and was merely re-entering my own flat from its kitchen entrance.

Once in the building, however, I rang the very first bell in the very first hall—making sure, of course, that it was not the door of the apartment where the illegal meeting was to take place. A Jew opened the door. He was the householder—a tailor by profession, I later learned. The day happened to be a Saturday, and he had just come back from his synagogue. His wife and his pretty daughter stood behind him, both with puzzled expressions. Quickly I explained to them who I was and the danger that threatened me. "Let me stay here until the police go away," I pleaded.

At first the man and his wife were terrified, but they calmed down and even grew bold. I was installed in one of the inner rooms and began to play the role of the young girl's tutor. There we sat, surrounded by her textbooks, and listened to the heavy footsteps of the police stamping up and down the stairs and halls outside the apartment.

Two hours passed in this suspense. Once a gendarme opened the door, but, seeing an old Jew in a skullcap in the first room, he did not bother to investigate the rest of the apartment and left. Even after the police had finally departed, the tailor and his wife would not let me go but kept on peeking out repeatedly. Only much later did they decide that the coast was clear.

The sequence of this episode was rather interesting: the young girl became intrigued, started to read revolutionary literature, and soon joined our movement. It was through her that I met my future wife, a girl who was also helping the common cause of the revolution.

Another time I was detailed by the committee to deliver a speech at a secret assembly of soldiers in the summer camp of a tsarist regiment. The meeting convened at night, in the reception room of a local doctor. But hardly had I started my speech when our sentry rushed in: gendarmes of the tsar were approaching the building! If I, a civilian, were caught in the act of propagandizing His Majesty's troops, severe punishment would be my lot. Nor would the soldiers escape easily. But the soldiers thought first of me. Quickly tying together their leather belts, they lowered me from a second-story window into a back yard, whence a reliable guide took me into an adjacent grove. I was saved.

I was deeply touched by this thoughtfulness on the part of the soldiers, these simple sons of the long-suffering people, who made my rescue possible before they took care of themselves.

After this episode, however, I realized that my remaining in Odessa would do the cause no earthly good. I left for my native village.

My parents were glad to see me and forgave me for running away. They were resigned to my independent existence and were delighted with my visit, however short it might be. I did not stay with them for long. Having found a tutor's position in the home of a near-by landlord, I moved there.

I led a peaceful life in that mansion, except that on one occasion, upon returning home from a walk in the fields, I saw that all my papers and books had mysteriously disappeared. Soon I learned that a detachment of Cossacks had just arrived in the nearest village and that some of the local peasant lads, who by then were among my staunchest friends, had decided that the tsar's horsemen must be looking for me. Fearing that the Cossacks would search my room, the boys had made a beeline for the mansion, climbed through a window into my chamber, and removed everything which they thought might compromise me. After the Cossacks were gone (without even inquiring about me), I asked my friends: "But where are my papers and books?"

Shamefacedly they confessed that in their excess of zeal and caution, they had dumped my little library into the nearest pond. This included even such innocent works as my books on physics and geometry. But, of course, I could only laugh and thank them.

All such episodes made me feel with an especial poignancy the bond between myself and the people—the very people in whose name, for whose sake, we wanted a revolution and an overthrow of tsarism. And though the revolutionary wave of 1905 was put down and the tsarist reaction that followed was long and severe, we knew that the people would again be with us when we were ready for the second and final attempt.

(8)

NO TSARIST

IN THE SUMMER OF 1907 THE TSARIST GOVERNMENT PUT AN ABRUPT END TO THE Second Duma, the young Russian parliament. Throughout the land scores of thousands of people were imprisoned. Punitive expeditions and death sentences terrorized the nation. In this period of furious reaction the revolutionary organizations of Russia suffered greatly. The sheer physical defeat brought with it inner disappointment and moral fatigue to the underground workers. Intellectuals were depressed and apathetic; some socialists were "liquidating" their maximum demands, their enthusiasms. Under such circumstances it was difficult to continue revolutionary propaganda. Connections between many fighting groups and individuals were broken. Friends were torn apart by the whirlwind of tsarist persecution and police searches.

My personal position was not too hopeful. To avoid being arrested, I had to flee to Kiev. Separated from my fellow-combatants, I was at a loss to know what to do next for the defeated but still beloved cause. I had no money, no means of livelihood; hence the first task, while waiting for the revolution to gather its strength once more, seemed to be to find a job, to make a living.

A friend of my cousin in Zhitomir gave me a letter to the owner of a timber-exporting firm in Kiev, and I got a minor job. At that time I knew nothing of woods except their poetry; but here was the practical, commercial side of the sylvan beauty of Russia. I quickly became completely engrossed in the duties of my new clerical berth with the timber concern.

At first my interest was purely in the scientific, technical features of the lumber business. I was struck by the tremendous amount of mathematical calculations, as well as expert knowledge of woods, required in the timber operations as they were being planned beforehand in that office. Each oak called for a masterful analysis before it was chopped down and transformed into salable boards. The analysts, the calculators, the merchants, and the exporters dealing with Russia's wealth of forests had to be virtuosos—and they were.

From the very beginning I wanted to be no less expert than these men at this unique art and science. I plunged into the mathematics of timber areas and sawmill capacities. As I ate and dreamed, as I dressed and walked and talked, my thoughts were with the woods and their output. Soon I gained my goal: I

49

was a recognized specialist in the most complex timber calculations of the day. I even compiled a table of timber calculations, which was published as a manual for the trade and in time was used by timber men the country over.

Starting at a small salary, I advanced rapidly enough to be able to attend the University of Kiev in my spare time. Within a few years, although still a college student, I was on the boards of directors of several timber companies. The university sent me abroad to study European markets for Russian lumber, and I found myself a member of a special commission of the Timber Department of the tsar's Ministry of Agriculture. This commission had been appointed to review and improve Russia's trade agreement with Germany, then about to expire.

On the eve of World War I, in 1914, I was at the head of three large timber companies of Russia. The works I managed were scattered from one end of the empire to another, and I had to travel now to the Urals, now to the Caucasus, then to Siberia, and back to the western borders of Russia. As I journeyed, I met outstanding representatives of the nation's landed aristocracy, also various financiers, industrialists, and bureaucrats of tsardom.

It seemed impossible. Here I was, fresh from the revolutionary underground, working and making friends with the masters of the tsar's economic and political regime! And yet, despite this new life and notwithstanding my novel and astounding earnings, I doggedly stuck to my radical views. If anything, my encounters and collaboration with the mighty of tsarist Russia further strengthened my feeling that cardinal changes of social and political conditions in the empire were inevitable. For now, more clearly than ever before, I saw the horrible width and depth of the chasm separating the masses of the Russian people from the handful of landlords, bankers, and court officials ruling the country and enjoying all the rights and privileges on earth.

Kiev was the social and commercial center of the entire southwest of Russia, with its plenitude of great manors and estates belonging to certain prominent members of tsarist aristocracy. I worked at the estimating and improvement of the wooded riches belonging to Durnovo, a former minister of the interior. On another occasion I was engaged to make calculations and do marketing for the forests of Brasovo, an estate of Grand Duke Michael Romanov, the tsar's brother. Still later, I was asked to form a chamber of foreign commerce for the magnates of the southwest, with special reference to timber-export possibilities. While establishing this organization in Kiev, I came to know the Balashovs, one of the wealthiest families of old Russia.

The Balashovs were noblemen, as were their kinsmen, the Vorontsov-Dashkovs and the Shuvalovs. The three clans were among the staunchest pillars of the tsarist regime, economically as well as politically. The Balashovs especially were an enterprising breed who loved to plan and scheme on a large scale. In particular, this family was partly responsible for the Russo-Japanese war of 1904-5—their fondness for forests led them to seek and gain the ill-famed timber concessions on the Yalu River in the Far East, the concessions that alarmed the Japanese to the point of eventually attacking the Russian fleet at Port Arthur early in 1904. Ivan Petrovich Balashov was the chief concessionary. Such court families as the Oldenburgs never forgave him and his kin these concessions and their sequel, the unfortunate war with Japan; and the Balashovs were blamed for the war by practically the entire nobility of the tsar.

These Balashovs had a truly remarkable weakness for forests and their exploitations, and they preached a singular "historic mission" as their alibi. According to this theory, the nobility of Russia *had* to change over to an industrial leadership so as to obviate the otherwise unavoidable conflict between the landowning aristocracy and the rising business class. Only such a peaceful evolution of the nobles into industrialists and businessmen, said the Balashovs, would save Russia from an impending revolution. And, they went on, what could be more logical and natural for the nobles, as their first industrial and commercial pursuit, than this exploitation of their own abundant woods?

Ivan Petrovich Balashov was the more energetic of the two brothers, who had been schoolmates of Tsar Alexander III, the father of Nicholas II (or the Last); they had also been among the closest advisers of Alexander III up to his death in 1894. The Balashovs owned vast properties: some 2,700,000 acres of land throughout Russia; sugar-mills in several corners of the Ukraine; saltworks at Solikamsk in the north; timber areas in the Urals; and, in the same Ural hills, the entire Simsky region, one of the richest mineral fields in the country, a gift to the family from Catherine the Great, I believe.

Before the end of the nineteenth century, the enormous forests of the Balashovs in the Urals had been hardly touched. Now, however, whatever wood was need for the family's metalworks and mineral works in the Urals was chopped down regardless, and some of the most valuable kinds of wood known to man thus perished senselessly.

Only a small part of the chopped wood was rafted down the Kama River for the outside market. But because of the long distances, the rafting took two or three months, and poor management brought the Balashovs nothing but losses. Because of this they engaged me to survey and improve their timber operations—to teach them practical methods of carrying out their newly conceived "historic mission."

When I traveled for this family, sometimes a whole month was taken up by a trip through their forests. Pillows, huge loaves of bread, and many hard-boiled eggs were part of my baggage, for there were stretches without any human habitation or food for three and four days at a time. Even when I found a forester's hut, the insects in the little house were usually so overpowering that I preferred to use my own pillows outdoors, in winter as well as in summer. On occasion my fellow-travelers and I shot a hare, and this was the extent of our provisions for a day or two.

At times we rested in a monastery or a nunnery. The monks and the nuns

51

were most hospitable, and we talked with them for hours. These people were almost completely cut off from the rest of the world; scarcely any news ever reached them except through such rare travelers as ourselves or a visiting petty official of the region. To me these stopovers were romance itself—because of my feeling of being so far away from the main stream of life, because of the stern yet handsome faces of the nuns, because of the deep silence of the endless forests all around me.

The customs and psychology in these nunneries and monasteries were truly of another Russia—of ancient times or at least the Middle Ages. The nuns and monks often spoke of "innovations" with a horror amazing to behold. They hated everything "rebellious"—that is, whatever seemed to be the consequence, in fact or spirit, of the miscarried revolution of 1905. And yet in their time, centuries back, these retreats had been established in this wilderness by men and women who were, in a sense, revolutionaries. Their founders had been either religious rebels or freedom-loving people who fled to the borderland from the persecutions and injustices of the tsars and the boyars. Here again I saw the many-faceted paradoxes of Russia—the peculiar amalgam of her backward ignorance and her forward drive, of her immobility and her rebelliousness.

After such trips into the wilderness of forests and narrowness of human thought, I sometimes happened to come into the town of Perm, which was then one of the clearing houses for revolutionaries being shipped from European Russia to the prisons or exile of Siberia. The contrast between the motionless crust of the monasteries and the ardent spirit of these revolutionists was even further heightened.

I tried to help the revolutionaries in chains as much as I could. I used my new contacts with the powers that were, suggesting to the latter that certain exiles be permitted to settle down in the larger towns where life would be easier for them, and seeing to the convicts' supplies of warm clothing and medicine and better food. Some revolutionaries were brought by the tsarist police to settle down as exiles in the Cherdyn country of the Urals. The Balashovs owned huge forests and saltworks out there, and this gave me an opportunity to find agreeable work for the exiles in the estates of my new friends and employers.

In Perm I sometimes met old friends, both Bolsheviks and Mensheviks, as they made their chained or police-escorted way east. Such encounters moved me deeply, bringing forth not only memories of the recent past but also the renewed hope for a better future for these people—for the whole of Russia. And then back I would go into the world of my aristocratic employers who did not seem even to suspect that deep beneath the surface of Russia the first tremors of an earthquake were rumbling, bringing doom for all the splendor of the autocratic empire.

Many a time I saw plainly that the nobility realized little of what was going on around them. With the rebellion of 1905 put down so luckily, they now believed in the unshakable firmness of the tsarist regime, which gave them their riches and their position. Yet, eighty years earlier, the ancestors of some of these very people had been the recruits of the Decembrist revolt against tsarist absolutism and for a constitutional government. And often, even now, their children were to be found in the ranks of the new revolutionists.

In this connection I vividly recall one such feudalistic gentleman, Prince Oldenburg, an uncle of the tsar. I met him in his great Caucasian estates, where he followed his old-fashioned way, using his cane upon those of his subordinates who happened to displease him. Even if a person was not a subordinate but merely a visitor, by appearing within the confines of the Oldenburg estates or the nearest town of Gagry the stranger exposed himself to whatever course of action the prince deemed necessary. Witness the following instance:

In the midst of World War I, a newlywed pair of high-society folk came down from Petrograd to spend their honeymoon at the seashore of Gagry. The beauty of the young bride attracted an officer staying with Prince Oldenburg. Honeymoon or not, the young woman yielded. Soon the story made the rounds of the town and reached the ear of the prince, who, however, did not think it funny. Outraged in his feelings of propriety, the prince ordered the immediate departure of the woman and her luckless husband. The next steamer was leaving at six o'clock in the morning, and the prince's aides rushed the couple to the dock at that hour. Mortified, the bride broke away from the guards and jumped into the sea. She was at once pulled out and revived. Prince Oldenburg was not only the satrap of the region but, as was the custom in those days, the chairman of the local Society of Rescue on the Waters; notified of the near-tragedy, he hastened to the dock, placed the woman in his carriage, carefully covered her with his greatcoat, and took her back to the city, chiding her on the way in unprintable language and with the constant refrain: "And how could you, in my Gagry, dare to pull such stunts!" I heard this story, in all its comic detail, on a visit to Gagry a few days after the couple had been successfully removed from the town.

My own journey to this sunny, subtropical region of the Caucasus was made for two reasons. One was the new railroad, then being constructed along the Black Sea shore and in need of ties and other timber which I was to estimate and supply. The other reason was an investigation I was to make of the sanitary conditions of a camp for some two thousand German and Austrian prisoners of war laboring in the timber areas and sawmills near Gagry. It so happened that these timber-works and mills were leased in Prince Oldenburg's domains by a company headed by the man he so disliked—Ivan Petrovich Balashov. And so here I was, the company's manager, in the principality of my employer's foe.

It was my duty to call upon the prince the very first thing on my arrival in Gagry. Some of my friends who accompanied me to Gagry were worried, for all of us had heard of the prince's eccentricities. We had enough cause to worry,

53

but I had no choice. Bidding goodbye to my friends, who were plainly trembling for my fate, I went to see the prince.

I was ushered into his presence, and as we began to converse I mentioned two new small woodworking machines which, I had learned, had been recently installed in a plant on one of his estates near by. Actually the machines —as well as the prince's few plants and mills—were nothing remarkable. One turned out plywood screens for the prince's beloved tangerine trees; the other peeled wood and manufactured excelsior for packing these tangerines as they were brought in from the local groves of Gagry. No startling mechanism, either one of them, but the prince was immensely pleased with his technical achievements on the primitive cliffs of the Caucasus. The fact that I knew of them and mentioned them in my first breath flattered him; he at once felt that he was way ahead of his enemies, the Balashovs, and that I, a valued employee of his rivals, must be recognizing this superiority in this very remark. As if to say, "Ah, but you've seen nothing yet," he forthwith took me to his kitchen to show me a very modern electrical stove. It was indeed a rarity for the Russia of the time.

This first audience granted me by the satrap lasted ten minutes. Such was the customary ritual. Safe and sound, I returned to my hotel. Within a half-hour the prince's chamberlain called upon me with his master's invitation to come to luncheon in the castle. When I arrived, I found about thirty other guests, all of them military men of various ranks.

Some time later the prince himself rode over to my hotel with a friendly summons to join him in his carriage for a tour of his forests and other properties. My stay in Gagry lasted several days, and not a single one passed without a meeting of one sort or another with the old man.

When the time came for me to start back to Petrograd, I was given a practical demonstration of the limitless extent of the prince's power. Because of a military emergency, all passenger traffic had just been suspended for a fortnight by the tsarist government. A special permit was needed if one wanted to travel. Upon hearing of my difficulty the prince telegraphed the right quarters, and I was given not only the necessary permit but also a special compartment and entirely too much care and civility all the long way to the capital. In Rostov, for instance, despite the early morning hour at which the train arrived, a military gentleman entered my compartment to click his heels, salute, and inquire whether everything was to my satisfaction. A similar performance awaited me at each important step. The last of the series was staged when the train finally reached Petrograd—much to my relief.

All this was on the very eve of the revolution of 1917. In fact, the great upheaval was but a few days in the offing. The Mad Monk, Gregory Rasputin, had been assassinated the preceding December, and the air was charged with the expectation of a terrific political storm. The mood of opposition to the

54

tsar's court, to the entire inept government of the Romanovs and their nobles, could be felt even in the hitherto moderate circles of Russian society.

And yet, at the topmost rungs of the Russian ladder, among such exalted persons as the Balashovs and Prince Oldenburg, a curious feeling of self-confidence and complacency prevailed. These men understood nothing. However, the tycoons of Russia's industries and finances were not distinguished by any gift of clairvoyance either. As the angry people began to rise, the businessmen no less than the court's nobles were certain that one or two hundred Cossacks could easily quell the rebellion.

Two or three days before the overthrow of tsarism, I was at a conference of the board of directors of the Sormovo-Kolomna metalworks, one of the largest combines of its kind, which also owned certain sawmills, then under my management. As we sat and deliberated, we suddenly heard rifle shots. Rushing to the windows, we beheld detachments of soldiers firing at a workers' demonstration. One volley was enough to disperse the crowd, and yet it was evident that the workers were not running away for long, that many of them were turning back to re-form their ranks under their red banners, shouting for bread and urging their fellows to rejoin them.

Alexis Meshchersky, director-in-chief of the metalworks, was standing by my side and gazing at the unique sight in no particular alarm. Nevertheless, he seemed to dislike the slow movements of the troops on the street below. He said to me: "It's too bad the authorities are acting with such caution, afraid to shed blood. We need a real blood-letting, to put a quick end to all these disorders."

I was shocked, for Meshchersky was generally considered one of the most progressive industrialists of Russia. He was not a powerful and wealthy magnate in his own right. Still an engineer, it was with the help of his own brain and brawn and not of any inherited riches that he had reached the top of the social ladder in old Russia. The metalworks, which he was then running, did not really belong to him but were controlled by Russian and foreign capital, which, in fact, controlled and bossed him, too. In private conversations he would often wax indignant over the stupidity of the tsarist regime and was not averse from welcoming certain reforms. But when he said "democracy" he really meant "anarchy," and this he feared and hated.

In tsarist times I was a frequent participant in the conferences of sundry councils of Russian industrialists. Some of the latter had come up the hard way, beginning as poor and radically inclined university students and attaining their commanding posts after many years of intellectual and physical sweat. A majority of them were opposed to the tsarist regime, seeing in it as they did a feudalistic encumbrance. They felt that industrial capital was the lawful heir of this regime and should take over. But it was the working class that represented the only real and fighting force of the revolution against tsarism and its feudalism. The industrialists were afraid of the workers and also of the peasants. They declared openly that they were ready and willing to make

55

their peace with the tsarist regime in order to withstand the desires and demands of the working class and, in part, of the peasantry, too.

In the more progressive strata of Russian society we could discern awareness that the revolution against tsarism could triumph only if Russia's most active classes—the workers and the peasants—received some social boons in the process. Some Russian capitalists would not have minded seeing the workers and the peasants overthrow tsarism—but they would not allow for one moment the unpleasant thought that capital, too, would have to make concessions to those very classes which might make this revolution a success.

The more I observed this state of affairs, the clearer my realization became that the coming revolution could not be bloodless. I also felt that the blame for such bloodletting would properly be affixed, not to the cruelty and sternness of certain elements among the revolutionaries, but to the egotism and greed of the dominant classes. The latter apparently could not be expected to sacrifice even a small part of their privileges for the sake of a bloodless success in the impending revolution.

When the revolution of February and March, 1917, finally did arrive, I hailed it with faith and enthusiasm. Here was my youthful dream come true! For me there could be no question of whether or not to join the revolution. At once I would place myself—all my strength and knowledge—at the disposal of the freed people.

One of the very first nights of the revolution I was coming home past the burning precinct stations of the tsar's police. All that I saw around me reminded me of descriptions of the taking of the Bastille. The same night, on reaching my home and desk, I wrote letters of resignation to all the industrial companies in which I served as a director. I wanted to be free to serve the revolution. The next morning I was in the Taurida Palace, the center of the revolution, to offer my services to the new government.

I was appointed to the Economic Branch of the Petrograd Soviet of Workers Deputies, also to the vice-chairmanship of an organization which was to insure a supply of wood fuel to the railroads of Russia.

There were troubles. I recall with what hatred the prominent engineers of Russia, still identifying themselves with capitalism but not with the people, met the first workers deputized by their comrades to confer with the management. This was, in embryo, that struggle which later developed full-blown between the Soviet workers and the specialists and which, at least in part, was responsible for the disorganization of Russian industry. It is noteworthy that the hostility between the capitalists and the workers sharpened in 1917, the year when the tsar's bureaucrats were replaced by the capitalists delegated by the Provisional Government.

I remember, too, with what little understanding certain men of the old regime faced this great upheaval of 1917. A few days after the overthrow of the monarchy, a smartly dressed officer came to see me in the Economic

Branch of the Petrograd Soviet. He handed me an application. I read it and looked up in surprise. This was the Grand Duke Michael Romanov, the brother of the last tsar, who only a few days before this had himself refused to occupy the vacant throne. His application dealt with hunting: he wished us to permit him to go after some game in one of his wooded estates near Tsarskoye Selo. We gave him the desired permission, but we certainly were astonished— astonished to see the tsar's brother turning to thoughts of hunting when the entire nation was concerned with its very fate.

Then on the third day of the revolution I was invited to the house of Nicholas Petrovich Balashov, who was, among other things, a former member of the tsar's State Council. When I arrived I found a family conference in full swing, with some of the employees participating and voicing their respectful opinions. My advice was also solicited. And what was the burning topic of discussion? Nothing more or less than the problem of what to do with the Balashovs' celebrated wine cellar, which included a number of bottles from Napoleonic times. The wine cellars of the tsar's Winter Palace had just been broken into and taken apart by a mob of thirsty soldiers; the same fate might strike the Balashov cellar. The final decision of this unique council was to distribute Balashov wines and liquors among relatives and friends. But it was reached only after a long and passionate discussion, as if the fate of these wines was more important than the fate of the Russian nation.

In July, 1917, I was again in the Balashov house, this time looking out of its fine windows together with one of the younger Balashovs, a former leader of the conservative nationalists in the Duma. We were watching one of the first armed Bolshevik demonstrations against the Kerensky government, the so-called "July Insurrection." Balashov, the son, remarked to me: "I pray to God for one thing only: that the Bolsheviks do seize power. We will then have a brief blood-bath, and the revolution will be over."

Five years later I met his father at the German spa of Baden-Baden. Nicholas Balashov was then an octogenarian. Both the years and the revolution had left telling marks on his once hardy physique, but he still hoped for a return of the past. "How soon will those accursed Bolsheviks be kicked out, how soon, ha?" he kept asking me.

I had an acute feeling of wonder, mixed with pity and ire, when early and late in the Russian revolution I saw this lack of understanding, this mental dulness—nay, blindness—of many who had been pillars of the old regime. They simply could not believe that an end had come to their position, their might, their privileges.

In contrast to this outlook, the rosy, holiday-like mood that had embraced us, the supporters of the revolution, had vanished a few days after the February revolution of 1917. We knew there were hardships and tumult ahead. The struggle of the various parties threatened to bring on a civil war and a series of new upheavals, and this indeed happened in time. With every new day there appeared among the seemingly united Russian people the widening fissures of class, race, and economic disagreements. The Russian army did not want to fight; the front against the Central Powers was melting away. Germany and her allies were awaiting the best possible moment, now not too far off, to jump upon a weakening Russia. The situation was becoming increasingly complex and depressing.

And yet one thing was plain to me. Whatever ties bound me to the Mensheviks, I must not tear myself away from the Russian people and its destiny. I must remain a servitor of the revolution within my modest capacities, no matter what the circumstances and consequences. And this decision I carried out at the price of many sacrifices and hardships. It shaped my life after the Bolsheviks came to power in the fall of 1917.

But I was not and could not be a Bolshevik. I was not born—I was not reared by the forces that molded me—to be a Bolshevik. And even many of those who, unlike me, were born Bolsheviks died without seeing the triumph of their ideas and emotions—died, in fact, with a bitter feeling of being hounded to death by the very forces which they had believed in and had brought to a powerful existence.

(9)

KRASSIN, GENTLEMAN OF THE SOVIETS

AMONG THE MEN OF THE EARLY SOVIET PHASE WHO WERE NOT DESTINED TO SEE the promised land of their dreams and work, Leonid Krassin was surely one of the most brilliant personalities. And though he labored in the common vineyard, he was certainly in a class by himself, one of those men of whom it is said that the pattern is thrown away by his Maker after his creation.

Even in his appearance Krassin was quite unlike the general run of Lenin's Communist aides. Perfect taste always distinguished his attire. His necktie matched his suit and shirt in color, and even his stickpin was stuck with the special jauntiness of a well-dressed man. No matter how bitter the weather, he avoided wearing felt boots. Nor did he favor the sheepskin coats which his colleagues found indispensable in the unheated Soviet offices during the winters of the civil war.

Tall and swarthy, with lively sweeping gestures, he drew attention wherever he went. His wedge-shaped, neatly groomed beard lengthened his already oblong face, with its high forehead beneath the smoothly parted, gray-black hair. When he smiled, his mouth grew wider, revealing his beautiful white teeth, and the dimples on his cheeks became deeper, adding to the attractiveness of his face. His eyes were intelligent and sly and reflected now his utter seriousness, now his impetuous gaiety. When Krassin was merry, you inevitably thought what a mischievous lad he must have been in his youth.

Krassin had been an active Bolshevik even before the first revolution of 1905, and it was during that abortive upheaval that he became a close friend of Lenin. In the years of reaction that followed he forsook active revolutionary work, serving, from 1908 on, as a high-salaried electrical engineer in Berlin, with the firm of Siemens and Schuckert. This concern had factories in Russia as well, and in 1912 they sent Krassin to Moscow. In 1914, at the outbreak of the Russo-German war, the tsar's government removed all Germans from leading posts in Russian industry, and Krassin became the manager of the extensive Siemens and Schuckert plants in Russia. His headquarters were in Petrograd, and that is where the revolution of 1917 found him—holding a responsible post and enjoying a large income.

In the spring of 1917, soon after the overthrow of tsarism, I often met Krassin in the home of some mutual friends of ours. At that time he spoke with emphatic disapproval of the political stand taken by Lenin and his group, even though he still retained his personal contact with Lenin; for he was an old friend not only of Lenin himself but also of Lenin's brother-in-law, M. T. Yelizarov (who was married to Lenin's sister Anna). During the few months of the Kerensky government, Krassin regarded Lenin's idea as "the delirium of a utopian" and predicted a terrible catastrophe for the Bolsheviks. In his anticipation of bloodshed and chaos in Russia, Krassin sent his wife and children away to Norway as early as July, 1917.

In the spring of 1918 he went to visit them, and on the way back stopped in Berlin. Just then Adolph Joffe, the first Soviet envoy in Germany, was negotiating various economic matters with the German government. On beholding Krassin, Joffe begged him to be his consultant, for Krassin knew both Germany and economics.

Later Krassin told me that before leaving for Russia he was called to the imperial staff headquarters, for General Ludendorff himself wanted to see him. Blindfolded, Krassin was taken in an automobile hundreds of miles back of the German-Russian frontier. His conversation with Ludendorff lasted two hours. He spoke to the war-lord of a number of Soviet objections to the not-too-smooth course of relations with Germany that followed the Treaty of Brest Litovsk. Ludendorff was chary of words. The substance of his remarks to Krassin was: "We need your grain. If you want to exist, you must see to it that our armies are well fed."

In August, 1918, on returning to Moscow, Krassin began to work actively as one of the main leaders in the Soviet government. The Bolsheviks were delighted. Proudly they said that in Krassin they had gained an outstanding Communist, as well as a first-rate businessman. He started out in the Soviet government by managing the Red Army's supplies; later he shifted to the post of people's commissar of communications.

By nature Krassin was an industrialist. He felt that Russia's main trouble lay in her industrial backwardness. In his impatience with the country's uncouthness and clumsiness he shared some of Gorky's views. When projects of nation-wide electrification came to the fore, they pleased Krassin as much as they fired Lenin. I remember that in the beaming presence of Krassin and other approving aides, Lenin once said: "With the peasant, electricity shall take God's place. Let the peasant pray to electricity. It will make him feel the power of our government rather than Heaven's."

Soon after his return from Germany, I saw Krassin in his room at the Metropole. He told me that he knew how difficult it was to work with the Soviet government at that time but that the revolution must take its course—there was no other path for Russia.

"The country needs a strong government!" he exclaimed. "The Russian peasant must be cleansed of his age-old mange. Can't do it with kid gloves, you know. We have to persecute as well as persuade. And all the economists, engineers, and other experts must give us a hand in this work. Boycotting and sabotaging of all kinds will help no one but the enemy."

In conclusion he declared that his new assignment from Lenin was to enlist all the non-Communist experts as loyal employees of the new government and that I must help him in this recruiting.

From the very beginning the man was successful in his novel activities. He was intimate with Lenin, and, on the other hand, he had a multitude of contacts in a wide range of social strata, including the former tycoons of Russian capital. The freedom with which he continued to criticize the powers that were, the easy manner and the general skill with which he handled all sorts of people, soon won him a unique position in Moscow. He was very popular, a magnetic center for individuals and groups of highly varied tendencies and characteristics.

Lenin valued Krassin above all as a rare blend of the true Bolshevik and the expert businessman, something that he had sought long and, on the whole, unsuccessfully. Lenin was impressed with the fact that the capitalist world had paid Krassin a large income for his talents and that it was "quite something" for the Soviets to be able to appear with Krassin in the bourgeois world. "See," Lenin would boast to his intimates, "for the outside world Krassin will be one more proof that we are not exactly a bunch of visionaries, bookworms, and sans-culottes."

Gradually Lenin referred to Krassin an increasing number of problems of economic policy, both foreign and domestic. Later their scope widened to include general political questions. Lenin's high opinion of Krassin was soon adopted as their own by the entire inner sanctum of Communism. The Communist leaders bragged, "Ah, but our Krassin is an expert, too. *Our* expert, not a stranger, not a bourgeois, but a stonewall Bolshevik."

Krassin, on the other hand, always emphasized his foreign experience and contacts—his cosmopolitanism. He often broadly hinted that he had accepted hardships and privations by returning from Germany to Russia of his own free will; that he had even parted with his family, who would not accompany him back to the torn, bleeding, upset, and upsetting homeland. Also, he let it be known that he was not one of those Russian intellectuals like the non-Communist experts, jellyfish individuals who had many duties and no rights; that he had been among the earliest instigators of the Bolshevik theory and practice of revolution while many of the others were "knee-high to a grasshopper."

Nevertheless, Krassin's influence was felt most among precisely these intellectuals outside the Communist party. First of all, he rallied the engineers and economists who once upon a time, in their youth, had sympathized with Bolshevism but had later drifted away from it. They now found it much easier to deal with Krassin than with Lenin or Trotsky. In Krassin's home and office I met many such former Bolsheviks. In 1918, thanks to Krassin, they returned by easy stages to active collaboration with the ruling party. Presently many of them were given high posts in the new government. In addition, to Krassin came most of the outstanding engineers who had not dabbled in politics but who at this time were anti-Communist. The revolution had thrown them overboard—they had lost their fine jobs and ample incomes and were now eking out a bare existence on the fringes of the newly woven economic fabric, as meek consultants, second-class assistants, and so forth. Many had known Krassin in the old days, having met him in this bank or that, in this directors' boardroom or that. On entering his Soviet office they began by reminding him:

"You remember me, don't you, Leonid Borisovich? We met at the Russo-Asiatic Bank, also at Putilov's....."

Before the revolution Krassin had been not only the No. 1 man for Siemens and Schuckert in Russia but had also been on the board of the great Baranovsky machine-works. Through a bank which in those years was financing the works, his connections had become amazingly far reaching. Now his new reception room in Lenin's Moscow was thronged by such demoted aces of Russian industry as the chairman of the Kazan Railroad board, the head of the Nizhni-Novgorod Fair Committee (an especially powerful figure in old Russia's merchant world), or the chief engineers of the Sormovo-Kolomna works, or all the top leaders of Petrograd's heavy industry.

Milling around in this same anteroom, too, were not a few shady characters, wartime fly-by-nights, and former profiteers. Until the revolution these individuals had been busy running errands behind the scenes of important industrial establishments, serving as contact men or brokers in settling all sorts of affairs with the War Department and other ministries, securing orders, purchasing materials, and so forth. In the new era they were looking for something new to do and so parked at Krassin's doorstep.

Krassin was also surrounded by the leading stars of Russia's artistic world, particularly since his brother Boris was connected with the theater but also because the Russian actors and artists of the period were eager to restore their old ties with western Europe and Krassin was their "window to Europe." Through him it was possible to meet the various Europeans who came to his office or house the moment they arrived in Russia. In 1918 and 1919 many Russian actors and artists nursed plans of showing Europe what Russian art was and what it could do. This, in their opinion, would help to break the Allies' blockade of Russia. If I remember correctly, Catherine Geltser herself, the most famous of Russian ballerinas, worked energetically toward that end.

Many of these theater folk, incidentally, came to me, too—with little notes from Krassin. They needed fuel, and I was it. And so they sat in my reception room, awaiting their turn to implore me, these stars old and new, these prima ballerinas, and some of the latter's aristocratic husbands. They begged me for wood and tried to soften me by inviting me to share a bowl of borshch with them. There were among them many unfortunates whom the Cheka had managed to enlist as its spies. And every time I received such an invitation to share their borshch, I thought to myself, "Is this a trap?"

Krassin had a special knack for talking to each one of these people in just the right terms and tone, so that they melted and poured their hearts out to him; for they saw in him not a Bolshevik but "one of ours." He really helped many of them in their troubles with the Cheka, which was then on a rampage. His own attitude toward the Cheka was extremely independent. While visiting in his office, I often heard him demand imperiously over the telephone: "Release X immediately. I need him in my work, and I vouch for his loyalty."

When talking with his non-Communist visitors and aides, he spoke of them and himself as "we" and of the Soviet government as "they." (Of course, he reversed the process in his conversations in the Kremlin or the Cheka or other Communist institutions.) But even in his private chats with non-Communist experts, he liked to emphasize the fact that Lenin was in a category all his own, that one could trust Lenin. "Lenin is not one of those blunderhead Communists, I assure you," he put it.

Krassin's popularity among non-Communists sometimes led to unexpected results. One day the wife of an army officer came to Krassin in tears: her husband had just been arrested by the Cheka on charges of collaborating with the Whites. Woudn't Krassin please help? Krassin would and did. The officer was released—and the grateful woman moved into Krassin's apartment (his own wife was still abroad).

Because of that woman, Krassin was among the few people's commissars who lived outside the Kremlin; and for the same reason he would not receive any of his official visitors in his house. The only exception was made for Abel Yenukidze, the secretary of the Cental Executive Committee of the Soviets. Krassin and Yenukidze were old friends, ever since the time—some fifteen years before the revolution—when Yenukidze had worked for the engineer as an electrician in Baku.

During the first stages of his work with the Soviets, Krassin often protected certain former capitalists, who in their turn could do a few things for the new government in its most critical moments.

Most members of the prerevolutionary capitalist class had scattered. Many had fled to foreign lands; some had become petty employees of the new Soviet state and now tried to be inconspicuous. But among those private entrepreneurs who were willing to work with us, not as the state's employees but as semicapitalists, there were a number of dexterous fellows, not to say sharpers and double-dealers. They took grave risks cheating both the government and the consumer. Their aim was to make money quickly and disappear with it, leaving no traces. Though not all of our semicapitalist employees were of this ilk, still a spirit of frivolous and unashamed fortune-hunting characterized the whole group of them.

And yet it was necessary to use their services at certain crucial times. When Krassin was the people's commissar of communications, he appointed to the chief post in his firewood supply department a former vice-minister in the Kerensky government. This man called upon private entrepreneurs to help him, and they were given far greater liberties of action than I, for instance, granted similar persons in my firewood supply work. Since the activities of Krassin's men interfered with my department, I tried to regulate and control them, but they opposed me in every way possible and attacked me for my "Communism."

Later, Krassin had to pay a high price for the confidence he had placed in these men. A number of his firewood contractors sometimes took joyrides on the trains, their pockets filled with paper money, their supplies of food even more impressive, special petty commissars accompanying them as their guards and factotums. Some of these men worked their way close to Poland and, at the first opportunity, deserted to the other side of the border, with the state's money, food, and in some cases with their commissars, who had turned out to be their partners in crime and treason.

It was still 1918 when Krassin was given a new post, that of people's commissar of foreign trade. There was hardly any foreign trade at the time: Soviet Russia was still blockaded by the Allies; no important transactions with either the Allies, neutrals, or Germany were possible. But Russia's need of many commodities was great. To relieve the acute shortage, several Soviet offices resorted to contraband dealing at the borders. The Cheka was especially active in such smuggling activities.

This is how it was done. Daring young men were sent to the border regions. They were furnished with considerable sums of paper money, and the more reliable Communists among them were also given diamonds and other precious stones and jewelry to be used instead of currency. Engaging the services of professional smugglers, the young messengers bought with this money and jewelry whatever foreign goods they could get. Inevitably, all such "foreign trade" was of a hit-and-miss nature. It could not be seriously controlled or guided, and even its extent was miserably slight.

When placed in charge of this field, Krassin began by centralizing the work

of all the Soviet agencies then involved in this work. He became the head of
government-sponsored smuggling, so to speak. As his next step he assigned to
his young agents, as their companions, a few old businessmen whom he had
known in prerevolutionary years. These old-timers added knowledge and
experience to the ingenuity and hardihood of the young men and soon proved
their worth. They displayed astonishing talent in helping the Soviet state
break the Allied blockade—and soon you could find them working in practically every Soviet department: in the Commissariat of Finance, in the
Cheka, everywhere. And everywhere their zeal was commendable, although
no one ever asked whether it was entirely unselfish.

(10)

RYCKOV, ECONOMIC CHIEF

BETWEEN 1918 AND 1920, DURING THE ERA OF THE SO-CALLED "WAR COMMUNISM,"
one of my two or three immediate chiefs was Alexis Ryckov. As I write this
I realize that his name is now only vaguely remembered abroad. In Russia it
is accursed or, at best, taboo; for its bearer was shot during the purges of 1937.
Nevertheless, Ryckov, who for a time held the post of Soviet prime minister,
was a significant personality in his heyday—the early phase of Bolshevik
power. At one period he was very close to Lenin.

I had known Ryckov long before the revolution. It was in 1906, in Odessa,
that I first met him: we belonged to the same Social Democratic organization.
A party convention was in the offing, and Ryckov was a candidate from the
Bolshevik faction, while I worked with all my might to elect as our delegate
a printer who was a Menshevik. Despite the pre-election struggle, Ryckov and
I became friends.

Several times he stayed overnight in my home. We spent a number of
evenings together over red wine in a little tavern near the Odessa campus.
This wine cellar was frequented by other Social Democrats as well, among
whom I recall Pavel Yushkevich, who later wrote a well-known book on
historical materialism, and Nicholas Maliantovich, subsequently a lawyer and
a perennial Social Democrat candidate for the Duma. In the same tavern I
made the acquaintance of a man known cryptically as "Comrade Myron."
Sixteen years later I met him again—in London, where he wore in his lapel
the rosette of the Legion of Honor and pontificated as an intimate friend and
collaborator of Gaston Painlevé, the French minister. Only then did I learn
that his real name was Rechsthammer. By that time he had grown fat as well
as important. In 1922 he was in London on an unofficial mission from the
French government, sounding out Krassin, the Soviet envoy in England,
to the Kremlin's willingness to pay old tsarist debts to France.

But after those early days in Odessa, I did not see Ryckov for a long time. It was not until the fall of 1918 that I spotted him as both of us were leaving the Moscow Art Theater. I recognized him at once, in spite of the passage of time. How could one forget his short, squatty figure, his thoughtful, intelligent face, with that thick hair and little beard of his? Under his leather jacket one could see that his suit was threadbare. His shoes, too, were badly worn.

We were glad to see each other—very glad, in fact. After some joyous shoulder-slapping, he invited me to visit him at the Supreme Council of Economy, to the chairmanship of which he had been appointed by Lenin a short time before. This is how I learned that he was really my chief; for my timber department, like many other economic organizations, was under his jurisdiction.

I called at his office the very next day. From that moment on and for many years to come we were in close contact and trusted each other completely. In every difficult situation—and there were many of them in my work—I found a true friend in him. It was mainly because of his friendship that I could and did continue my service with the Soviets for five years more than would otherwise have been humanly possible. To him, and him alone, I could speak my mind and heart with entire frankness. Even with Krassin my relations were not so completely and mutually friendly, although Krassin and I were bound by a friendship of many years, had worked together a great deal, and had been of the same social origin (as Ryckov and I were not).

My relations with Ryckov, on the one hand, and Krassin, on the other, were such that I was in a position, and often was called upon, to make peace between the two. My very work was on the border line of their two commissariats. While the production of lumber and firewood, being a domestic economic function, was within Ryckov's sphere of authority as chairman of the Supreme Council of Economy, the selling of Soviet lumber on foreign markets had to be supervised by Krassin as commissar for foreign trade. Generally speaking, Krassin jealously guarded his prerogatives in his field of foreign trade; yet, by virtue of a special, though tacit, agreement with Ryckov, he left the sales of lumber abroad entirely in my hands.

For a number of years I was able to observe Ryckov in his office and at the sessions of the Council of People's Commissars and the Council of Labor and Defense. Ryckov was a disciple and an admirer of Lenin. He himself was neither a leader nor even an important political figure, but Lenin valued him as a loyal man, a faithful member of the policy-making top of his party. It was plain to all how highly Lenin esteemed Ryckov. There was only one other Bolshevik occupying the same place in his regard: Alexander Tsuriupa. Both Ryckov and Tsuriupa had identical official positions—they were Lenin's vice-chairmen of the Council of People's Commissars (of which council Lenin was the chairman). Tsuriupa, however, constantly ailed and was frequently absent; Ryckov, on the contrary, attended practically every session and took part in the discussion of most economic problems.

All, but especially Lenin, carefully considered Ryckov's opinion on each economic matter in question, although the vice-chairman had received no formal training in economics and, to boot, had boasted of no practical business experience. He had a great deal of common sense—what in America is called "horse sense" and in Russia *russkaya smekalka,* or "Russian shrewdness" —and his remarks either in formal debates or in informal conversations were meaty, to the point, and, by and large, very valuable.

I remember that at one of the meetings of the Council of Labor and Defense, the old troublesome question of what to do to increase firewood supply had come up. In each locality, when peasants were hired by the Soviet state to act as lumberjacks, they were required to come with their horses and to use the latter for hauling logs to the railroad stations. It was necessary to pay these peasants in food supplies, as I have explained, and it was also necessary to feed the horses.

Both food and fodder were hard to get, and even the state officers had trouble in replenishing the stock piles. Tsuriupa, who was the people's commissar of food supplies, zealously hoarded the few reserves he had. He was up in arms when I suggested that he part with some of his department's food and fodder for the good of my timber operations.

"It will deprive our city workers of the meager rations they now have!" he protested.

Argument pro and con ensued, and when all the objections and counter-claims had been exhausted, Ryckov spoke up. With his customary stutter, he slowly said:

"We, luckily, with our revolutionary pathos, can make our workers and peasants work even without bread. But, unfortunately, we haven't as yet succeeded in a similar training of horses. Of course we could denounce the horses as a bunch of counterrevolutionaries. But it won't help. They'll still want oats."

Turning with a sly grin toward Dzerzhinsky, of the Cheka, he added: "Even you won't achieve anything. Just try to take a few dozen horses before your firing squads!"

This decided the whole matter. Lenin at once, without letting the debate drag, began to dictate a resolution of the Council of Labor and Defense, ordering food and fodder for the timber operations. The order was binding upon all the commissariats involved.

There was an essential difference between Ryckov and the other members of the Communist élite who played important roles in Soviet economics. Take, for instance, Lev Kamenev, Trotsky's brother-in-law. Kamenev was in charge of a number of economic agencies, yet Lenin did not hold too high an opinion about his practical sense. He preferred to intrust Kamenev merely with the drawing-up of projects, resolutions, decrees, etc.—a well-nigh mechanical task, not requiring much originality.

The difference was also apparent between Ryckov, the business-like doer of

66

things, and Larin, the visionary. Finally, between Ryckov and Trotsky not only a great difference but sheer antagonism existed. This stemmed, on the one hand, from the conflict of two separate departments and, on the other, from the clash of two sharply contrary human characters.

Trotsky was by nature, and remained by choice, a chief who loved to give orders. Even with his closest collaborators he would not be on personal, friendly terms. In his own reminiscences Trotsky later noted that in the three years of his work with his most intimate aide, Emphraim Skliansky, he talked of nothing but the Red Army, its supplies, its equipment, and so on. Ryckov, on the contrary, was a fine type of warmhearted Russian intellectual, somewhat in the style of the kindly doctors of the old-time provinces. He was gregarious and hearty and would often visit his subordinates in their homes, even if they were not Communists. He loved to take a glass with them and have expansive talks with them. His slight stutter made him a good deal more human than most of his forbidding colleagues, and, in conversations with his subordinates and friends, Ryckov would permit himself the good-natured irony that is so characteristic of some stammerers, as he told stories about the work of his comrades of the Kremlin.

With all that, Ryckov had great respect for the duties assigned to him and to his organization, the Supreme Council of Economy. According to Lenin's theory, which was then widely accepted, the development of the Soviet state would inevitably lead to a "withering-away" process and to abolition of all the governmental departments and organizations except those in charge of the state's economics. The state as such, as a weapon of coercion and force, would cease to exist the minute the struggle of the classes came to its natural end. Economic life alone would then need organized supervision and leadership. Ryckov was very proud that it was he whom Lenin and the party had intrusted with the foremost Soviet agency destined to survive in the halcyon world of the morrow.

But at the same time this gave Ryckov one more reason to view the other Soviet departments negatively, particularly the War Commissariat, the Commissariat for Foreign Trade, and the Cheka. Repeatedly, in private conversations, he stressed the idea that in his council alone the training of true Communist leaders was proceeding apace. He used to say that even nonparty members of his staff—nay, even Mensheviks and other socialists—were being imbued with higher, better thoughts. In particular, he pinned his hopes in this direction upon the middle and lower strata of his non-Communist employees.

"What do we see in the War Department and throughout the Red Army?" he asked, and answered his own question: "We see that officers of the old army, with their secret White Guard sympathies, play an important role. These officers are loyal to the old regime, really; it's practically impossible to re-educate them. That is why the new Soviet state won't be able to use them beyond the duration of this civil war."

As for the officials of the Commissariat of Foreign Trade, according to

Ryckov, they were corrupted by the life they led abroad, where they were kept by their duties. He said that they plainly and quickly degenerated into typical bourgeois once they crossed the border into foreign lands. Only in and around his Supreme Council of Economy could you feel the genuine atmosphere of socialist construction—the healthy influence of workers' organizations and Soviet science. So said Ryckov.

Last but not least, Ryckov had his run-ins with the Cheka. When the Cheka began one of its periodic waves of arrests among nonparty employees of the economic agencies of the government, it did not inquire beforehand whether or not this pleased Ryckov. Naturally, Ryckov's own council would suddenly lose some of its most valued experts and other staff members. Ryckov in great indignation would rush to their rescue. If he failed, he would apply to Lenin himself. I was once present when Ryckov, in much irritation, shouted at one of the leading Cheka officials: "So what if I do keep a few Mensheviks on my staff? At least they work! But you—your Cheka staff is full of secret White Guards who only use your organization as their shield and shelter and are preparing all sorts of unpleasant surprises for you. Just wait and see what they will yet do!"

After a glass or two in good company Ryckov invariably selected the Cheka as the target for his quips and anecdotes. He was especially pleasant and cheerful when slightly under the influence of liquor; his friends knew this well and often arranged little parties in their homes, "bachelor-boy get-togethers." Generally speaking, it was not very easy to obtain hard liquor in those days; but an old Bolshevik, who was an understanding soul, happened to be in charge of the Liquor Administration. Armed with a special permit from the Supreme Council of Economy, a man would come to him to beg some vodka for an illness. The old liquor chief would glance at the "patient's" name on the permit, recognize it, and fulfil the request at once.

One Alexander Kviatkovsky, a personal friend of Lenin, was especially enterprising in this matter of arranging get-togethers. He had been a Bolshevik in his younger days, but now for some reason was not a member of the party. The evenings arranged by him and others were always marked by true camaraderie: men lowered their ever present guards and became natural, talkative, frank. Ryckov himself was in a great measure responsible for this—with his jests devoid of malice, his cheery garrulousness, his utter simplicity.

There is a well-known Russian saying: "What a sober man has on his mind, the drunkard has on his tongue." This was strikingly applicable to my good friend Ryckov. But even as he tipsily complained about the difficulties of his position and work in the Soviet government, he remembered to keep himself within the limits of caution. He praised Lenin even as he criticized him. Ryckov would say:

"Yes, look at me: I am at the helm of socialist construction. I am the head of the Supreme Council of Economy. Ilyich believes in me, trusts me. And yet, how uncertain he is! I can't depend on him one hundred per cent, oh no. I

68

come to him, I discuss things with him, and he and I reach an agreement. He tells me: 'Bring this subject up at the next meeting, I'll support you.' But the moment he feels that the majority of the conferees are against my proposals, he betrays me. Yes, Vladimir Ilyich Lenin will betray everything, will recant everything—in the name of the Revolution and Socialism. He will remain true to one basic idea alone—Socialism, Communism.....".

Several months before the New Economic Policy of 1921 was introduced, signifying a retreat from pure Communism, Ryckov and I had an earnest talk. I poured out my heart on a variety of subjects, chiefly on the economic and other policies of the Soviet government. I spoke of the economic chaos in the land and expressed my surprise over the stubborn refusal of the Kremlin to co-operate with other political groups which could have given it a number of valuable experts. As an example, I mentioned Ryckov's own Supreme Council of Economy.

"Why not offer some of the Mensheviks leading posts in the Council?" I suggested. "They have shown their willingness to collaborate. In the summer of 1919, when General Denikin's troops threatened Moscow and were already near Tula, the Mensheviks mobilized their members to join the Red Army against the Whites. The Mensheviks have tremendous influence with important groups abroad. Working with them at this point would be of value to the Soviet government in so many respects."

This conversation took place at one of those historic junctures when the situation both at home and abroad was most unfavorable for the cause of Russian Communism. And it was one of those moments when Lenin himself showed a modicum of willingness to accept the collaboration of other socialist parties.

Thus, in 1917–18, the Bolsheviks believed no more than their opponents did that the Soviet government would actually last. On more than one occasion in that period Lenin said in his own close circle that Bolshevik power would not survive more than three or four weeks. And Trotsky threatened that if the Soviets fell, they—the Bolsheviks—would "slam the door so that the whole world will tremble."

This pessimistic appraisal of our chances of survival gave place to a very optimistic one by the end of 1918, when, following the end of World War I, central Europe was in the throes of a revolution. Lenin and his party were afire with the high hope of a quick success for Communism all over Europe.

Depending on the changing situation, the Mensheviks were now jailed, now courted and asked to help the Soviet government. When the sanguine expectation of a general European upheaval did not materialize, when the Communist revolts in Bavaria and Hungary were quelled, there was a great deal of ill-concealed depression in the Kremlin. This was the moment to broach to Ryckov and others my advocacy of collaboration with the Mensheviks.

Ryckov carried the gist of our talk to Lenin. Within a few days I heard from George Lomov that Lenin was favorably inclined toward my proposals and wanted me to open negotiations with the Mensheviks. He was willing to bring into the presidium of Ryckov's Supreme Council of Economy one of the outstanding Menshevik leaders, Feodor Dan. Dan was a physician by profession and, as such, had already been called to the service of the Soviet state. His promotion to the higher post would have been technically easy of accomplishment.

Later I learned that the situation was being explored by other men as well. Communists like Larin, Kamenev, and Bukharin took tentative steps in the same direction. There was a general feeling in the highest stratum of the Bolsheviks that it was time to bring other socialist parties into the picture.

But nothing came of all this. Lenin was willing to give a few leading posts to the Mensheviks but was far from any thought of really sharing power with them. Actually, all the power in the state was to remain in the hands of the Central Committee of the Communist party. Naturally enough, the Mensheviks declined this collaboration whereby they would share in responsibility but not in rights. Thus there was no change in their status. The Mensheviks allowed their members to work in the various governmental organizations as experts and other employees, mostly in economic posts, each of his own private choice.

As for Ryckov, he was against offering Dan a leading position in the Supreme Council of Economy. According to Ryckov, Dan was too much of a politician. Dan would draw to himself all the various Mensheviks already employed in the several branches of the Supreme Council of Economy, and a regular Menshevik caucus would be formed. This would hamper the entire work of the council.

There the matter rested. Everything remained as before. And, as a matter of fact, it could not have been otherwise. In the course of those unsuccessful negotiations I felt with especial clarity that not merely differences of opinion but a deep psychological chasm, almost hatred, separated the Bolsheviks and Mensheviks, once members of a united Social Democratic party. This was a blood feud, of the kind that first breaks up, then ruins, families. As it is written in the Bible, "And brother rose against brother." The Bolsheviks hated the Mensheviks with special violence precisely because of their common origin and mutual past. They hated the Mensheviks because both groups were Marxists and, in arguments against each other, both used practically the same terminology and based their sallies upon the same class-struggle analysis of events. Reconciliation was out of the question. Only death or an indisputable triumph of one of the rivals could put an end to this internecine strife.

I felt this with a renewed sharpness when I realized that the rulers in the Kremlin were at times more conciliatory in their relations with the bourgeois world than in their negotiations with the moderate socialists. They often tried to find some common ground with the bourgeois, but when dealing with other socialists they first of all looked for points of disagreement.

70

The full force of this antagonism is apparent in Lenin's writings. For example, his hatred for the so-called "Renegade" Kautsky, the German Social Democrat, was far more virulent than his hostility toward Winston S. Churchill (then an active leader of anti-Soviet interventionist groups abroad). The Soviet government found it more difficult to come to an agreement with Rudolf Hilferding, the Social Democratic leader in the Weimar Republic, than with Joseph Wirth, the Catholic party figure of the time. While the names of Ramsay Macdonald or Hermann Mueller were uttered with contempt in the Kremlin because they were "social-betrayers," I often heard in the same chit-chat that Lenin himself wished to satisfy certain wishes of Herr Wirth and his emissary, Dr. Haas—nay, the wishes of Hugo Stinnes, too—as Wirth and Stinnes and Haas negotiated with us about the very first timber concession granted by the Soviets to the Reich's lumber interests.

One is inevitably reminded of war and the military. Warriors respect those of their enemies who openly say that they are enemies. But they are merciless to those foes who were friends only yesterday and who do not seem to be fighting them openly, yet annoyingly disagree with their strategy and tactics.

In the field of socialistic theories the Bolshevik-Menshevik conflict had a precedent in the story of the First International when, in the 1870's, Karl Marx and Michael Bakunin fought each other tooth and nail while seemingly remaining in the same fold of socialism. Verily, the war of ideas is a total war.

Much later, in 1935–36, in France and other countries of western Europe I saw something of the same fratricide in episodes accompanying the rise and death of the Popular Front. As I witnessed and took part in the western European events of 1935–36, I once more saw with an awful lucidity how impossible it is to bring about true collaboration between groups that, starting at the same point, with the socialist platform, have with years grown apart. One might as well try to mix fire and water. Collaboration can be achieved only at the cost of mutual concessions and compromises—the implacable reality of history compels such mutual concessions—but on many crucial occasions men comply with the dictates of history only when it is too late.

Of the two social philosophies in question, one has in the course of its historic evolution adopted the principle of class collaboration, but the other has stood for the idea and practice of ruthless class struggle. Without reciprocal concessions they cannot unite. Can they ever find a common line, can they come to mutual understanding? To me it often appeared that Marx himself may have practiced more flexibility and tolerance than was shown by his disciple Lenin. Alas, zealous students, in trying to spread the mentors' teachings, are frequently more crude and brutal than their teachers.

(11)

TROTSKY, THE WAR-LORD

ONE DAY IN 1920 I WAS SUMMONED TO TROTSKY'S TRAIN, WHICH WAS ABOUT TO pull out for the Urals. He was then still the people's commissar of war. But the civil war was over, and his was the task of transforming a part of the Red Army into labor battalions. The metal plants of the Urals had come to depend on wood as their fuel; and, as Trotsky's new labor battalions were to lend a hand in the metal industry of that region, he wanted me to accompany him on his journey east.

I nevertheless declined to join him—for the simple reason that my job was to provide fuel not for the Urals alone but for the entire country. I had to remain in Moscow, and therefore I sent a representative. My brief visit to the train was interesting, just the same. The train was a veritable Noah's Ark, what with its staff of specialists from a wide range of Russia's economic institutions, its military experts, instructors, Communist party leaders, and so on. Soldiers and laborers were busily loading food supplies, lathes and other machines, rifles and machine guns. Red Army officers were in charge of all this activity. They worked fast and feverishly, no doubt wishing to prove to us civilian slackers the true efficiency of front-line fighters now reconverting themselves to peaceful economy.

The train was famous. Only a short while before, in October, 1920, on his way to the Crimea to battle and defeat the last White Guard army of General Peter Wrangel, Trotsky had issued his celebrated order:

"Once more our train is on its way to the front.

"The fighters of our train were at the walls of Kazan in those trying weeks of 1918 when we were wresting from the foe his control of the Volga River. That struggle has long been ended. On that front our Soviet power is now nearing the shores of the Pacific Ocean.

"With great honor the fighters of our train defended the city of Petrograd. We saved Petrograd. In the last few years numerous representatives of the world's proletariat have visited that city.

"Not once but many times our train was at the Polish front. By now a preliminary peace treaty has been signed with Poland.

"The fighters of our train were also in the steppes of the Don when first Krasnov and then Denikin pushed their offensives from the south against Soviet Russia. The days of Krasnov and Denikin are gone.

"There remains the Crimea which the French government has transformed into a fortress of its own. A German-Russian general, Baron Wrangel, is in command of the White Guard garrison of this French fortress.

72

"A new campaign is awaiting the harmonious family of our train. Let us make it our last campaign!"

And, indeed, the Crimean campaign did prove to be the last chapter of the Russian civil war.

When Trotsky was asked what name he would choose for his train, he replied: "The Train of Victory."

And now he wanted the fame of his train to be as resounding on the economic front as it had been in military campaigns. Hundreds of Communist commanders, returning from the theaters of war, were being distributed throughout the nation's most important offices of civilian administration. They had little patience for those of their Bolshevik brethren who had not been at the front. And these civilian functionaries, in their turn, were soon antagonistic to the Trotskyites with their military uniforms and their high-handed ways.

This was the first time that the term "Trotskyites" had been used in Russia. Of course, at that time it had a far different, prouder ring than it acquired later on. But even then many Bolsheviks, not in Trotsky's entourage, were puzzled and resentful. They saw that Trotsky wanted to militarize Russian economics rather than demobilize Russia's armies. The entire Red Army was to become one huge industrial organization.

It should be noted that even these 'Trotskyites'—the Communist commanders in Trotsky's organization—had once begun by mistrusting and disliking this man; for they remembered his past; they recalled that for years, until the spring of 1917, he had strenuously opposed the Bolsheviks. But this memory became dim and nearly disappeared as, through the tough years of Rusia's civil war, these Bolsheviks assigned to Trotsky's staff learned to work with him. Actually, in many cases it took but a few months for their hostility to vanish without a trace and for a great pride in their "Trotskyism" to arise. And yet they had a fear as well as a fondness for him!

That day, late in 1920, as I was sitting in George Piatakov's compartment in the far-famed train, the telephone rang. Piatakov was then a Bolshevik with a long and distinguished record. When a few years later, after Lenin's death, Lenin's will became known, we found that Piatakov was mentioned there as one of the great hopes of the Communist party.

As he picked up the telephone leisurely and listened to the message on the telephone, Piatakov's whole manner changed. It became quick and nervously abrupt. He said, "Right away!" and after replacing the receiver began hurriedly to put on his military equipment—all of it, it seemed. Tightening his belt sprucely, fastening his saber and his holstered revolver, he explained without looking at me: "Lev Davidovich loves the 'pathos of distance' between us and himself..... Probably he is right."

Indeed, Trotsky sternly preserved this distance between his subordinates and himself. He stressed the gap. This is not to say that he was motivated by his personal superiority complex alone; perhaps he wanted respect for his post

73

more than for his own person as such. On several occasions I chanced to observe this trait of his—especially at the sessions of the Council of Labor and Defense that he attended on his trips to Moscow from the front.

My first personal contact with Trotsky and his peculiar ways took place late in 1920, some time after my visit to his train. In the years before the revolution I had heard the name of Leon Trotsky; yet, while he was often discussed, nobody ever expected him to be one of the top leaders of the Bolshevik revolution. His position in the prerevolutionary era was not one of leadership. Lenin was the acknowledged chief of the Bolsheviks, as Martov was the acknowledged chief of the Mensheviks. Trotsky at that time was a Menshevik, and his fame mainly derived from his extraordinary ability as a pamphleteer who pulled no punches and, above all, was a truly inspired orator. All these factors contributed to make him widely known and talked about, but not necessarily a candidate for such a high position.

My interview with him, in this problem of fuel for the metalworks of the Urals, finally occurred in his town office. I was to report at the Commissariat of War. The instruction read: "Be there at noon, and remember to be prompt." On arriving, I discovered that it was more difficult to reach Trotsky than to see Lenin. I had to pass through five rooms, all swarming with neatly dressed military people. The fifth room was Trotsky's anteroom. The door to the war-lord's private office was guarded by two sentries. As I entered, I beheld a tremendous desk, every inch of it of ministerial stature. And there was the man himself, sitting behind the desk.

Every movement and word of his revealed that Trotsky felt his historic and revolutionary importance; that he was certain that the eyes of all the peoples and all the succeeding centuries were fixed upon him; that, in short, he deemed himself to be a great man, like any of those painted on the canvases hung all around the room.

Whereas Lenin was simplicity itself, Trotsky was cool, snobbish, formal. Trotsky's appearance was characteristic: his thick, black-gray hair was combed back, yet looked stubborn; his wedgelike beard was well groomed yet sharp; his eyes glinting behind his pince-nez were wise but harsh; his long fingers were nervous. He was dressed in semimilitary khaki clothes of a good cut. His boots were high and of the officer's model. Yes, here was a minister of the state, a real war-lord.

The desk, though all orderliness and discipline, was crowded with too many writing materials and other knickknacks. I was especially intrigued by the numerous pencils and crayons, of all shades and hues, all sharpened and arranged in strict sequence.

"Sit down, please," came from Trotsky.

I lowered myself into a soft chair, but the desk between the two of us was so wide that I at once felt the "pathos of distance" to which Piatakov had referred on my recent visit to the train. Years later I remembered all this, and so was not especially surprised to hear that in his will Lenin defined Trotsky as a talented leader who nevertheless paid too much attention to details of sheer organizational work.

True, Trotsky could and did move vast masses of people—but only in extraordinary times and unusual situations. In normal everyday life he was clearly handicapped by his deference to the formula in preference to reality, by his fussy insistence on theory rather than on practice. That was why, at the crucial point of his struggle with Stalin, he could not adapt himself to the circumstances which demanded a give-and-take policy, an opportunism of a kind, a hard-boiled realism certainly. His closest aides admired him, to be sure; but even at that, he was always a lonely figure.

Together we talked about the Urals, the fuel problem, the reconversion of Soviet Russia to peaceful economics. Actually we talked for half an hour without establishing any genuine contact—any warm meeting of minds. All the time I felt that he was a minister of the state and that I was making my formal report to him. Perhaps, as we had both been Mensheviks and he had eventually joined the Bolsheviks while I had not, he wanted to underscore the difference between us.

Raising his tone to that of a man in authority, he tried to prove to me that, from this point in Russian history on, the Red Army was going to be the main source of wood production. His labor battalions, he said, were going to solve the problem which the Russian peasant found too difficult.

Cautiously I suggested that perhaps we should give the peasant a little more time; that perhaps the peasant, rather than Trotsky's soldier, could yet prove himself the proper laborer of Russia's woods. The forests of our country, I pointed out, were distributed throughout the land too unevenly to be tackled by soldiers who would have to be, in many cases, brought long distances. The peasants, on the other hand, were already on the spot, close to the forests that were to be exploited. Our chief handicap, I remarked, was our lack of food supplies for the peasant-lumberjacks and of fodder for the peasants' horses needed for the timber transport. Were soldiers to be used as lumberjacks, they would require far more food and fodder. Besides, these soldiers would inevitably be concentrated in certain areas, whereas other regions would prove to be far away from their reach. This, I said, would lead to an overproduction of timber in some forests and an underproduction in others. The overpiling of timber in the areas reached by the soldiers would cause added difficulties in the already disorganized field of transport.

Trotsky listened impatiently, then declared: "All your arguments are nothing but an echo of the old-style bourgeois thinking, of capitalistic inefficiency. The work of my battalions will be one giant stride forward, along the path of Russia's sovietization. My battalions will help to free the peasant from his ignorance and inertia. We will show the peasant the proper way to work. It is absolutely necessary to instil some discipline into our apparatus. This will be our first important step toward socialism."

As he spoke, I felt helpless to offer any more arguments. The war-lord of the revolution had the upper hand, and that was that.

And yet the events of the very next few weeks and months put an end to Trotsky's plans. His idea of militarizing Russia's economy proved stillborn. Even Lenin, who had at first supported Trotsky's ideas, gave them up. The cessation of the Russian civil war terminated those very military impulses in Russian life which permitted extraordinary measures for the army. Those impulses held for the duration only, no longer. The plea that the revolution was threatened by the foe, effective only such a short while before, was of no further use. The Communists could not employ it to get food out of the countryside by force alone. They realized that chaos reigned in the economy of Russia and that coercion or military orders were not enough to revive the normal processes of the nation's life. Other stimuli were sorely needed. Trotsky's ways were being fast discarded.

But in his own time—in the era of the initial revolutionary work of the Bolsheviks—Trotsky was in his element and triumphant. I recall being present at one of the first meetings addressed by Trotsky in Petrograd. This was in the summer of 1917, when Kerensky's government unsuccessfully attempted to rule Russia. The meeting brought together not ordinary soldiers and officers but chairmen of revolutionary military committees, who had come to Kerensky's capital from the front, which was as yet sustained against the Germans. Most of the deputies from the front were sharply opposed to the Bolsheviks, who were then being accused of trying to demoralize the Russian war effort against the Central Powers.

Trotsky, who had just recently returned to Russia from North America, was among the chief speakers at the meeting. As his views were known to the audience beforehand, he was greeted with hostility. There was much tumult; soldiers and officers talked and yelled unpleasantly. And yet Trotsky kept on talking, and soon the hall began to quiet down. The orator's words were like whips. His criticism of the helpless, vacillating regime of Kerensky was cutting, bitter, to the point. Toward the end of the speech, the deputies from the front either stood in silent gloom, their heads lowered, or were applauding heartily.

The audience won over, the Bolsheviks pressed home their advantage. The next Bolshevik orator, an army officer named Nicholas Krylenko, found the men in the hall far more receptive than they had been when Trotsky had first begun to work on them.

Trotsky actually did not have much respect for the human mass. His theory was approximately this: the overwhelming majority of human beings are inert, indifferent, indecisive; the rest are the active extremes on either flank of the majority—one extreme being good men, the other extreme bad men. He proudly felt and said that he could prevail upon the "good" extreme to assert itself over both the listless majority and the "bad" extreme. This was his vaunted "influence over the people." He maintained that he could and did excel

76

in his ability to lead the masses, to propagandize. Leadership and propaganda, according to him, were the main factors in life and politics.)

Such a theory, purporting to deify the human mass, is, of course, in reality fraught with much scorn of man as an individual. Trotsky loved distant men and things. He was cool to men and things which the rest of us consider near and dear. You felt this immediately, in your first encounter with Trotsky.

Trotsky, like Lenin, took very lightly decisions to execute this man or that. To Lenin there was, in such terrible decisions, something abstract and necessary—a necessary evil, essential to all revolutions. Trotsky regarded the same death sentences differently. To him each sentence was a revolutionary act, to be viewed even at the time of its signing and execution as part of a historical process. He was always conscious of being in the limelight, in the center of the world stage; and he played his role accordingly, feeling upon himself the eyes of the other participants, as well as the eyes of the spectators watching this great revolutionary drama.

The contrast between the two leaders of the Russian upheaval, when they were in action side by side, was fascinating to observe, and I had an excellent opportunity for such observation at the meetings of the Council of the People's Commissars and the Council of Labor and Defense.

Naturally, the most important decisions of the Soviet state machine were made not at those sessions but at the more restricted meetings of the Central Committee of the Communist party or of the Politbureau, the inner sanctum of that Central Committee. As for the Council of the People's Commissars and the Council of Labor and Defense, these two organs of Soviet power were one notch lower than the Central Committee and the Politbureau, although actually the two councils together constituted what in Western countries is known as the "cabinet of ministers." Current or business problems were decided by the councils. Paramount questions of supreme policy were settled beforehand by the Central Committee and its Politbureau; but on occasion the procedure was disrupted, and matters of policy broke through from these inner chambers of the Communist party into the more prosaic and workaday councils. This was inevitable in connection with certain crucial questions of that era. At such times we, the non-Commuist experts present at the council meetings, witnessed something of the acute disagreement, the gigantic strife, going on behind the scenes of the Communist party. We heard echoes of passionate arguments between Lenin and some of his collaborators.

Lenin himself always occupied the chair at the sessions of the Council of Labor and Defense, the membership of which consisted exclusively of those commissars who were in charge of economic or military affairs. They were mainly Lenin's old-time associates in the Bolshevik group of the pre-revolutionary underground days: Ryckov, Kamenev, Tsuriupa, Sheinman, Sokolnikov, Tomsky, and others. As usual, they brought along to these meetings some of their aides and associates, Communist and non-Communist, to make reports, supply figures and facts, and generally act as consultants and experts.

These commissars and their aides made a rather homogeneous group, whereas such personalities as Trotsky and Dzerzhinsky and, in a way, Krassin too, did not exactly fit in. Each one of these three somehow stood out from the rest.

This was especially apparent in the way the agenda were altered the minute either one of the first two appeared in the room to join the session. Other affairs were dropped forthwith, and whatever question had brought either Trotsky or Dzerzhinsky to the meeting was taken up. This may have been done because the military and other matters in which these men were concerned were far more weighty than many of the other current problems—but, nevertheless, it must not be forgotten that these three individuals, each in his field, were of the utmost significance in the life-and-death struggle of the Soviet republic.

Then, too, each one of these leaders was addressed by the others in a special fashion, and the manner of this address was truly a mirror of their standing in the Communist party. Dzerzhinsky, for instance, was addressed rather officially, by his name and patronymic. Yet some colleagues who had known him well in the old days of the underground employed the more friendly or familiar "Comrade Felix."

But no one used a comradely approach toward Trotsky. The formal use of both his name and his patronymic, Lev Davidovich, prevailed at those sessions always. For his was a singular position: he was still a stranger in the ranks of the Bolshevik party of which he was one of the highest leaders! The other Bolsheviks well remembered that only a short time before—for many years prior to 1917—he had opposed Bolshevism. Trotsky was always a forceful individual, too much so to be forgiven all his past deviations from and disagreements with the Bolsheviks, despite his recent transformation and collaboration with Lenin. And so he was addressed formally as Lev Davidovich, for his fellow-committeemen wanted to emphasize in this subtle fashion a certain distance still existing (in their minds) between Trotsky and the Communist party.

In any gathering of those old Bolsheviks, Trotsky remained an alien. It is true that, for the sake of his present service in the revolution, some of the commissars were willing to forgive some of his past sins. But, though forgiving, they were not forgetting. Trotsky compelled them to respect him, to pay heed to every word he spoke. Yet they resented it bitterly, or a least were dissatisfied and jealous, whenever Lenin saw fit to defer publicly to Trotsky.

Lenin valued and lauded Trotsky's military talents and his general ability as an organizer and seemed to appreciate Trotsky's revolutionary temperament above all his other qualities. He remembered the man's tremendous role in the preparation and carrying-out of the Bolshevik coup d'état in October, 1917. And Lenin, as well as everybody else, was perfectly aware that it was Trotsky who actually created the Red Army in 1918–20—that it was Trotsky with his fiery spirit and inexhaustible energy who insured that army's victory over the White Guard movement.

Generally speaking, in that struggle against the counterrevolution and against foreign intervention, Trotsky was constantly in the foreground. While Lenin was called "the brain and the will power of the revolution," Trotsky was often referred to as "the slashing sword of the revolution." Such dramatic expressions as these appealed to Lev Davidovich; they were quite in line with his theatrical predilections.

Because Trotsky felt sure of Lenin's support, he conducted himself at our council meetings in a distinctive manner. He was aloof, spoke with brusque authority, and, the greater his successes at the front were, the more snobbish his words and actions at the council meetings became. He was particularly arrogant as he addressed, or mentioned, the commissars of our various economic departments. On the economic front in Russia, not very many triumphs had been noted for several months or even years; for the economists had to supply the army ahead of the civilian population, and neither the military nor the civilians considered the work of these commissars halfway satisfactory. Trotsky's oral barbs seemed to have this undertone: "Just wait. I'll finish the White Guards at the front, and then I'll tackle the home front—I'll tackle *you!*"

The difference between Lenin and Trotsky and their respective brands of leadership was plain for anyone to see at a council meeting. Lenin was spoken of as "Ilyich," a somewhat familiar appellation, certainly, yet one with much fondness in it, too—and this fondness, as well as great and genuine respect, could be sensed at any meeting of either of the two councils. Every Bolshevik had a personal attachment for Lenin, and thus an intimate tie was felt between the party and its founder and organizer. It was partly because of this that Lenin's authority in the affairs of the party proved to be so extraordinary.

As the leader whose word was actually law, Lenin had not only to lead these men but also to iron out all the tangles and rough spots in the living fabric of his party. In fact, at times it appeared as if his whole activity were a series of compromises and concessions. Karl Radek, the celebrated wit of the Communist party, once said of him: "As a true Marxist, Lenin makes his decisions on the basis of facts, and only then builds his theories explaining those decisions of his."

Trotsky, to the contrary, never bent this way or that; for he was always confident of being right. He was sure that he knew what he wanted and, moreover, that he also knew which way lay the best and the shortest road to the achievement of his wants. When Lenin heard a report, he carefully listened and really profited. Trotsky, on the other hand, listened superficially and often impatiently. In any conversation he liked to make the other man (or men) feel that he, Trotsky, knew better.

In the years 1921–23, it was no longer a secret that Trotsky was in frequent opposition to the basic policy of the Communist party and, to a degree, to Lenin himself. We all knew, too, that a number of outstanding Communist leaders found themselves disagreeing increasingly with Trotsky and his ideas. Everybody talked of this rift, quite freely. Even the Soviet press published items and articles about it. And yet almost everyone, with the exception of a handful of Communists who actually knew, thought that Trotsky's position in the party and the government was solid. More than that: the general impression was that, with Lenin's eventual passing, Trotsky would step into his shoes as Russia's first leader.

Toward the end of 1923 Lenin's illness became so serious that no hope at all was held out for his recovery, and the Politbureau earnestly discussed the question of his successor. I had just returned to Moscow from one of my prolonged trips to London, and when I called on Ryckov at his home I was told that he was away at a Politbureau meeting. Since he was due to return shortly, I decided to wait. But instead of Ryckov, George Lomov appeared in the apartment. I thought that he knew the impending solution of the problem under discussion. "Tell me, George," I asked, "who is elected or to be elected as Lenin's successor? Trotsky, of course?"

"Not at all," was the quick answer. "We prefer three men with a modest head apiece to one man with that swelled head of his."

I must have had a surprised expression, for he explained: "The revolution has by now found its proper track. We don't need geniuses any longer. We need good and modest leaders who will take our locomotive farther along the same track. But as to Trotsky, as to our Lev Davidovich, why, we would never know our destination if we gave him the controls!"

The trio that succeeded Lenin were, of course, Zinoviev, Kamenev, and Stalin.

(12)

STALIN, THE RISING STAR

I HAVE ALREADY SPOKEN OF MY ONE MEETING WITH STALIN, WHICH WAS BRIEF AND wholly accidental. During the course of all my work in Soviet business organizations I did not happen to see the man at close quarters; but, despite my lack of personal connections with him, I do have a few words to say about Stalin. I recall, for instance, the talk which throughout the early 1920's was heard increasingly in the governing circles of Russia, on the subject of this rising star of the Communist party. And at the time I had, at first hand, a certain amount of information about Stalin's personality and activities. Together these two sources gave me a picture of his first political ascendancy though, of course, I do not pretend to present an exhaustive outline of his meteoric career.

Stalin's role in the history of Russia and her revolution has been too decisive for any one of his contemporaries to be able to tell its full story; meanwhile, the data that we do have begin with his birth on December 20, 1879, in the village of Gori. The son of a Georgian cobbler named Vissarion Djugashvili, the boy was destined for the priesthood, at the desire of his family and especially of his mother, Catherine. At the age of fourteen Joseph entered the theological seminary of Tiflis, but a secret society of Marxists converted him to the cause of the revolution, and when he was nineteen he joined the Russian Social Democratic party.

Expelled from the seminary "for political unreliability," young Stalin plunged into revolutionary work. For a number of years he was destined to live and labor underground; to suffer prison and Siberian exile; to undertake clever and successful escapes, only to be caught by the tsar's police again and again. His real name was seldom mentioned and little known. The party called him "David," "Koba," "Nizheradi," "Chizhikov," "Stalin"—conspiratorial pseudonyms all.

The Caucasus and other Russian provinces were the arena of his activities. At times he published heavy-footed discourses in the underground press of the Bolsheviks, Russian and Georgian; but his main strength was his organizational ability, not his theories and ideas.

After 1905, during the years of tsarist reaction against the temporarily defeated revolution, Stalin displayed his considerable stubbornness, not to say fanaticism, in the building and safeguarding of the Bolshevik apparatus, in the restoration of the underground nuclei, unearthed and destroyed by the tsar's gendarmes. Stalin also found new connections of value to his party. He obtained new money, not stopping even at armed expropriation: once he actually held up a convoy of the tsarist treasury in Tiflis. All the singularities of his one-track mind, his wilful nature, found outlets in his new activities.

The revolution of 1917 saw Stalin in the first ranks of the Bolshevik party, with a well-formed reputation as a practical and active leader. Following the October–November upheaval of that year and the establishment of the Soviet government, Stalin became the people's commissar of nationalities (national minorities of Russia, that is). Soon afterward he was taking an energetic part in the civil war.

I remember that the very first conflict between Trotsky and the Politbureau occurred over Stalin. Trotsky complained that the local army staff at Tsaritsyn (now Stalingrad), headed by Klim Voroshilov and Josef Stalin, was deliberately disobeying his orders from headquarters. As the conflict progressed, assuming ever sharper forms, Trotsky demanded Stalin's recall from the southern front. At first the Politbureau would not satisfy Trotsky's request; but he persisted, and finally Stalin was recalled. The majority of high-ranking Bolshevik leaders sided with Stalin in this argument, but, irritated by Trotsky's superiority complex, they were anti-Trotsky rather than pro-Stalin. Even at that time I heard remarks in some circles to the effect that Trotsky was "beginning his counterrevolutionary work of disorganization," that he did not want to carry out the party's decisions.

At the same time, the top stratum of the Communist party of Russia did not have any real love for Stalin. Rather, it was respect. In and around the Kremlin, men and women referred to Stalin as "he," and this pronoun was used simply yet with overtones of restrained awe, as well as with a certain tinge of alarm or fear. "He" was pronounced in a lower voice than the rest of the sentence, whatever it was.

Admittedly, Stalin was an old and prominent Bolshevik, but the channels of his work in those underground years had led away from the guiding circles of his party; so in a way he was a new man to many in the party as he advanced to its foreground. There was, too, a forcefulness bordering on aggressiveness in him, and his party comrades did not know just what his ascendancy might portend for the party and Russia. There was an air of the unknown, of vague dangers, wherever he appeared.

Beginning with 1919, while still running his Commissariat of Nationalities, Stalin carried the added duties of people's commissar of state control (later called Workers' and Peasants' Inspection). At this new post, however, he confined himself to general policy-making. The detail work was done by his deputy chief, Avanesov, whom I often met on business. It was Avanesov who represented Stalin's control (or inspection) department at the sessions of the Council of Labor and Defense.

The Workers' and Peasants' Inspection had important functions. It examined with a stern eye all the economic units of the Soviet republic. Although Stalin seldom appeared in the open as the chief of the inspection, his instructions guided all its work from behind the scenes. By giving Stalin such a responsible post, Lenin clearly demonstrated his high opinion of the Georgian's organizing talents.

Thus, gradually, Stalin was concentrating in his hands all the valuable information available on the personnel of both the Communist party network and the Soviet governmental apparatus. This gave him ample weapons for the future—when he was to need them to combat his rivals in the party.

As Stalin's influence grew, his name was heard in the Communist circles of Russia with increasing frequency. Some spoke of him with hope, and almost with affection. They beheld in him the only man capable of halting "this stranger Trotsky" in his upward rush—especially after the Tsaritsyn argument between the two. Others, to the contrary, referred to Stalin with ill-concealed fear and hostility. These were the people who had spoken or acted against him in the past; it was realized by then that Stalin never forgot an offense.

Neither one of Stalin's two commissariats—nationalities and inspection—was much in the foreign public eye; and if the new leader's name appeared seldom in the newspaper headlines even of Russia, abroad it was hardly known. In actual practice, however, Stalin was already gathering into his capable hands the main levers of the state machinery in the Soviet republic. His duties as the head man of the state's inspection gave him a chance to study in detail the entire structure of the people's economy. When Lenin wrote the outline of the inspection, as it was to function after its reorganization, he declared that this department was to be the chief tool in improving the Soviet governing apparatus. The inspection, according to Lenin, was to be a model institution of the Red state. The best organizational talent available in Russia was to be drawn into its personnel. Much thought, care, and expert knowledge were to be invested in its framework from the very beginning.

Truly, all aspects of life in Russia came within the sphere of Stalin's Workers' and Peasants' Inspection: financial affairs, personnel matters, production problems, and so on. This was where Stalin gained much of that practical experience he was to display to the world in the years to come. This was where he found the resources and resourcefulness for his own later plans for Russia's far-reaching industrialization.

Nor should we overlook the benefit Stalin derived in those early years from his work as the commissar of nationalities. Back in 1913, Lenin had written: "Russia is a bright quilt of many nationalities. Despite this, the tsarist policy —the policy of the landlord-noblemen supported by Russia's bourgeoisie—is aimed at the narrow and reactionary glorification of the Russian nationality alone. Thus it is a policy directed against the majority of this country's population. Side by side with this, there rears its ugly head the bourgeois nationalism of the other nationalities—of the Poles, the Jews, the Ukrainians, the Georgians, and so on. This narrow nationalism strives to distract the working class from its class struggle."

In that same year of 1913, Stalin was laboring on his first literary experiment —an article entitled "Marxism and Nationalism." He had studied the nationality question in Austro-Hungary, which he now took as a negative example while developing the theses and conclusions of his essay.

Young Stalin's interest in this question was natural. He was born in a part of Russia where the problem of nationalities was a difficult one; where the workers of the province—the Georgians, the Tatars, the Armenians, and the Russians—had to solve the question quickly and efficiently in order to establish peace among themselves and thus have clear decks from which to fight together against their common political enemy, the autocracy of Russia.

Lenin, then living abroad, wrote to Maxim Gorky that a "wonderful Georgian" was with him, composing a remarkable article on nationalities for the magazine *Prosveshcheniye* ("Enlightenment"), basing it on the rich experience of Austro-Hungary and the fratricidal struggle between her different nationalities. This was Stalin's "Marxism and Nationalism," with its main premise that each nationality in Russia had the right of self-determination, up to and including its right of secession, but that the proletariat of all nationalities had the duty of organizing into labor unions and political parties common to all.

These early ideas of Stalin's served as the foundation of the celebrated decree issued by the Soviet government on November 15, 1917, under the title "The Declaration of the Rights of the Nationalities of Russia." The outstanding points of the decree were: (1) equality and sovereignty of the peoples of Russia; (2) their right to free self-determination, including their right to secede and form independent states; (3) abolition of all and sundry privileges, as well as discriminations of national and religious nature; (4) unlimited cultural development of national minorities and ethnic groups inhabiting Russia. The two signatures under this decree were Vladimir Ulianov—Lenin—and Josef Djugashvili—Stalin.

In time to come the Soviet government expanded this policy still further, particularly with regard to the raising of the cultural levels of the national minorities in Russia. And in the solution of the problem of Russia's nationalities, the Soviet authorities did indeed evidence statesmanship of the highest caliber. Stalin truly brought forth the inner untouched strength of the nationalities and tribes peopling the great expanses of Russia, especially her Asiatic lands. For many of the national groups this was more than an awakening from a sleep of many centuries; it was, in fact, being born into the modern world. And while working out his plan, Stalin saw to it that Russia did not become an arena of conflict among those nationalities—that it did not degenerate into another crazyquilt, as the Austro-Hungarian empire had in its day.

It should be noted, however, that while carrying out, through the Communist party, his ideas concerning the Russian family of nationalities, Stalin reminded the working class that the nationality problem, though important, was actually secondary to certain other political and social tasks of a more general character. Thus he kept within definite limits the nationalistic strivings of some groups in Russia. As a matter of fact, this was not, on the whole, so difficult a task as it might have been, for the majority of Russia's national groups and tribes were at a lower stage of cultural development than, say, Velikorussia (Great Russia), Belorussia (White Russia), and the Ukraine. The Russian culture proper—that is, the language and literature of Great Russia—proved to be the magnetic, cementing, and dominating element in this conglomerate of nationalities.

Stalin made sure that this element had every chance to grow. He felt it would be unstatesmanlike to allow boundless play to the separatist tendencies of such parts of the Soviet republic as the Ukraine or his own native Georgia, with their highly sensitized national consciousness. At one time or another, however, some Communists of those lands attempted to foster such nationalistic movements—they paid dearly for their efforts. Alexander Cherviakov, the chief of Soviet Belorussia, committed suicide during the purges of the 1930's. Suicide was also the fate of Skrypnik, the chief of the Soviet Ukraine. And a group of the highest-placed Communists of Georgia—Stalin's own fellow-fighters in the old days of his struggle against the Mensheviks of that region—

were ruthlessly liquidated by the new leader when they showed signs of wanting more national independence for their region than he was willing to grant.

As for the Jews of Russia, they were soon emancipated, within the confines of this new national policy of the Soviets. However, scattered as they were all over the country, the Jews were to a degree assimilated as well as emancipated.

In short, then, Stalin had through his control of nationality affairs an early and extensive opportunity to become acquainted intimately with the problems, interests, and possibilities of each of the many nationalities to be found on Russian territory, including those national groups which in the past had been only feeble currents in the main stream of the nation's life. And through his command of the inspection—the control agent of the state apparatus of the Red republic—he acquired a thorough knowledge of all the weaknesses, no less than all the strong features, of Soviet Russia. These two circumstances were to play a most important role in the subsequent political career of Stalin—they made him what he is today, the leader of the Soviet Union.

The turning-point in that initial phase of Stalin's ascendancy in the 1920's was his appointment to the post of secretary-general of the Communist party. This added to his two other advantages a third and most significant one, that of controlling the state organism *politically*. As secretary-general of the party he effected this new control through the secretaries of Communist cells the country over. This armed him with a tremendous amount of actual power over the workaday governing business in Russia.

The other old Bolsheviks, outsmarted and outmaneuvered by Stalin through this strategic acquisition of the three posts, began to fear for their future, even for their lives. Krassin, for instance, would exclaim in despair: "Oh, but what am I to do? Stalin hates me, you know!"

Or take Karl Danishevsky. This old and daring Communist suddenly re-called an old sin of his own—the time, long before the revolution, when he had sympathized with certain of Trotsky's ideas and, besides, had labored to bring the Bolsheviks and the Mensheviks together. He now trembled at Stalin's excellent memory and steely eye. For months he begged for an interview and a "chance to explain," and finally the request was granted. With much satisfaction, almost happiness, Danishevsky came back to his friends saying: "Stalin has forgiven me!"

Everyone knew Stalin's stubbornness and harshness. This supreme master of politics marched toward his dictatorial power in an assured and implacable manner, overcoming whatever handicaps and opposition were in his way. Trotsky's fiery aggressiveness was smashed by the cold, shrewd craftiness of the imperturbable Stalin. And the victory remained in the grasp of this unique secretary-general, of "this steel-like, unbending man," as he was defined by one Soviet writer.

On one occasion I came pretty close to making Stalin's actual acquaintance.

My candidacy for a certain post in the North Timber Trust had to be approved by the Communist party, which meant that Stalin as its secretary-general had to pass upon my reliability. In this connection I was informed that Stalin was aware of my existence and activities, that he viewed my work favorably, and that soon I would have an opportunity to be presented to him. But this was at a time when I was about to break with the Soviets, and shortly after Stalin's word had been brought to me, I left to go abroad and never again returned to Soviet Russia.

Legends are likely to grow around the successful personalities of revolutionary eras, and flattering legends about Stalin are already galore. In the eastern part of the Soviet Union especially, there are folk tales which almost deify him. These legends are encouraged in the "interests of the revolution." The American writer John Scott (who worked as a machine hand behind the Urals) remarked, apropos of this phenomenon, that the Communist party of Russia, though atheistic in its essence, did not mind creating the "cult of the leader"—for the sake of strengthening the party's authority in the land.

Just for once I should like to tell a different sort of story, which I once heard from a political opponent of Stalin. This man was, like Stalin, a Georgian and a Social Democrat, but, on the other hand, he was a Menshevik. I met him abroad, in the middle 1930's, at the time of the sensational trials in Moscow.

"In the old times, before the revolution," I said to him, "you as a leading Georgian Menshevik knew Stalin far better than many others did. As a revolutionary, Stalin is sincere, isn't he? Well then, speaking frankly, can you tell me how he can believe his own accusations against Bukharin, Ryckov, Krestinsky, and many other defendants now standing trial in Moscow? How can he honestly believe that they were traitors, that they acted as Hitler's and Japan's agents? Surely down deep in his heart he knows that all such charges are utter lies!"

My friend was thoughtful and silent for a while, then he replied: "It's really difficult to explain such a man as Stalin, with all the good and bad interlarded in him in a complicated pattern. But I'll tell you of an episode in his early life which will reveal his character to you as hardly anything else can.

"You will remember that at one time, long before the revolution of 1917, the two factions of the Social Democratic party—the Mensheviks and the Bolsheviks—got into quite an argument over the problem of our attitude toward the liberal elements in Russia. We, the Mensheviks, tried to convince the Bolsheviks that it was imperative to continue our collaboration with the liberal bourgeoisie in the field of our common struggle against tsarism. The Bolsheviks, on the other hand, stood for boycotting the bourgeoisie. They didn't trust even the liberals among the bourgeois.

"Finally, it was decided to hold one final meeting of the underground leaders, in order to listen to one Menshevik speaker and one Bolshevik orator, and then put the question to vote. After much effort the two factions found an apartment which seemed safe enough from the prying eyes of the tsar's spies, and the best brains of both sides gathered to tackle the question. The Bolshevik spokesman rose first. When he was through with his exposition, our Menshevik representative began his talk. From the very beginning of the Menshevik's address it was apparent that most of those gathered in the apartment shared his, not the Bolshevik's, viewpoint. Our victory was imminent. Soon both sides were ready for the vote.

"But just before we were to begin casting our ballots, two revolver shots rang outside, in the courtyard of an apartment building. The police! The highest leaders of the party, assembled for the occasion, were to be arrested in the raid! All hurried and scurried in this direction and that, trying to escape. No one thought to go on with the vote.

"There were no arrests, however. It was a false alarm—deliberately caused by Stalin. Earlier in the evening, when he had first noticed the effect of the address by the Menshevik, he had slipped out of the apartment into the courtyard and fired his revolver into the air—to prevent the unfavorable resolution from passing.

"It was a risky thing on his part, to do this impromptu shooting. We all knew very well that Stalin was not an agent-provocateur, yet there is no doubt that such shooting was usually done by provocateurs. Someone could have shot back at him without realizing who he was and why he was shooting out there in the dark. But, as you see, he would not stop at risking his own life and the lives of all the leaders of both factions of the party—just to see his viewpoint prevail! Here is the genuine Stalin for you. Draw your own conclusions....."

I do not know to this day how true the story was. It may have been just another of the many legends, good and bad, that have grown around Stalin's early life. And yet it is typical of the man who, to safeguard socialism in one country, did not hesitate to sign a pact with Hitler and shortly thereafter to lead the Russian people in its heroic defense of its fatherland—in its determination to annihilate this very same Hitler.

We must remember, however, that on countless occasions Stalin has discounted his own achievements by referring to himself as merely the disciple of a great master. As he put it many times: "Where I am in doubt, I try to think of what Lenin would have done."

In view of that, it becomes important to remember Lenin's own statement: "For me, theory is only a hypothesis, not the Holy Scripture; it is a tool in our daily work." The sudden shifts in Stalin's policies that mystify foreign newspapermen now become understandable. Stalin is really Lenin's pupil, and if he discards today what he worshiped yesterday, it is only because it has ceased to serve the supreme interest of Soviet Russia.

(13)

LENIN CONSIDERS A CHANGE

The so-called war communism of Russia embraced a period of nearly three years—an era of stormy upheavals; of ruthless fighting on the home and foreign fronts; of desperate attempts to activate the people's economy through the stern measures of terror and other coercion; of stark ruin, unemployment, starvation, and epidemics. The three years began in the middle of 1918 and ended in the spring of 1921, when the Communist party, through its leader Lenin, announced its New Economic Policy.

For several months before this period, up to the Treaty of Brest Litovsk in March, 1918, Soviet Russia was still at war with the Central Powers. The treaty was a signal for the German occupation of the Ukraine, the Crimea, and Russia's Baltic region. Then Russia's civil war began in earnest—in the south, the north, and Siberia. The years of 1919 and 1920 were bloody and tragic, not alone with the battles against the White generals—Denikin, Wrangel, Kolchak, Miller, and Yudenich—but also with the struggle to repulse the foreign interventionists who were aiding the White Guards: the British in Archangel, in south Russia, and in the Caucasus; the French in the south; the Japanese in the Russian Far East. And this was also the period of a life-and-death struggle against the blockade, wherewith the Allies nearly strangled the Soviet regime in Russia.

In 1920 there was, besides, the Soviets' unfortunate war with Poland, as a result of which Russia lost to Poland the western Ukraine and western Belorussia. The Baltic provinces, Estonia, Latvia, and Lithuania, separated from Russia and became independent states at about the same time.

It was against this gory background that Russia was endeavoring to carry out a tremendous revolution in her politics, economics, and social structure. Abolition of private landownership came first, with its mass confiscation of landlords' property. This was followed by a sweeping expropriation of banks, railroads, factories, and plants and all kinds of corporations. Smaller enterprises had their turn, too; they were not spared.

The Soviet government groped as it proceeded to build a new economy on these ruins. The workers' management of the sequestered factories and mines responded but little to directives from the Kremlin; the workers' effort was mostly spontaneous and unruly, bringing in its wake disorder and at times complete chaos.

Because of the shortages of raw materials, of fuel, and of food, the industrial output fell to about 26 per cent of the pre-war level. And even this scant yield was earmarked for the needs of the Red Army; civilians got practically nothing. In many cases factories stood idle or diminished their production because there were not enough workers—the latter had been disappearing into the countryside to save themselves and their families from the hunger that decimated the cities.

Lenin realized that the chief source of his power lay in skilled industrial labor and that he therefore had to prevent this labor force from melting away from the factories to the fields to grow their own food. The same consideration prompted him to refrain from including too many such skilled workers even in the armed forces defending the revolution. Although such labor was willing, often eager, to fight, Lenin endeavored to have this social and economic force preserved as much as possible. Thus the army of the revolution came to consist mainly of young enthusiastic Communists as yet untrained in the field of industrial labor and of those former members of the tsar's army and navy who had spearheaded the revolution.

To add to the confusion, illnesses and malnutrition resulted in absenteeism among the workers who still remained in the cities; and when they did come to their lathes, production per man was very low. In the country, too, the picture was far from cheerful. The fields in crops were only three-fifths of the pre-war norm. Yield per acre diminished catastrophically. Hundreds of thousands of people died of famine. A two-year drought in the Volga region in 1920–21 cost millions of lives. Transportation was completely ruined; 60 per cent of all locomotives were "sick."

To fight the general collapse of the country's economic life, the Soviet government resorted to compulsory mobilization of workers and to a labor draft of all citizens to help clear the railroads and prepare stock piles of fuel. The Kremlin ordered armed action to take grain from peasants, using labor battalions from the various industries in large cities to wrest it from the individual producers at the pistol point. Force and terror were common methods everywhere, for the era was one of a cruel and implacable dictatorship. Lenin himself defined the struggle as "a completely ruthless fight between the vanquished but not as yet annihilated capitalism and the already born but as yet weak Communism."

The Soviet authorities understood their task with a crude simplicity. "The roots of capitalism" were to be torn out with all possible force and dispatch. The very foundation of capitalism had to be blown sky-high. This, of course, often meant the physical destruction of men and women hostile (or allegedly hostile) to the new regime.

At the same time, for economic reasons, the peasantry was frequently at loggerheads with the Bolshevik government. The city failed to supply the village with manufactured goods. Private trade was forbidden. Requisition of the peasants' grain and other produce left the village bereft of its last reserves of food and fodder. The impression deepened in the countryside that the peasants had to give up everything without receiving anything at all in return —either nails or seed or agricultural machinery; for the state had little of such goods to give the peasants.

The result was that revolts flared up here and there, some of them assuming threatening proportions. There was, for instance, the peasants' rebellion in the Tambov province under Antonov and almost simultaneously the famous uprising at Kronstadt, where the insurgents—sailors and soldiers—rose against the Bolsheviks under the slogan of "Free Soviets." At Kronstadt the men, mostly of peasant origin, were actually expressing the dissatisfaction of the peasant masses of Russia with the practices of War Communism.

The Communist leaders realized that the economic life of the country was held together by the thin thread of old stock piles. But many of these reserves were being expended haphazardly and according to no plan. Soon the awful day would come when there would be no reserves left. The basic problem, therefore, was to organize new production in both industry and agriculture. Somehow labor everywhere had to become once more diligent and productive. In 1920 Lenin demanded from his associates that a plan be drawn up, "a great blueprint of economics covering not less than ten years in its scope." This was the beginning of the idea out of which the famous five-year plans were eventually born.

Lenin well understood the unavoidable and urgent necessity of transforming backward, rural Russia into a nation with a highly developed industry. He called this "the establishment of a new technical base" for Communism. He connected these plans with his pet plans for Russia's electrification, in which he saw the surest method of a quick shift to new paths in Russian economics and social order. However, both the vast industrialization and the electrification of the country were the "music of the future." Meantime, everybody had to work under the difficult conditions of the dreariest reality imaginable.

The so-called central or head committees (*glavki*) predominated at that time in every branch of industry. They were composed of delegates of labor unions for each field, working together with representatives of the Soviet government. In transport, for instance, the men were from railroad and water-shipping unions. These committees were in charge of their respective branches of industry the nation over; and all committees were brought together in Ryckov's Supreme Council of Economy, which was at the head of all industry, being in effect the Soviet commissariat of industry. Each provincial capital had a Council of Economy of its own and its own organization of trade-unions—all of which had to follow instructions from their central offices in Moscow—the Supreme Council of Economy, on the one hand, and the All-Russian Central Council of Trade-Unions (or of the chief body of a specific union), on the other.

In theory this scheme was quite plausible and attractive, but in actuality it worked badly. The organization of the people's economy was a horizontal one, in accordance with the administrative division of Russia into provinces; and, at the same time, a vertical one—for in all those provinces, and counties as well, the local provincial and county Councils of Economy intervened, wanting to have their say in the management of industry and agriculture. In the same spirit the local unions interfered, too, and as these councils and unions were further subordinated to the local Soviets, there was a dizzy complexity of governmental interrelations. Because local offices somehow or other depended upon, or were subordinated to, a wide network of other local offices, orders and instructions from Moscow often were set aside in favor of local orders. What with central decrees from Moscow, on the one hand, and the demands from the local authorities, on the other, factory managers found themselves between the hammer and the anvil.

Plants and factories in the provinces—or, to use the term of the period, "on the spot"—were completely in the hands of local authorities. The latter strove to gain the widest possible autonomy and to withhold part of the production for local needs. The central government in Moscow was not yet strong enough to combat and conquer these centrifugal tendencies.

A further complication was the indisputable fact that provincial workers were at a lower cultural level than the proletariat of Moscow. The best of provincial proletarians had by then become deputies to national organs, and had already moved to Moscow, with the result that in many cases plant committees were clearly unqualified to manage the enterprises falling into their hands. Nor could the officials of the local Council of Economy boast of stronger qualifications.

As a rule, local organs, when in need of food and financial aid from the center, would draw up very ambitious programs of production in the plants under their direction. They promised a wide-scale output of strategic goods and in return demanded advances of funds and provisions against their own industrial castles in the air. Supplying these committees and councils with funds was an easy matter, as Moscow's money-printing presses could be kept humming. But provisioning was quite another thing, and the central organs could satisfy such demands only in very limited quantities. Even these infinitesimal handouts, however, were of great importance to the provinces—but then it would turn out that the supply plans, worked out by the local authorities, were entirely impractical. Whatever output the local industries would finally deliver had to go mainly to the Red Army. Of the small part not claimed by the army, the local organs of the Soviet government kept for their own region all they could—a lion's share, really. The central Soviet authority received from these local bodies almost nothing to satisfy consumers' needs in other parts of the country.

Thus the economic catastrophe spiraled ever downward. Increasingly it became evident that some *new* way of saving the nation's economy must be found. As long as the civil war raged on, as long as the first duty of the government was to preserve and strengthen its political power, the Kremlin could somehow overlook the economic collapse—for the sake of and in the hope of future victories. But when the armed conflict ceased and the nation began to demobilize itself, economic problems became truly life-and-death problems. Before the Kremlin there loomed this choice: either to change its entire economic policy or to see its own and the nation's ruination as the result of this desperate crisis.

The thought that the course of Communism must be changed had long been in the air. In the Red Army especially, by its social origin closely tied with the peasantry, new and definite trends were taking shape. Red Army men demanded concessions for the village. They wanted cessation of grain requisitions from the peasants and of the armed expeditions to squeeze food supplies out of the countryside, which were actually pauperizing the village. But when Trotsky, one of the first among the leaders to do so, spoke in this connection of the necessity of "altering the system," he was charged by other Communist zealots with lapsing into Menshevism.

Ever since the critical days of the summer of 1919, when my name was included by Lenin in the list of those who were to be evacuated from Moscow in the face of Denikin's drive, I had been friends with a group of old Bolsheviks whose names were on the same list. That list was our bond; these leading Communists trusted me, partly because they knew I was to be in their company in the evacuation that never came. Once, in 1920, during a session of the Council of Labor and Defense, I had to wait in the council's anteroom long hours for my turn to appear at the session as an expert with a special report, and, while waiting, I talked with two of these old Bolsheviks, Andrew Lezhava and Gleb Krzhizhanovsky. The former was an assistant to Lenin; his friend was one of the earliest outstanding Soviet planners. We talked of Russia's dire plight, and this led to similar talks in the more private atmosphere of our respective homes. Presently we came to the conclusion that, in addition to the famous list of 1919, an identical attitude toward the events of 1920 united the three of us. And this was our common position:

we were (Striving to see Russia's economy improved speedily) we should draw the Kremlin's attention to the serious and sharp defects in its economic policy. The country's economy lay expiring in the death-grasp of War Communism, and the whole nation was fast approaching its end. All our private efforts to influence individual commissars into an early correction of the errors had been without avail; therefore it behooved us to bring our suggestions to the attention of Lenin himself.

We decided not to write any special memoranda or to draw up any formal programs but merely to work toward an interview with Lenin. Since, of the three of us, I was the only one who was an expert and not a Communist politician and could therefore speak to Lenin on such a subject more freely than the others, I was selected as the first one to address him. I also had the advantage of enjoying the trust of both Lenin and the non-Communists.

So once again I went to see Lenin. This talk took place in the same small reception room where I had been received the first time I met him. Lenin was waiting for me with an expression which told me that he had been advised beforehand by my friends of the subject I was to broach.

I began the conversation by stating our group's premises and then proceeded to illustrate the main points with examples from the practice of the Commissariat of Food Supply and of the local organs of the Communist party (the local agencies ruled even more strictly than the central government, as a whole). While at the center, in Moscow, the authorities were guided mostly by the considerations and needs of the civil war, the provincial officials thought and acted in terms of a 100 per cent socialism.

At this point I reminded Lenin that in my capacity as manager of supplies I was in constant touch with persons on the spot—with men coming to Moscow from all the nooks and corners of Russia. Our timber organization reached everywhere, and my work afforded me a contact with the peasantry, the industrial workers, and the party officials heading all manner of local organizations. I knew that all of them were dissatisfied, that all complained of the growing hostility toward the government even on the part of those citizens who had formerly followed the Soviets enthusiastically. And the cause of this hostility, the target of the complaints, was always the same: the fierce behavior of the armed expeditions roaming the countryside in search of the peasants' food.

But I never finished my speech. Lenin interrupted me:

"I understand what brought you here. I agree with you entirely. We are indeed in need of changes. We must broaden the base of our government. We should introduce economic relaxations and concessions. But don't forget, all you comrades, that the civil war is not quite ended yet. It still makes demands upon us. At Balashov a Communist division lost 60 per cent of its men. We cannot begin a retreat in our policy when hundreds and thousands of men continue to fall, continue to give their lives, while holding our banner in their hands. We cannot change our banner in the midst of this battle. The least change will kill our soldiers' enthusiasm. First we must vanquish the forces of counterrevolution, and only then will we begin to think of changes. Right now all of us must strive toward a sensible use of everything and anything that may help us in our fight against the Whites. However," he added later, "some of the measures you suggest will be adopted."

When it was time for me to go, he said by way of conclusion: "Leave it to us to decide the basic problems and to set the time and place and method for carrying out our decisions. You experts continue to do your work."

I felt that this was the boss talking; that Lenin could not only listen and argue but also order. And yet I felt, too, that a change was coming, that ideologically Lenin was preparing to change the system, but that he needed time—that he was looking for just the right moment and the most plausible excuse for putting the brakes on the revolution. He had talked to me the way he did on that occasion because he was the head of the government, which always had in store some logical explanation for whatever action it took.

Our conversation was not wholly fruitless. Within a few days it became known that the Commissariat of Food Supply had issued instructions to its officials to allow a certain easing-up in the demands made upon the peasants for their grain and other produce. Other changes were in evidence in other economic organizations of the Soviets. My friends and I were pleased with even such small victories for our viewpoint.

Several months later, toward the end of 1920, I happened to be on a mission to Berlin. There I met Y. O. Martov, the Menshevik leader who had left Russia a short time before and never returned. In utter confidence I told him of my conversation with Lenin. He became quite excited and exclaimed indignantly:

"How dared he answer you like that! This means that he sends Russian workers to die in battle for the slogans which he doesn't mean to keep!"

In this exclamation I once more felt the old, old argument between the two main currents of Russian Marxism: Who is to decide the fate of the working class? Is it the working class as a whole, after the pattern of Western democracies? Or is it the class-conscious vanguard speaking for the whole—the revolutionary political party, which, better than the nearsighted mass, understands the real interests of the proletariat?

Here were the two different approaches to this problem, expressed by the two outstanding leaders of the once-united Russian Social Democracy. One leader held that all was permissible in the name of the basic idea—the triumph of the revolution. The other maintained that even in the revolutionary struggle man must be guided by certain humanitarian principles. Perhaps that is why Martov was an *émigré* in Berlin while Lenin ruled in the Kremlin.

(14)

LENIN MAKES A SHIFT

EARLY IN 1921 LENIN REALIZED THAT WITH THE PEASANTS' UPRISING IN TAMBOV AND the sailors' rebellion in Kronstadt the masses of the Russian people had just about reached the end of their rope. The two rebellions showed him that he could procrastinate no longer. Now, at last, he would act.

Despite considerable opposition in his own circle, Lenin firmly resolved that Russia should follow his New Economic Policy, which meant an abandonment of "integral Communism," a partial re-establishment of free trade in small industry, and a whole series of concessions to the peasantry. Lenin, better than some of his aides, realized that agriculture and industry could not be revived if the old methods so loved by Larin were continued.

In March, 1921, the first new step was taken when the armed expeditions to drain the peasants' supplies were abolished in favor of "taxation in kind." The gist of this reform was that a peasant, having delivered to the state agencies a definite tax in produce, could do whatever he pleased with the rest of his grain, livestock, and other produce and property. He could even sell on the market the surplus yields of his acreage and labor.

With this came a general freedom of trade in country and town. The right of initiative, of private enterprise, was restored not to the peasants alone but also to artisans and even to middlemen and small industrialists. In his speeches of 1921, Lenin did not conceal that this New Economic Policy was a strategic retreat for Communism. He also defined it as a breathing spell, during which "there comes about, on the basis of an even limited freedom of trade, a resurrection of petty bourgeoisie and capitalism."

"The ruin and need in the nation," he declared, "are so great that we simply cannot undertake an immediate creation of large-scale industrial production on socialist principles. Consequently we must, up to a point, help to restore small industry which demands neither complicated machinery nor any considerable supplies of raw materials, fuel, and food from the state—which industry actually can give immediate and definite aid to the peasant's economy, raising its productivity."

Though capitalism was thus being revived, it was state capitalism. All the factories and plants—all large industry—remained in the hands of the Soviet government. The state also preserved for itself a complete monopoly of foreign trade. Foreign capital could be permitted via concessions only, and these were granted by the same all-powerful state, which controlled them every step of the way after granting them. There was no denationalization of any mines, forests, oil fields, or factories.

Still, the entire system of our economic life was being changed cardinally. We were soon to build a unique socioeconomic regime, where, side by side with socialized industry, existed certain elements of capitalism, thereby causing a competition between the socialist and nonsocialist sectors of economy. Because of this the socialist sector was also adopting the old capitalistic profit-and-loss way of looking at things—the state industry had to pay for itself, as Lenin taught his party. The socialist part of Soviet economy was to learn buying and selling at a profit—Lenin commanded its managers and directors. Because of that, the socialist element itself often adopted mixed forms of activity, that is, on occasion it resorted to the help of private enterprise, And, of course, the New Economic Policy was continuously creating an entirely new psychological atmosphere, new conditions of everyday existence. While releasing private initiative, it led to a new variety in life.

Naturally enough, this tremendous shift to a new policy was no easy matter. It met with opposition both at the center and in the provinces. Many Communists, having got used to the implacable ways of the first years of War Communism and having spent much time in the Red Army, would not even hear of this "descent with the brakes on." They regarded the New Economic Policy as almost a betrayal of the revolution and constantly put spokes in its wheels. In addition, the former bourgeois and the middle classes, while allowed a wide range of activity under this New Economic Policy, realized only too well that the breathing spell granted by Lenin was merely temporary. They knew that the Communist government was being forced by sheer necessity to give in here and there; that the government was doing it extremely reluctantly and would at the very first opportunity return to a radical and complete application of its original revolutionary program. Even Lenin's assurance that this change was "seriously meant and for a long time" they received with little faith, considering it a mere tactical maneuver.

This is why the changeover from War Communism to the New Economic Policy was such a complicated and prolonged process, marked by a struggle among various groups and by a multitude of inherent and insoluble contradictions. I had to witness all of this in my own field of work—the timber industry.

I have already mentioned the importance of the timber industry in connection with the fuel problem in Russia. The inauguration of the New Economic Policy brought many new tasks to the industry for this reason: Russia was to resume her old trade with foreign countries, and the export of timber had always had an important place in that trade.

Lenin, of course, realized very well that the introduction of the New Economic Policy was bringing the nation's economy back to the monetary system and that for the operations of the Central State Bank it was necessary to build up a sizable gold reserve. This was the bailiwick of Aron Sheinman, the acting commissar of finance and the future head of the State Bank. At Lenin's behest, Sheinman called together a special conference, in the course of which I voiced my thoughts on creating the needed gold reserve and laying sound foundations for Russia's foreign trade by way of timber export.

My suggestions were relayed to Lenin, and within a few days I was summoned to a conference of the special commission of the Council of People's Commissars sitting under Andrew Lezhava. The commission asked me: "In what degree is it possible to restore the timber industry, so as to make it a source of export and thus of foreign currency for the Soviet state coffers?" I asked for a few days' leeway to think it over, and on the appointed day I had my report ready.

In working out my plan I was guided by my knowledge of Russia's great timber riches and of their geographic distribution. The forest wealth of European Russia is distributed very unevenly: there are, for instance, districts in which woods occupy only 3–8 per cent of the area. And there are regions which are usually considered well wooded but which actually contain entire provinces without any timber whatsoever. Now it was necessary to rationalize the timber industry. The task was twofold: first, to increase the output of timber and, second, to put an end to the rapid deforestation of the most highly populated regions in European Russia. I proposed the following system: There should be less chopping down of our forests for fuel. We should begin to exploit some of our still untouched forests—those farther away from easy transportation. The centrally located forests should be used for domestic needs. Export needs should be satisfied out of the more distant woods, especially those in the north, with its river and sea transportation. For domestic uses we should chop our way from the west to the east, as the means of communication improved and as the far-off provinces were settled. Foreign concessionaires, on the other hand, were to be given easternmost areas, to move gradually from the east to the west.

From these fundamental premises it followed readily that the complex organization of Soviet industry, with its horizontal-vertical interdependence of all agencies, was not suitable for carrying out our new goals.)

My program of immediate and practical steps to be taken amounted to this: First, the old system of head committees—invented by Larin and the cause of all the irresponsible and uncontrollable excesses of War Communism in the timber industry—should be abolished. These committees, supervising and controlling in each branch of industry, created a topheavy organization unable to cope with the problems of factories of different size, scope, and facilities. They should be replaced by a system of "trusts," to be formed after the American or German pattern, with a stern eye kept on all profits and losses and with thorough supervision of all work done. Such trusts were to be regional groupings of the larger and most efficient plants, fed by the same or similar and adjoining areas of forests and served by the same transport facilities.

Second, the management of all the timber enterprises should be concentrated in the hands of a board, appointed by the government but intrusted with wide powers of action.

Third, the new board should be given the right—no matter what local feeling there might be against this—to transfer machines and workers from one plant to another, within the limits of each economic region.

Fourth, there must be a firmly maintained budget and a financial plan of production, in accordance with which the trust was to work—in contrast to the financial chaos of the preceding few years.

Fifth and finally, the State Bank, then in the process of formation, was to give this trust a special loan of one million rubles in gold, over and above the basic capital in Russian paper currency. The trust was to pay off this loan eventually with proceeds of our sales of Soviet timber on foreign markets. The loan, meantime, would give the trust a chance to purchase abroad additional food reserves to supply the workers and peasants of our north, with its great forests to be exploited for export.

To this I presently added one more condition, which at that time was considered quite "cheeky," especially since it was clear that I myself was meant to be the actual manager of the trust. (This was my demand that the plan of all such operations was to be confirmed by the government for one year, during which period neither the central nor any any local authorities had any right to interfere with our work. I announced my willingness to assume personal responsibility for that one year's activity of the trust, even though I was aware of the risks I was thus accepting in the Cheka-ruled life of the time.

(Later I suggested that certain former timber industrialists and merchants be added to the board.) On the one hand, I said, they knew this business; on the other, their very names would impress our foreign customers—would be a guaranty that the contracts would be carried out.

Foreseeing the determined opposition to all or most of my plans that was bound to come from the men in the provinces, I tried to checkmate it beforehand by offering to leave a certain proportion of the wooded area under the jurisdiction of the local Councils of Economy for the needs of the domestic market. We would not intervene in their timber operations. In return, they were to promise complete noninterference in our affairs.

The final decision was made after Lenin had called me to his office to discuss my project in detail. After first referring him to the chief principles of his New Economic Policy and to the prevailing or possible methods of their practical application in industry, I then stressed the peculiar conditions of the timber industry, especially in those regions where we had to work. Once more I emphasized the importance of timber export and spoke of the problem of supplying my timber workers with food and other necessities of life, as the forested north grew hardly any food of its own.

"And who is to make up the board of the trust you propose?" Lenin asked. My reply was that it was advisable to include men not belonging to, or dependent upon, the Soviet government—men well known abroad. I named Ivan Potseluyev, formerly head of the large timber concern of Gromov and Company; Ivan Pluysnin, a timber tycoon of Archangel; von Meck, the former head of the Kazan Railroad; Zaitsev, the editor of a timber trade journal; and Michael Nazvanov, a schoolmate of Lenin's, employed in Soviet economic agencies as an expert. Some of these men were at that time timber specialists attached to various Soviet government offices, but by their past records all of them belonged to that class of the upper bourgeoisie which was by now thoroughly declassed.

"If to all these men I have just listed," I said to Lenin, "you add about three outstanding Communists and several representatives of the Wood Workers' Union, you will have a board which will impress both Russia and western Europe. And if you should intrust me with this work for one year by giving me carte blanche, I will hope to justify your confidence in me."

Lenin thought a little, then answered: "Bring me a complete plan of such a trust, with all the by-laws it needs, and attach an explanatory report." Apparently he wished to avoid arguments with his closest aides. A detailed plan with absolutely all the necessary data might help him to meet their objections.

Once more I went to work. These were the considerations I laid down as the basis of the plan:

The industry was to be divided into regions, according to the proximity of their sources of raw materals as well as of their consumers. Among the latter there was the Red Army, as well as the foreign market and the domestic civilian need. Generally speaking, domestic need was to be subdivided into the calls from the central authority and those from the local population.

Sawmills working for export and situated in a certain economic region were to form one economic unit—just as the mills working for the domestic needs of the government were to form an economic unit of their own. Each unit was to be run by an administration appointed by the trust and subordinate only to the trust. The management of such units did not necessarily have to be quartered in Moscow but might conceivably have its offices in the provinces; this did not mean, however, that local Soviet economic agencies or local trade-unions could interfere with its activities. Whatever the criticism from such local agencies or unions, it should be sent directly to the central authorities in Moscow which might or might not recognize it as valid.

The sawmills were to have certain wood-reserve areas of their own, in ample quantities and located conveniently enough for the mills to have a closed and self-sufficient economy all their own. In many cases it was also necessary to attach to the sawmills certain food-producing enterprises—to insure proper nutrition for the workers occupied in timber-cutting and sawmill operations.

Each unit or combine of such timber areas and sawmills should be granted a definite sum of money as its basic capital, in accordance, of course, with the general program of timber output planned by the board of the trust.

The board was to be responsible for the capital and equipment intrusted to it, also for a rational organization of production, for the achievement of a self-supporting basis in each enterprise or unit, and for its workers' welfare. In some cases it was responsible for the quality of the trusts' goods, as well as for their sale.

The Soviet government, according to my plan, was to own and hold all the shares of the trust. It was to appoint the board of the trust for a definite term. The procedure of the appointment was to be handled officially by the Supreme Council of Economy, which would secure beforehand the approval of appointees by the Organizational Bureau of the Communist party—that is, in actuality, by the secretary-general of the party (the post to which Stalin soon came).

Strange as it may seem, the one-time capitalists I had suggested—these bourgeois who through nationalization had lost all their property and now did not even enjoy the ordinary Soviet citizen's right to a bread ration—presently became heads of the new timber combines! Alongside of these men there were also on the new trust board several prominent members of the Communist party and representatives of trade-unions; but, as a matter of fact, the Red officials were often in the minority.

The trust I had planned for the timber industry was soon the model and prototype of all or most trusts in various other branches of Soviet industry. It was to be created in the northern area encompassing the largest forests, those most accessible to export shipping points on the White Sea. This trust, when formed, was called *Severoles*, or the North Timber Trust. Similar trusts were later to group other regional areas on a horizontal, rather than a vertical, plan, thus making for efficient management and operations.

All boards and managements of trusts and their subordinate combines were, of course, subject to general Soviet Law. Once a year production plans had to be submitted to the Supreme Council of Economy for examination and approval. In time some such boards displayed enough initiative and energy to spend their entire capital in a year or so, and Lenin hardly approved of that. In a letter to one of his aides in February, 1922, he declared that when boards went bankrupt in such a fashion, their members should be arrested and tried.

"If, having created these trusts and enterprises on a commercial basis," he wrote, "we prove ourselves unable to safeguard our state interests in a business-like manner, we are nothing but fools."

The friends whom Lenin made overseers of the trusts were delighted with their chance, and soon saw evil intent where there was none. They would decline even the most legitimate requests for financial and other assistance, as I, among others, found out. Sheinman, of the State Bank, was the one who disillusioned me.

Being the manager of the very first trust in Soviet Russia, I once telephoned Sheinman what I thought was a legitimate and modest request for an increase of state credits already granted to our trust. In wintertime we would spend all these credits to stock-pile timber and lumber for our spring and summer export operations to England, but we needed the additional funds only until spring. I said to Sheinman, over the telephone and rather casually:

"Do help us out until then. We need a few extra million rubles in advance for our last remaining timber-cutting of the winter season. Meet us halfway, please."

I was startled to hear Sheinman's semi-ironical, semithreatening reply coming over the wire:

"Meet you halfway? Sure. Your office is in Lubiansky Alley, mine on the Kuznetsky Bridge. If we leave our offices at the same time, we are certain to meet at Lubianka Square. How do you like that as a meeting place?"

This was a blunt threat: Lubianka Square was the headquarters—and the symbol—of the Cheka. Sheinman's reply expressed the attitude toward the new trust boards which soon became common in the upper reaches of the Soviet government.

(15)

"LIBERMAN'S AGENTS"

When word of the new timber projects reached Archangel and other northern parts, which were the main region of our timber works, it caused much excitement among the local Soviet leaders. They began to say that "Liberman is smuggling in a restoration of the capitalist regime" and that all my projects were dictated by some special interests or other.

The Wood Workers' Union joined in spreading similar rumors. And then, from all over the northern region, telegrams of protest poured into Moscow, addressed to Lenin himself. At each step my friends, assistants, and I began to encounter stumbling blocks placed by those officials who, though forced to obey Lenin's New Economic Policy, saw a non-Communist hand in it.

Such men were constantly astir, suspecting everything and everybody. They investigated; they reported; they interfered with our work. At times their activities were actually the badly camouflaged protest of local officials against Moscow as the dominating center. More often, however, these activities resulted from the influence of the Cheka in Moscow, with its usual hostility toward bourgeois experts and with its omnipotent tentacles everywhere. If it had not been for the confidence and support we received from the highest authorities in the land, we should have made no progress in our work whatsoever. Lenin and his closest aides bolstered us continually, and we could and did start our novel undertaking despite all difficulties.

We began by abolishing the old names of the timber areas and sawmills, which were still called by the names of their prerevolutionary proprietors. Instead, we introduced consecutive numbers. In part this was imperative because of the lawsuits which might face us abroad if we exported timber and lumber under the old brands. (As a matter of fact, there were a few such suits at first.) Our other reason was that we had been shifting machines from one mill to another and were planning to do more of this; but with the machinery moved, the old names, often associated with the peculiar equipment of one mill or another, were losing their special meaning.

Opposition to such shifting and abolition of names came from an unexpected quarter: the old personnel of this sawmill and that. These oldtimers, the engineers and other employees, had for years been proud of their work for a boss whose name was known not in Russia alone but also abroad. They wanted to preserve the identity of their old employer's mill—machinery, name, and all. Some of them had actually promised the owner, on the eve of his flight, to try to preserve the status quo "until his return."

The main opposition, however, came from the sources already mentioned— the local Soviet offices, particularly the Cheka. The latter's officials saw plots everywhere. They accused us, for instance, of transferring better machinery to sawmills which had belonged to foreigners and which, because of the New Economic Policy and its concessions to foreign interests, might soon enjoy a privileged status. At one point the Cheka of Archangel nearly succeeded in building a case against "Liberman's agents" who had allegedly been moving good equipment to their "pet mills." The latter proved to be mills of former foreign ownership which, in truth, had always been equipped with better machinery than some native Russian plants—yet there it was, the charge that we were helping foreign capitalists, against the interests of our own Soviet industry.

All this might have been comic, except for the potentially tragic consequences to my collaborators and me. I was summoned for explanations by Michael Tomsky, who was the president of the Soviet trade-unions and had already begun to play an important role as a member of the Political Bureau of the Communist party, in addition to being Russia's No. 1 labor leader. In reply to his questions, I presented a detailed verbal picture of the chaos prevailing in the timber industry of the north. I also told him of our projects, which, I frankly declared, alone could save the entire situation.

The situation abroad did not favor us at the moment, I pointed out to Tomsky. It would not be an easy task to break through the steel ring of the Allied blockade. Foreign customers needed our timber but did not trust us, and their anti-Soviet attitude was encouraged by those Russian refugees abroad who had once owned our country's timber enterprises. England's skepticism was supported by a policy then pursued by the Scandinavian countries: Sweden, who had been Russia's competitor in the English timber market, was doing all she could to prevent our return to that market—to kill at their inception whatever deals England's merchants were willing to make with us. Sweden's agents in Britain warned the British that if the latter did business with the Soviet government, they, the Swedish and other Scandinavian producers, would refuse to sell their own timber in England. This threat made quite an impression, largely because few people in Europe felt sure that we would be able to fulfil our contracts. We had to remember the tremendous influence of the trade's brokers upon the British lumber market; they were middlemen, distributors, and financiers, all in one. We had to impress them and through them the rest of the European business world. We had to prove to them that we could really carry out fully whatever contracts and responsibilities we assumed—therefore the projects I had suggested had to be followed through.

Moreover, I went on, if my projects were carried out, they would bring about a change for the better in the mood of the workers of the north. (Early in 1920, after the withdrawal of the British and the Whites from Archangel, the local population had greeted the incoming Soviets enthusiastically, but soon the deteriorating food situation had led to wide dissatisfaction, which had resulted in a lowered production rate.) For these projects would mean, among other things, an opportunity for the Soviets, despite the Allied blockade, to buy food abroad for delivery and distribution in Archangel.

By the end of this long conversation I thought I had Tomsky's complete confidence and support. But I soon found out that this in no way altered the opposition to me on the part of the Wood Workers' Union and the Soviet officials "on the spot." Their stubborn antagonism had to be reckoned with for a long time to come.

At the risk of running ahead of my story, I want to note here that sometime later that year of 1920 we did manage, after selling some Russian lumber in England, to buy a quantity of foodstuffs and certain much-needed sawmill equipment, bringing all of it to Archangel before the autumnal ice stopped navigation for that year. This gave us the chance of distributing food rations not only among sawmill workers but also among the peasants usually employed as lumberjacks. Amid the poverty and hunger of that time, the appearance of this foreign food of good quality caused much excitement and approval; we regained good will, and work in the timber industry assumed a lively tempo. The workers dubbed this food "Liberman's rations."

Next year, during the first full season of navigation in the north, we succeeded in exporting lumber to the amount of several million pounds sterling, and at one of the sessions of the Council of People's Commissars, Sheinman, the head of the State Bank who had previously threatened me, declared: "The fund of the State Bank has, in fact, been created, thanks to the initiative and effort of Comrade Liberman and his North Timber Trust."

Many other obstacles, too, loomed ahead, and some of them remained insurmountable. Some were the result of the complex situation caused by the New Economic Policy. The state was gradually becoming a stern employer; its representatives and managers in Soviet trust and factory offices looked for bargains in goods and services, pinched pennies, tried to get from foreign customers all that the traffic would bear, and, in short, seemed in many of their functions and methods no better and no worse than so many private industrialists and merchants. Lenin called these men *Krasnyie Kuptsy,* or "Red Merchants." He openly and slyly urged them to learn the meaning of the old Russian proverb: "If you don't cheat, you don't sell." All at once we had before us also the old problems of labor and capital—of the workers' wage rates, of the workers' right to some of the yield and profit of their production— that is, the very same problems that are at the bottom of all social conflicts and movements in capitalistic countries.

For example, in a capitalist country each timber entrepreneur calculates the sales price of his product on the basis, first of all, of his expenditures. He has three main categories of expense: the money he pays the forest-owner for the right to chop and carry away the timber, the so-called land rent; the outlay for equipment, transport, and the like; and his workers' wages. Even a minimum sales price should cover all these expenses. Whatever the enterpreneur can get above this minimum is, of course, his profit.

But what about this profit if now the state is "governed by the proletariat" and private industrialists are no longer tolerated? That part of the sales price which used to be clear profit was free now. More than that, the first item of expense had been abolished, as private landownership was no more and no forest-owners had to be paid. It was plain that new calculations of the cost of timber had to be adopted in New Russia.

Workers and Communists held leading posts in each economic organization of the Soviets. When the question of the sales price of any product was considered, the vote of the trade-unions was decisive. And now the unions demanded both the forest-owners' rent and the entrepreneur's fee as the workers' increased share! It was a primitive point of view, yet quite understandable under the difficult conditions in which the workers of the time lived and labored.

Karl Marx, for that matter, had written that this was indeed to be the workers' share. The latter felt they needed and deserved this extra money. They could not and would not comprehend the fact that, in so far as the state took upon itself the capitalists' duties of enterprise and management, the state was entitled to a certain share of the industries' profits. The workers were indignant. They regarded as antilabor all such efforts of the state to earmark for itself part of the profits; and, when these efforts happened to be made by non-Communist employees of the state, the workers saw a reflection of bourgeois ideology. The state, nevertheless, having become an owner-employer, could not agree with the workers' contentions.

There were uncomfortable arguments from other sources as well. We had, in the offices of the Timber Trust, regular visitors from the People's Commissariat of Agriculture. These representatives felt that their commissariat inherited the rights and privileges of former forest-owners, and they demanded of us the rents which had formerly been paid to such owners. We were also called upon by representatives of the State Control Commission (then headed by Stalin), who were to examine all our operations, including our calculations of the cost and sales price of our timber and lumber. These men said to us, in half-irony, half-reprimand:

"See for yourselves what bad managers you are! What sort of 'Red Merchants' do you call yourselves? The oldtime entrepreneur and sawmill owner could and did get an adequate sales price for the lumber—adequate to cover the rent to the forest-owner as well as all other expenses, and enough to leave a sizable profit for himself. You people are free of the rent problem, and still you can't make both ends meet. You can't even pay your debt to the State Bank, as you promised you would."

After such criticism we had no choice except to economize in workers' wages; for otherwise it was true that we could not make both ends meet. But it was dangerous for me and other "bourgeois" experts to argue with the workers, so once more I decided to appeal to Lenin. Sometime in the latter part of 1921 I asked for an interview with him. He granted it at once, and I related to him the sad tale of our difficulties.

"On the foreign markets," I began, "we are faced with the competition of other lumber salesmen, particularly from the Scandinavian countries. That is why we cannot raise our prices any time we want to. Here in Moscow every step we take is watched sternly by our Soviet state organizations. The State Bank demands that we pay on time and in full the money we owe for the advances we received against our foreign sales. We have to pay the bank a rigid and unfair price, one English pound sterling for each Soviet *chervonets* we owe. That is why we have to be very careful in our own calculations of wage rates and other expense. But the trade-unions quote Karl Marx to us and demand that all the sales proceeds should go toward paying the workers. They allow only such items in addition as amortization of our machinery and transport expense, but nothing else. They say nothing else needs to be spent or allowed since both the timber tracts and the sawmills are now nationalized." I pointed out the primitive, provincial fallacies of such restricted thinking. The state should have its share of profits, of course.

Lenin listened to me with close attention. I could see that I was placing him in a grave dilemma. On the one hand, he well realized the soundness of our economic calculation—the importance of giving the state its share of the profits. On the other, he had little desire (and, under the circumstances, no chance) to come out against the workers and their standpoint. He could not tell them bluntly that their oversimplification of Marxism would only lead to economic disorder, that they must, despite their low wages, agree to these deductions in favor of the state.

He therefore tried to use the argument of "this transitional period." To his opponents it seemed a vague argument, but he often and ably employed it in order to carry out what he held to be necessary reforms. Lenin said to me: "After all, we live in a period of transition. We are only beginning to build socialism. To prepare our country for socialism, we must, first of all, introduce electrification. Now, this requires money. Timber is one of our natural resources which we will transform into money to carry out the electrification of Russia."

What he meant was that the Soviet state should receive from the Timber Trust the fees formerly paid to private forest-owners; he was agreeing with the argument of the Commissariat of Agriculture and of the State Control Commission. These fees would make up a special fund of the state, which the government would later return to the people's economy by way of the nation's electrification.

"We must calculate the prices of our products in a way different from the old one," Lenin went on. "We must proceed upward, not downward. Under the old system, the timber entrepreneur began with such expenses as the land rent, and so on, and only out of the remainder of his profit would he pay the workers' wages. But we must start with the establishment of a minimum needed by the workers for their necessities of life. To that we must add all other expenses of the timber industry. And only with whatever money remains after all these expenditures can we compensate the state. From that balance of the sales proceeds, the state is to get money for the purposes of the restoration and amortization of the plants and their machinery, and, last but not least, deductions in favor of the electrification fund. You will soon be going abroad again—this will be your chance to watch the Swedes and the Finns in their methods of calculating the cost of their lumber. We can and must learn a few things from them."

When, in the course of our conversation, I mentioned that the Soviet State Bank was demanding the payment of our debts on time and in full, Lenin commented: "The State Bank is right, of course. Business is business. But, if at the end of your operations, you come out short, then naturally we will have to re-examine the whole situation. But we will do so only in case your difficulties can be traced not to any lack of business ability on your part but to our general economic backwardness as a nation and to the inability of our labor to work as well and swiftly as the labor in western Europe can."

It so happened that I had already collected the Swedish and Finnish calculations to which Lenin had referred, so a few days later I came back to him armed with neatly prepared diagrams and tables. They could demonstrate to him whatever essential difference there was between the Russian and the Scandinavian systems of reckoning the sales prices of lumber. The main point was that the Scandinavian figures were based on the latest, swiftest, and generally most perfected machinery available at the time. For this reason alone, the Scandinavian lumberjacks and sawmill hands were able to produce far more per man-hour than the Russian workers could; consequently wages in the Scandinavian industry, although considerably higher than corresponding wages in Russia, represented a smaller percentage of the cost of the lumber. All of this was the result of the general technical backwardness of Russia, and for this we could find no swift and truly effective remedies.

Lenin pored over the diagrams and tables for a long time. He scribbled all sorts of notes and interesting calculations of his own on the margins of the documents. (These tables with Lenin's marginalia remained behind among my other papers when I left Paris in the late 1930's; it is impossible to say whether or not they are hopelessly lost.) He then shifted to another facet of the same problem:

"We must really tackle this question of a more economical and rational exploitation of our forests. In tsarist times no one was interested in a rational exploitation of these riches, especially of the large state-owned forests. I know that the average timber entrepreneur often threw away, right there in the woods, many by-products of his operations. Some of those by-products were very valuable, but he saw no profit in having them hauled to the railroad stations or river docks. Now we must point out to the workers that the forests are the people's property and that all of us must try to get the maximum yield out of each tree. We must by all means increase the yield of every single wooded acre. Our workers must realize this."

He took his notebook, wrote a few sentences, tore the page out, and rang for his secretary. "Send this immediately to the Commissariat of Agriculture," he said. Within a few days I saw an item on the agenda of the Council of Labor and Defense: "*Re.* changing the system of timber works." And I found myself commissioned to prepare a report for the council's deliberations on the subject.

Lenin was in the chair at this particular session of the Council of Labor and Defense. Again and again he returned to a theme which obviously worried him—the neglect of by-products. In the old times (he and I explained to the council members) the average timber entrepreneur cut for the market the lower part of each tree, no more than 15 or 20 feet of the trunk, this being the best part of the tree. The rest of the chopped-down tree was left to rot on the spot. We now had to impress the timber industry of the Soviets with the importance of saving, transporting, and utilizing the remainder of each tree as well. Repeatedly, Lenin said: "The workers must be made to understand this. After all, this is common property of the people."

Among other problems connected with the introduction of the New Economic Policy was that of unemployment in Soviet industry as a whole and in our timber-works in particular. Again Lenin and I discussed this question during one of my talks with him.

"In a way," I said, "the unemployed are a ready pool of labor—ready for the industry whenever it needs more workers. In our sawmills we install a six- or seven-horsepower motor when we really need a five-horsepower one, so that we will have an additional reserve of energy in case of emergency. Similarly, to be able to expand at a moment's notice, the industry needs a reserve of manpower. Don't you think we should figure this necessary reserve at 10 per cent of the total personnel normally employed in a given industry? If so, these 10 per cent should be regularly and officially attached to each plant. The plant should pay them a living wage. Moreover, they should be given a chance to work from time to time, replacing the permanent workers of the plant. In this way these reservists would not become demoralized economically and morally. And as the other workers leave the plant for good because of illness, death, and so forth, the reservists take their places permanently. If we inaugurate such a method, we may be able to solve, at least partly, the problem of unemployment."

I added, as if thinking aloud: "Why is it that other countries haven't relieved their unemployment in this simple way?"

Lenin had been listening carefully, but, at this last remark his lips spread in a sardonic smile. He said:

"The capitalist world cannot use this method of yours without disturbing its own foundations. Out there they aren't interested in solving the problem of unemployment. They *want* lines of unemployed to stand in front of their factory gates. They want this because it makes the employed workers fear for the safety of their jobs. It makes those workers do their work for less money and with more speed and other effort."

Again he marked something down in his omnipresent notebook. Then he raised his head and said he agreed with my proposal to add the unemployed to the pay rolls of our timber-works in the north. Emboldened, I advanced another suggestion.

"Wouldn't it be sensible," I asked, "to include in each plant's expenditures certain sums for the manual training of young people—to prepare in this way the cadres of future workers for each plant and industry?"

"Oh no!" Lenin exclaimed. "The Soviet government itself has the duty of educating the new generation! It has no business handing this over to individual factories or trusts. In America, some clever capitalists give such training and other similar concessions to their workers—in order to keep the workers quiet and obedient. We don't need such a method in Soviet Russia. We have the People's Commissariat of Education. We have the People's Commissariat of Social Welfare. They are in charge of this problem. But your first proposal—to attach the unemployed to the plants—is all right. Talk it over with Tomsky in detail."

At my next meeting with Tomsky I explained my idea to him, and he, too, liked it. The Timber Trust was soon among the first to put the plan into actual practice.

Later a surprising consequence of my innovation appeared to plague us, one I had neither expected nor wished for. This was an overoptimistic and completely incorrect appraisal of unemployment in Soviet Russia. Since so many of the unemployed were attached to this or that plant as its reserve, it seemed, on paper, that there was a great decrease of unemployment in the land. Of course, this was only a technical drawback, and the use of the system itself was undoubtedly a step forward.

(16)

SORTIE TO STOCKHOLM

IT WAS ON JANUARY 16, 1920, MORE THAN A YEAR BEFORE THE ANNOUNCEMENT OF the New Economic Policy, that the Supreme Council of the Allies decided to lift the blockade of Soviet Russia. This was an event of supreme importance to the Soviets, although it could hardly be said that with this change for the better all the difficulties of our country were solved.

The civil war was not yet over in Russia. Both France and Britain pursued a wavering policy toward the Soviets. For the time being, there could be no possibility of gaining diplomatic recognition of our government on the part of the Western powers or of exchanging envoys and resuming political collaboration with France and England. The lifting of the blockade meant trade only.

And even this trade was to be restricted, according to the same decision of the Allied Council, which permitted "exchange of goods on a mutual basis between the Russian people and the Allied and neutral countries" via the narrow channel of "the co-operatives having direct contacts with Russia." By the latter the Allies meant the foreign offices of the old Russian co-operative combines as yet unconnected with, or only slightly dominated by, the Soviet government. The decision of the Allied Council also clearly stated that this step "did by no means signify a change in the policy of the Allied governments toward the Soviet government."

Lloyd George was willing to trade with Russia in a rather condescending fashion. He said to his people, by way of an excuse, "After all, we deal with cannibals, too."

Thus the lifting of the blockade was a great advance for the Soviets, but still far from a complete triumph. What to do next? Lenin strove for a full recognition of his government by the Allies. The decision of their Supreme Council he regarded as the first breach in the wall of Russia's isolation. Political aims were foremost with Lenin, and the economic opportunities now opened to him by the Allies' decision were mainly another step toward the realization of his political goals.

But there was another point of view in Russia, shared to some extent even

108

by the circles of the Communist party. Since the Allies were allowing us to take up commerce with foreign lands, why not develop this channel itself to the utmost? Economic collaboration, if properly developed, would almost automatically lead to political concessions in favor of Soviet Russia on the part of the outside world. According to this viewpoint, these new economic possibilities should assume more importance in Russia, should become important per se. The two opposing trends clashed behind the scenes, in the Kremlin and in the Commissariat of Foreign Trade. I happened to observe this particular struggle at rather close quarters.

Irrespective of which point of view was to prevail eventually, the thing for the Soviet government to do was to establish the initial commercial relations. For this it was necessary to send a Soviet delegation abroad. This was naturally the task of the Commissariat of Foreign Trade, and just as naturally it was Krassin who should head the delegation. By his past record of business connections in foreign countries, as well as by his present leading position in the Soviet government, he was the only suitable person for the novel job. Still, some of these same business ties abroad made his candidacy rather questionable! Would not his German connections be a source of trouble between him and the Allies, who would look at him askance for both his "German orientation" and his Russian origin? It was finally decided in the Kremlin to disregard this fear entirely, and subsequent events showed that the decision was wise.

Because the Allies allowed this new trade with Russia to be conducted via the co-operatives only, officially the first delegation had to be sent by the Moscow headquarters of the Centrosoyuz, or the All-Russian Union of Co-operatives. The executive board of this organization was mainly either non-partisan or definitely anti-Communist, which was precisely why France and England wanted to do business with the co-operatives. But Lenin had other ideas, of course. He wanted to send a delegation of a political character, guided by outstanding Communists. In the end, the Soviet government compelled the leaders of the Centrosoyuz to agree to a delegation of some twenty men who had never had much or anything to do with co-operatives. Chief among these were Leonid Krassin, Victor Noghin, and S. Rozovsky.

The other delegates were prominent experts in economics, none of whom had ever participated in the co-operative movement. Among them were Ivitsky, a well-known railroad specialist and the chief engineer of the Sormovo-Kolomna works, and another railroad expert, Voskresensky. The machine-building industry was represented by Kirshner, the manager of some large mills in Petrograd. Professor Volkov was the delegation's expert in grains. A member of the old Russian aristocracy, Bellegard, was the financial specialist. Vasily V. Starkov knew the electrical works and needs of new Russia. I was added to the delegation as its timber specialist. The chief secretary of the delegation was one Grozhan, a friend of Krassin's and formerly, but no longer, a Bolshevik. A certain Miss Luntz, who was a talented musician, came with us as our interpreter and stenographer. (Later, in London, while we negotiated lumber and machinery, she married Semion Orlov, a real leader of the Centrosoyuz, and did not return to Russia.)

A trip abroad was a great event in those days, and for many of the delegates this was the first journey to England. Most of us became friendly in no time at all, and yet there was a natural and almost instinctive process of selection from the very beginning: we, the non-Communist experts, rather kept away from the Communists. Four or five of us—Starkov, Kirshner, Ivitsky, and I, and later also Bellegard—headed the non-Communist contingent of the delegation, with the tacit agreement of the other non-Communists, of course. We became a center which guided the non-Communist delegates in questions relating to the delegation's internal problems and our general conduct and which dealt with the chief Communists for the entire group. All of us bore in mind that we had to return to Russia some day and that perhaps we would be grilled by the Cheka. We were therefore atremble with apprehension and kept reminding one another: "Walls have ears, you know....."

We left Moscow in March, 1920. The train left in the evening, about eight o'clock. Some four hours later we were all awakened by a terrific bang and clatter. An iron rod had been pushed into the window of our car, but since the compartment it struck was used for luggage only, no one was injured. Later we heard that this was an attempt on our lives; that the unknown criminals had shoved the rod from a train going in the opposite direction, in the hope that it would derail and smash our car with all of us in it. The next morning Krassin said to me laughingly, "All of us should really thank God for our miraculous deliverance. We could have been smashed to smithereens."

On reaching Tallinn (Reval) in Estonia, we boarded a steamer for Copenhagen, where special emissaries of the British government were to await us. In Copenhagen, British visas were to be issued to us. It was in Tallinn that we first heard disquieting rumors that opposition to our coming had been manifested by the old representatives of the Centrosoyuz co-operatives residing abroad, mostly in London. Having learned of the Communist leadership of the delegation, ostensibly representing the Centrosoyuz in Russia, these men voiced their protest in England and began to work energetically against the issuance of British visas to all of us, but particularly to our Communist superiors.

The rumors were confirmed when we reached Copenhagen. We learned that the British government was willing to give visas to the non-Communist delegates among us, the economic experts, but not to some of the leading Communists. The Soviet government, however, insisted on the right of the entire delegation to enter England, and thus began negotiations which were carried on for two months after our arrival in Copenhagen. All that time we most uselessly waited in the Danish capital.

Maxim Maximovich Litvinov, who was then the vice-commissar for foreign affairs (under Commissar George Chicherin), arrived in Copenhagen to join Krassin in the latter's negotiations with the representatives of the British government on the subject of our journey to London. Litvinov's knowledge of the English language was fuller than Krassin's, and he was better versed in British politics. He was married to an Englishwoman and had for a time lived in London, whence he was deported to Russia "for Bolshevism."

While in Copenhagen, the delegation dealt with a Mr. Weiss, who was sent there by Lloyd George. Later Weiss played an important role in the field of Anglo-Soviet *rapprochement,* and still later he gave up his official position as a British civil servant and entered the London agency of the Centrosoyuz as one of the directors of the board. I came to know him during our sojourn and in time invited him to be a director of the agency of a Soviet lumber company in London.

Another British representative in Copenhagen was there in an unofficial capacity. He was of Russian origin, a clever adventurer who, on the one hand, managed to convince Lloyd George that he had for years been close to Krassin and, on the other, succeeding in impressing Krassin with the story of his being Lloyd George's unofficial representative in the British Intelligence Service.

A difference of opinion between Litvinov and Krassin became apparent while we waited at Copenhagen; it was the political versus the economic approach to foreign trade. Krassin was more the practical businessman, ready for compromises of all kinds, so long as they would give us our British visas. Litvinov wanted England to make certain concessions in principle in this matter of our visas. Above all, he wanted to be in the delegation himself, despite the British refusal to admit him. He was motivated by his desire to see revolutionary principles triumph via his own presence in London. Krassin's conciliatory attitude went against the grain with Litvinov, who felt that such an attitude was in contradiction to the basic policy of the Communist party.

Krassin, too, toyed with the idea of outwitting the bourgeoisie, but he thought he could achieve this end by way of Soviet Russian trade with the rest of Europe. He was convinced that trade, not diplomacy, would prove the decisive factor. Therefore, to the British he talked less of his political views and more of his role as a guiding spirit in Russia's new economics. His line was something like this: "Our political platform is not too important, you know. Let your people and ours sit at the same table and tackle our practical questions of concrete business."

Such talk irked Litvinov, a party leader from top to toe, who implacably declined any compromises which seemed to lower the prestige of the Soviet government. It should be noted that as a 100 per cent Bolshevik he was appointed by the government to assist Foreign Commissar Chicherin because the latter was never really forgiven by the Communists for either his former Menshevism or his aristocratic origin. Litvinov was detailed by the party to be its watchdog in Chicherin's commissariat. Much water flowed under the world's bridges until, instead of Litvinov the stubborn Communist, there emerged before Europe's chancelleries Litvinov the cautious diplomat.

In 1920 Litvinov felt that, on the basis of his past experience, he ought to have been the titular foreign commissar. His main ambition was to further the interests of the revolution, and his devotion was such that he was known among his party comrades as *papasha* or "Daddy," and all troublesome matters were given him to be straightened out. This was because he enjoyed Lenin's fullest confidence as a comrade who would put the good of the party above everything else. Litvinov therefore could not be satisfied with a compromise that did not recognize the prestige of the new regime.

Because of Litvinov's revolutionary past and because of his present position in the Foreign Commissariat, ardent Communists all over the world, some of them old friends of his in exile, felt that they were his unofficial, even if illegal, foreign representatives. They spontaneously assumed the duty of sending him full information about goings-on in the various countries and thus enabled him to amass invaluable records which often proved more accurate than those obtained by the commissars. Litvinov kept up his contacts through the 1920's and 1930's, and it was his wealth of private information that gave him a correct appraisal of Europe's main popular currents and in time made of him, the formerly uncompromising revolutionary, the latter-day spokesman of the common man of Europe in the halls of the League of Nations.

In 1920, as we non-Communists cooled our heels in Copenhagen, our sympathies were naturally on the side of Krassin, not Litvinov. This was apparent at the meetings of our delegation each time Litvinov was present. We were as icy toward him as he was toward us.

One insignificant episode aroused much laughter, especially on our side. The British representatives in Copenhagen had invited both Krassin and Litvinov to dinner, and several members of our delegation were sitting in the lobby of the hotel where all of us were stopping, when Litvinov and Krassin came down, ready to depart for the solemn occasion. Litvinov, at first supposing that ladies would also be present, had put on his tails and white tie but later, following Krassin's suggestion, had changed into his tuxedo. But he had forgotten to change ties; and so here he was, coming down in his tuxedo and white tie, which was, of course, the official uniform of a headwaiter. Krassin, without saying a word, stepped toward him and pulled him by the ill-starred tie. Much embarrassed, Litvinov took the elevator back to his room to change the tie. We non-Communists were much pleased that our chief Krassin was so thoroughly conversant with bourgeois etiquette!

While thus idling around in Copenhagen, I got to be rather intimate with another member of the Communist trio heading our delegation, Victor Noghin, who in those days was decidedly influential in Soviet affairs. Soon he and I were great friends and spent a number of evenings together. I can still see him—tall, stately, with his little red beard and his thick hair, combed back *en brosse*. By origin he was a textile-factory worker, but he had received some education along the way, of which he was proud, often reminding his listeners that he had had some schooling. As a political *émigré* in tsarist times, he had lived in England before World War I. What really marked him apart from other Bolsheviks was his sense of proportion and tact, particularly in his relations with us, the non-Communists. He never boasted to us of his party membership and position. He deeply respected Krassin for his business abilities but disapproved of the third Communist chieftain of our delegation, Rozovsky, for that official's lack of cultured habits and for his "Communist snobbery."

Noghin and I took frequent walks around the Danish city. One Sunday, as we strolled along the neat, pretty streets of that cozy little capital, I said to Noghin: "Look at these food-store windows. This decaying capitalist Europe can certainly feed itself! Compare this with our socialist Russia!"

At first Noghin did not argue. Later, watching the throngs of people leaving the churches, he replied: "And still Europe has grown poorer, and workers are worse off than they used to be. I can tell this by the shoes of the churchgoers —look at all the worn tops and torn soles! And the stores which fascinate you so—those are for the bourgeois, not for the workers." He spoke softly, as if begging my pardon for the things he had to say.

Because of the negotiations with the British, which seemed to drag on without end, it was finally decided by our chiefs that several members of the delegation should in the meantime go to Stockholm, to make certain purchases for Russia. Four or five of us went, with Krassin at our head.

There were several reasons for this journey. First, the authorities and businessmen in London well knew that the appropriation in gold, given the Soviet delegation by the Kremlin for purchases abroad, was rather limited. Were we to begin to spend it in Stockholm, the gentlemen of London might become afraid that there would not be much left as their share. Indeed, on hearing of our subsequent purchases in Stockholm, certain London firms began to exert pressure on their government to give us our British visas.

Second, by making those purchases in Stockholm we were proving to the world of commerce that, despite what was said about us in foreign newspapers, we were busy not with propaganda alone.

The third reason was a personal one with Krassin. He simply wanted to get rid of the monitoring presence of Litvinov. Indeed, Litvinov could obtain neither the Swedish nor the British visa and was thus forced to stay behind in Denmark.

Our first task in Stockholm was to buy such goods as were most urgently needed by Soviet Russia at the time, from the military as well as from the purely economic viewpoint. We needed and bought railroad equipment, especially locomotives, and various other machinery. Locomotives, of which we bought some two hundred and fifty, were our main acquisition. But, unfortunately, we spent almost all the gold reserve of our delegation, and there was hardly anything left for our purchases in the other countries we meant to visit.

The business and political circles of Sweden were of several minds toward us. It all depended on the specific interests of the groups in question. The machine-building industry, for instance, courted us attentively, in the hope of capturing the great Russian market formerly dominated by the German machine-makers and exporters. On the other hand, the Swedish timber men, seeing in us nothing but competitors, referred to our mission skeptically, gossiping that we were bluffers, that Russia had neither the man-power nor the special technical personnel to operate these new Swedish machines we were trying to buy.

Among the machines we finally bought in Sweden were a number for our sawmills. It must be noted here that, in that particular period, sawmill machinery was being rapidly perfected and the latest models of the time, capable of an astonishing speed, were gradually replacing the old equipment. Certain Swedish machine-building firms were endeavoring to sell us the very latest and swiftest models—perhaps under the sly influence of our Swedish competitors, for both the competitors and we knew that we lacked the extra-well-trained operators needed for such machines. We skirted the temptation and solved the problem, buying very little of this most perfected equipment—just enough to establish one large mill in Russia that would be a model mill, a school, so to speak, for our entire north. For the rest we bought older machines, which did not cost us so much.

At least, we thought, this was a sensible solution. But later—much later—it occurred to someone to "make a rope" for me out of these purchases. This was either in 1921 or 1922, when the Cheka charged me with sabotage! I was accused of buying all the older models for the express purpose of wrecking the Soviet industry! I first learned of these charges when, during one of my periodic reports to Lenin, he suddenly asked me: "Tell me, why did your delegation buy those old models in Stockholm?"

Recovering from my momentary surprise, I replied: "The technical development of a country is never ahead of that country's worker, of his mental development. The Swedish mills achieved their gradual transition from the machines making 150 revolutions per minute to those making 375 revolutions. Gradual, I say, not sudden, because the workers, too, had to get used gradually to the change. Their eyes, fingers, and all reactions and movements had to make this gradual adjustment to the new speed. But if we, now, place our Russian worker in charge of a machine making 375 revolutions a minute, and if we expect him not to be automatic about it but bear in mind that each tree, each log requires special thinking and calculation as he works it with that machine, he will either smash the machine or cut his own hands. Besides, half of the product will be defective and will have to be thrown out. And another thing: Our wage rates are not so high that we must be in a hurry and get the maximum of production per man-hour by using those high-speed machines. If you want to base all our industry on such high-speed machines, well then, let's import the foreign workers who know how to run those machines."

I further explained to Lenin that Sawmill No. 6 was going to be equipped with the latest machinery only, for the purpose of training young workers in better and quicker methods. We must engage a few foreign technicians, I said, to help us run this model mill. Lenin was listening carefully, scribbling notes the meantime. He finally announced that, on the whole, he agreed with me.

In Stockholm, however, our main purchases were the locomotives. We even opened a special Soviet office in the Swedish capital for the inspection of those locomotives and the settlement of our bills, which were to be paid over a considerable period of time.

This office we placed under the management of a well-known Russian engineer, Professor George Lomonosov, who had earlier served with the Russian Railway Mission in America. He was an extremely fat man, with a huge, black, well-groomed beard, and soft, catlike movements. Some of his old students insisted that in his university days he had been a monarchist. Now, however, he proclaimed himself not only an expert most loyal to the Soviets, but a Communist to boot. He was a descendant of Michael Lomonosov, the great Russian savant of the eighteenth century—a source of pride to him, often manifested in public.

Lomonosov liked to invite us to share his luncheons—veritable feasts beginning at noon and ending at about three o'clock in the afternoon, abounding in fish and wine. His dinners lasted well into the night. He was patriarchal in his relations with the employees of his Stockholm office, but actually his secretary held sway over everything and everybody.

Although Lomonosov was a great favorite of Lenin's, in a few years he became one of the "nonreturners" to Soviet Russia. He first declared his decision to break with the Soviet government by one day calling together his entire staff, treating the men and women to a fine dinner, then asking them to rise and form a semicircle, which he faced as he delivered his speech, revealing his decision to quit the Soviets and giving his reasons. Then, tears in his eyes, he bade goodbye to each employee separately. He made the sign of the cross over some of them, as a special mark of his love and blessing, and walked out of the room.

But he came back the very next minute—to take his rubbers off, place them in the middle of the room, and say: "I have shaken the dust of my country off my feet." Then he walked out again, never to return.

(17)

MATCHING BRITISH WITS

AT LONG LAST, BY THE END OF THE SUMMER OF 1920, THE ENTIRE DELEGATION received British visas. All efforts, however, to have Litvinov, the diplomat and the assistant foreign commissar, included in the delegation, failed completely. In its note of July 1 the British government demanded the right to declare *personae non gratae* certain individual members of whatever Soviet delegations might in the future be sent to negotiate either trade or peace. On July 7 Moscow accepted Britain's basic terms. Suddenly, however, Downing Street broke off these negotiations and began to support Poland in its war against the Soviets. Not until March, 1921, was the first trade agreement signed between Soviet Russia and England. The diplomatic recognition of the Soviet government by the British government came much later, in February, 1924.

In the summer of 1920 we were the first Soviet representatives to be allowed to come to England. We boarded a steamer at Bergen, Norway, and from the very start felt surrounded by surveillance and suspicion—in the persons of specially detailed men, all in mufti but all unmistakably in Britain's official service.

On arriving in London, we were given rooms in the First Avenue Hotel, which was far from first class, but we were obliged to live there and nowhere else. Some of us had friends and even relatives in England, but none received permission to move from the hotel to private homes. It took me months to secure leave to move to another hotel, and I was the first one to do this. In the lobby of the First Avenue Hotel we soon spotted the several police inspectors assigned to watch our every move.

We got busy quickly. The first move was to change or replenish our wardrobes. In addition to the usual clothes and footwear, we ordered the inevitable tuxedos for official appearances. The London press, nevertheless, ran stories and even photographs about the "Soviet savages who eat with their knives," who "clear their noses into their fists," and so on. To counteract this propaganda, we were urged by our Soviet superiors to be on guard—to get acquainted with English customs, to observe and follow even the superficial forms of good conduct in London society. And there was no lack of volunteer instructors to teach all of us good manners.

At first, however, there was not much activity in store for us in the commercial sphere that interested us most. Our purchases in England could not be expected to amount to much after most of our resources had been spent in Sweden, and there was hardly any immediate chance of selling anything Russian on the British market. Nonetheless, from the moment of our arrival, the First Avenue Hotel was swarming with second- and third-rate businessmen, some of them with grandiose projects for breaking through the blockade. There was a plenitude of schemes and a dearth of actual business.

At that time Krassin could not speak a word of English, and the entire delegation boasted but two or three persons who could somehow make themselves understood in that language, so our chiefs were always surrounded by interpreters. Actually, however, I had the greatest number of visitors—because Russian lumber industries had traditionally been connected with the British market. There was the added circumstance that certain British funds had been marooned in the north of Russia as a consequence of British investments in our lumber mills before the revolution; all the stock piles of timber and lumber, upon which these British interests had once counted, were by now nationalized by the Soviets. The British who had once owned (or considered that they owned) the wood in question now approached the delegation in London with an offer to sell that wood for a moderate price. They watched me carefully to see that, on behalf of the Soviet government, I did not sell to someone else the timber that had belonged to them.

The day after our arrival we were approached by a very important English lumber importer, who was also a whiskey king, and one of his business partners, a Canadian general who during World War I had been in charge of his country's lumber supplies. Krassin and I were invited by the two of them to lunch.

Our first meeting with these British industrialists took place in an atmosphere of secrecy. A special room was engaged by our host at the Carlton, one of the most fashionable hotels of London. The entrance to the room was from a side staircase. The room was semidark; the walls were paneled in dark wood; and the draperies were also dark. My English was very poor, but here I was appearing as the chief Soviet lumber specialist, so I came to this lunch with some misgivings.

Krassin luckily spoke some French. The Englishman knew a few French words, but they had been picked up on his periodic trips to Paris and were mainly the lingo of houses of joy and gambling dens. The Canadian spoke French, but it was Canadian French and very difficult to understand. There were just the four of us—no interpreters.

The table was magnificently set, with an impressive assortment of forks and spoons. I handled them gingerly, afraid of using the wrong ones and giving the British a chance to talk of us as a pair of muzhiks who did not know how to employ cutlery properly. We were also on pins and needles as we beheld the waiters serving us: were they truly waiters, or were they disguised agents of the intelligence service? Krassin spoke to me jestingly:
"Let's have a look first. If they are agents, these fellows may shove some subversive literature under our chairs, and then we'd be in a fine mess!" He then went around the room touching draperies and murmuring, to whoever might be concealed behind them, to come out!

We took our seats at the rich, round table and at once plunged into food and conversation. We talked about Russian lumber, particularly railroad ties, since one of our two hosts was then supplying British railroads with ties. We used both French and English, and several times the lumber-and-whiskey man broke off his discourse on railroads to reminisce fondly about *chemin de fer* and other games of hazard and gay adventures in which he had indulged during his junkets to France. The mixed talk rather bewildered me, but Krassin constantly nudged me, demanding that I keep up the conversation.

Meantime we were being served roast chicken with English peas. I was very tense anyway, and became more so when Krassin, stumped for an answer because of his trouble with English, looked to me for help. Trying to

117

aid him, I made an awkward movement and, much to my horror, saw my chicken and peas being pushed by my elbow down into my lap. Fortunately a napkin lay spread on my knees, and, as luck would have it, Krassin and the two Englishmen were so absorbed in their conversational effort that they noticed nothing. Desperately I pretended to eat some remnants of fried potatoes still on my plate, while actually I got busy tying the napkin around the chicken and lowered it stealthily to the floor beneath my chair!

For three days afterward I feared to look into London newspapers. I expected to see a photograph of my chicken in its napkin, with a caption explaining that I had intended to take the food home from our sumptuous banquet. Not only would this have been a horrible disgrace, but the Cheka would have decided that I had acted deliberately to make the Soviet government look utterly ridiculous.

Soon thereafter I told Krassin about the entire episode, and when, three months later, I returned to Russia and attended my first session of the Council of Labor and Defense, I was greeted with much laughter. The story had already reached Moscow via Krassin; amid loud guffaws it was told and retold how "Liberman ate chicken in London." The Communists especially relished the tale, for they knew that I attached much importance to outward forms.

A few days after our nerve-racking luncheon, Krassin was received by Lloyd George, then still the prime minister of Great Britain. Lloyd George, on the whole, favored the establishment of Anglo-Soviet trade; but, knowing the mood of the main influences in British business, he suggested to Krassin that Russia *prove* to British buyers that she really meant to abide by her contracts with foreigners.

Krassin agreed with this suggestion. In order to break the wall of distrust facing us when we tried to deal with private British firms, we signed our first contracts with Britain's governmental organizations, formed during the war and still functioning. One of these was His Majesty's committee in charge of purchasing railroad ties. I succeeded in getting out of it a contract for one million ties, but in the course of the negotiations the committee's members, among them several English industrialists, kept asking me whether the Soviet government could guarantee the delivery of the ties, without which the British railroads would have a rather difficult time. I continually assured them that the very first shipment, 200,000 ties, would leave Archangel for England the moment the next season's navigation started.

I knew that there were that many ties in Archangel. But I also knew that, at one of the recent sessions of our Council of Labor and Defense, representatives of Soviet railroads had demanded those ties for their needs. In order to make sure that my London contract would be fulfilled, I telegraphed Lenin a request that he cancel the resolution of the Council of Labor and Defense releasing those ties to the Russian railroads. I pointed out that the entire contract, involving 1,000,000 railroad ties, would stand or fall on the delivery or nondelivery of that first one-fifth of the quantity contracted for. Soon the news reached me from Moscow that the council's resolution was canceled; all was well.

Even after the navigation season of 1921 opened, however, we had other troubles. The port of Archangel proved to be so disorganized as the result of the recent civil war that only a part of the first promised shipment could be made ready for export.

There was also a threat from Holland which hampered our initial efforts at exporting lumber. Some Dutch timber merchants, who had previously had investments in the north of Russia, went to court in the Netherlands with a complaint that the lumber, recently brought in Soviet ships to Dutch ports, was actually their property. The court laid an injunction on the lumber, forbidding us to sell it. We now feared that the Dutch complainants would reach into British courts, too, and secure an injunction against our ties and other lumber shipped to England.

In Moscow a great struggle seethed around the work of our delegation while we were in London. In essence, the problem was the same one over which Krassin and Litvinov had split while waiting for British visas in Copenhagen. Only now, in Moscow, it had grown into a serious conflict.

The entire Commissariat of Foreign Affairs, and especially Litvinov as its vice-commissar, were inclined to view the delegation as a Trojan horse, inside which a political embassy of the Soviet Government was to be smuggled into England. In their opinion the commercial side of our work was just a clever bait. They did not expect from us any real commercial accomplishments, and they did not want such commerce. Rather, they wanted to show the British that truly great vistas of trade would open up only after Britain consented to a political understanding with Russia.

Krassin, of course, regarded the whole matter quite differently, and set as his goal the conclusion of tangible commercial deals with the British. He wanted to convince these stubborn, practical-minded Englishmen that, even at this early date, the Soviet government was an earnest and a necessary buyer and seller. He believed that political relations with England would come by themselves, gradually, with the development of trade between the two countries.

But in Moscow, many of Krassin's ill-wishers explained his policy as a "lack of principles" and chided him for his alleged indifference to the basic ideas of the Soviet government. Among his foes were such outstanding personalities as Sheinman, the head of the Soviet State Bank and Krassin's vice-commissar in the Commissariat of Foreign Trade; Litvinov, of the Commissariat of Foreign Affairs; and certain Communists recently installed in the Centrosoyuz offices. As proof of Krassin's failure they pointed out that, having expended a goodly part of our gold reserve for the deals just concluded in Sweden, he had not so far secured any political recognition from Sweden in return. His sole defender of any importance in Moscow was Avel Yenukidze, his old friend and secretary of the All-Russian Executive Council of Soviet Deputies. But

119

Yenukidze was a steady, true defender, making up in the intensity and wisdom of his effort on Krassin's behalf what Krassin lacked in numbers on his side.

Hearing of the charges brewing in Moscow against him, Krassin decided to send Starkov and me, his two best friends in the delegation, back to Russia with detailed explanations of his work and aims. For some reason, he deemed it advisable for Starkov and me to travel separately, and as Starkov was a personal friend of Lenin's he left ahead of me, intrusted with a special letter from Krassin to Lenin. I started out a little later, bringing with me the first contract for the sale and delivery of railroad ties to England.

To reach Moscow from London I chose the route through Sweden and Estonia. But at that time there was no regular steamer connection between Stockholm and Tallinn, so I was forced to wait in the Swedish capital about two weeks before I finally received a telephone call from a local lawyer, which sent me on my way. He was a prominent figure in the Swedish Communist party, and he was now advising me of a berth on a freighter bound for Tallinn.

It turned out to be a tiny 100-ton ship, and I was its only passenger. The voyage was difficult and took three times as long as originally expected; several times the going was so rough that I was told to wear my life-jacket. Later the captain told me that the little vessel belonged to the Swedish Communist party and was engaged in illegal munitions traffic with Russia—that is, illegal from the viewpoint of the Western powers but not of the Soviets. The captain's main concern was to evade the sea patrols of the Western governments; that was why the ship zigzagged this way and that, taking "safe" routes known to the captain and his crew. The captain remarked that he made these trips frequently but seldom took any passengers along. I was given my berth as a rare exception and only because "we knew that your journey was an emergency one in the service of the Soviet government." Frankly, I was vastly relieved when we finally reached Tallinn and I stepped ashore.

The day after my return to Moscow, I reported to Lenin. We talked for two hours. His very first question was: "What are the British saying about our war with Poland?"

I told Lenin that in this conflict almost all popular sympathies in England were with Russia. These sympathies, I hastened to add, had their roots not in any love for the Soviet state but in the negative attitude of the British toward Polish expansion. I mentioned the powerful impression made by the special appeal issued by General Alexis Brusilov, who was famous for his brilliant service in the old tsarist army and who now called upon his former officers to join the Red Army as their patriotic Russian duty. Brusilov's statement, I went on, also caused certain individuals and groups among the Russian *émigrés* abroad to waver in their hatred of the Soviets. In this connection, Krassin's position in London was steadily growing stronger.

At the same time, I did not want to conceal from Lenin a few important changes for the worse in Soviet stock abroad. I mentioned among the bad points the formation of the so-called Revolutionary Committee of Poland, headed by Dzerzhinsky and Markhlevsky and brought by the Red Army to Belostok ("Bialystok" in Polish), the city we had just won from the Poles. This committee was regarded everywhere as a ready-made Communist government for Poland, in case that country should be overwhelmed by Lenin's legions. I told Lenin that the establishment of the committee in Belostok made for a certain coolness toward Russia in Britain, and I cited to him the opinion of many English friends of Soviet Russia, to the effect that this committee would eventually prove the undoing of Russia's own plans in Poland.

At that time, I did not know that Lenin himself was the author of the Soviet policy in Poland! I was somewhat surprised to see an expression of displeasure on his face when I mentioned the negative reaction in England toward the formation of the committee in Belostok. That was the time when Moscow was, on the whole, most sanguine in its hopes for a Red Europe. In 1920 the Kremlin felt that great, and perhaps decisive, revolutionary battles were about to flare up in Europe, and Lenin and his followers viewed the Russo-Polish war as one of the important links in the European chain of social upheavals. It was in the summer of 1920 that the British transport workers' trade-unions resolved against working on shipments of munitions to Soviet Russia's enemies, an incident that coincided with a number of others reflecting the growing class-consciousness of European workers. But these facts were relayed to Moscow in a rather exaggerated form and among the Russian leaders gave rise to a mistaken notion about the scale of the mass movement in the West.

In the course of my conversation with Lenin, I showed him a clipping from a conservative British newspaper, the *Evening Standard,* known to be the mouthpiece of Lord Curzon. The clipping was that of a cartoon by the now famous Low, representing a small-statured Pole and a large-sized Britisher standing on two sides of a globe. The Englishman was asking: "And what, after all, does Poland demand?" In reply the Pole was pointing: "All of the globe."

Lenin liked the cartoon very much indeed. He looked at it for a long time, studying all its details, and finally asked me to leave it with him.

The next step in our conversation was to report on our transactions in England. I stressed our obligation to deliver to Britain a considerable shipment of railroad ties with the very first navigation, and asked for Lenin's help. He complied with my request by ordering that these ties be definitely set aside to insure the fulfilment of the first trade contracts of the Soviet government with England.

At the same time, I touched upon the dilemma in which Krassin found himself in England. Krassin, I related, carried on his negotiations with the British on matters purely economic and was often successful, winning agreements or concessions from the English—and yet, almost nothing concrete resulted from these *pourparlers*. The reason for the failure, it seemed to me, was Moscow's insistence that a political point or two be included in the negotiations at the very last moment, so to speak. A commercial deal was complicated and confused by Moscow's raising far wider issues than mere

121

trade. To us in London it had seemed as if Krassin's foes in Moscow were bent on charging him with an excessively narrow viewpoint—and the result of such charges and of the political pressure on Krassin was a fiasco in this commercial deal and that. The situation was difficult, almost unbearable, for the leader of our delegation.

"Yes, Krassin's job is, in truth, hard," Lenin agreed. "However, he and you must remember that Soviet Russia is not only a merchant but also the first revolutionary government in the world. Therefore we must view all our steps and actions abroad in both their aspects, political as well as commercial. One element may prevail over the other, depending on the circumstances of the moment. At the present time, if England wants to maintain normal relations with us she must first of all recognize the Soviet government."

My final recommendations to Lenin boiled down to two points. One was that we could still buy abroad whatever goods we badly needed as long as we had some gold left. Foreigners would sell their goods to us willingly, despite any and all political agitation centering around Soviet Russia; in fact, they would be only too glad to pump the last remaining gold out of our country. They were quite sure that they could handle us without any trouble, as they did not believe in our ability to use the newly bought machinery with any degree of efficiency. Selling all this machinery and other equipment to us did not appear to be of any dire consequence to foreign industrialists and merchants, who thought that Russia would not become industrialized and would not grow into a new competitor of the Western World. So let us buy, I said to Lenin, all we could while the foreigners did not mind selling to us.

My second recommendation was that we had to sell some of our raw materials abroad, in order to build up a fund of foreign currency for our further purchases of Western machinery. England, I said, would be happy to buy some of our goods, particularly our wood products—but in this field we would probably have to reach some compromise or other with British capital. The stumbling block was the attitude of those London brokers who not so long ago had handled large British investments in the timber industry of the Russian north. They adamantly refused to consider these investments nullified or sequestered by the Russian revolution, but without these brokers and their good will it was impossible for us to resume Russia's trade with England. That is why, I concluded, a compromise was imperative.

"Do you trust me, Vladimir Ilyich?" I asked. "If so, here is my thought—we must settle this problem by creating mixed companies. These should be concessions, frankly granted to foreign capital by the Soviet government. Our state should for the time being join forces with foreign capital. That is how we'll be able to navigate the dangerous passage between the Soviet Scylla and the capitalist Charybdis. This idea, believe me, was not instilled into my mind by perfidious Albion; it came to me after I had left England for Russia. There is no crafty English design behind it to destroy our Soviet state.

"There are great stock piles of lumber at Archangel—sold to the English importers in the pre-Soviet period by Russian lumbermen. The sawmill proprietors have already received payment for that lumber, but their sawmills stopped working after the owners had fled to foreign lands. The lumber-yards are chock full of those old stock piles, and there is no new activity—the entire timber economy of our north is in a chaotic condition, as you know. We must come to some agreement with the British if we want to move things off their dead center. If we begin to export those stock piles without first reaching such an agreement, we will run the risk of having court injunctions used against our sales abroad by the former owners of that lumber. Those former owners, whether British or Russian, will cause us many difficulties abroad if we don't do something about the 'legality' of our sales beforehand."

The concessions I proposed were to be in the form of stock companies, with the Soviet government and foreign capital sharing in the stocks half and half. When appointing its representatives to such companies, too, the Kremlin could include delegates from Soviet labor unions, who would see to it that the interests of the Russian workers were not impaired by these foreign concessionaires.

Lenin considered the idea carefully. He nodded his consent as I spoke, and by the end of the interview he said:

"Fine. I approve of the general principal of the thing you suggest. But while carrying it out in practice, we must avoid such steps as might create an impression abroad that the Soviet government is weak, that it is forced to make concessions. For we are not weak, and we are not forced to do anything against our will."

(18)

WELCOME IN BERLIN

OF COURSE, SOVIET RUSSIA WAS NOT BUILT BY ECONOMICS ALONE, ALTHOUGH THAT was the side of which I saw most. But in the various positions I held both before and after the advent of the New Economic Policy, I also witnessed the Kremlin's diplomatic negotiations with more than one of Russia's neighbors.

First, on June 12, 1920, peace was signed between Russia and Latvia, and one of the clauses of the pact obligated the Soviet government to grant Latvia a concession involving 2,700,000 acres of Russian woodlands. Some days before this, at midnight, I was summoned by Foreign Commissar Chicherin who wanted to know: "How should we write this particular clause into the treaty so as to safeguard Soviet Russia against any impairment of her sovereignty whatsoever?"

At once I called a conference of experts, among whom were Kutler, of the tsarist ministry of finance; Tal, a professor of international law; and Markov, an old official of the Forestry Department of the tsarist ministry of agriculture. All of us together drafted the clause. We knew that the Latvian government itself would not have the means necessary to exploit the concession, but we feared that the men of Riga would bring in a group of foreign capitalists who would want to exploit the Russian forests in competition with Russia herself. And, in time, that is exactly what happened.

Within three years an understanding was reached between Latvia and the timber interests of Sweden. With the Swedish contract in its vaults, the Riga government then insisted on bringing to life the "woodland clause" of the Lettish-Russian treaty of 1920. The Moscow government said, "all right, here is your concession"—and placed at Latvia's disposal the stipulated 2,700,000 acres, designating them in several widely separated provinces at varying distances from the Lettish border. Moscow claimed a strategic reason: a desire to safeguard the young Soviet republic against possible aggression. The result was that the Swedish concerns were deprived of a real opportunity to exploit these Russian woodlands.

There were also the Polish-Russian negotiations, which finally led to the Treaty of Riga in 1921. I recall that the fate of that part of Volyn which the treaty of 1921 gave to Poland was decided by considerations having nothing to do with the ethnic character of the countryside. One important reason (aside from the obvious ones) why the Polish government insisted on that section of Volyn was the fact that the largest estates of the most influential Polish aristocrats happened to lie in that region. This aristocracy was connected by marriage with many of the royal families of Europe, including the Romanovs of old Russia, and in 1920 the Polish nobles used their connections at all the surviving courts of royalty, and even at the Vatican, to put additional pressure upon the Russians to surrender this area of Volyn to Poland and so save their great estates.

It was during our first trip to London that a number of these blue-bloods invaded Krassin's reception room to see what they could do. They offered to bring about diplomatic recognition of Russia by this European government and that; the cancellation of tsarist debts, which were then still demanded from the Soviets; and what-not—if only the Kremlin would stop being so stubborn in this question of handing western Volyn over to Poland.

Since most of the immense manors of the Polish noblemen were in the wooded area of Volyn, all documents containing promises and requests eventually reached my hands. In these documents I beheld far-famed names of Polish and other aristocrats—and even of Russia's Grand Duke Nicholas (Nikolai Nikolaievich), the commander-in-chief of the tsarist armies in 1914–15, now an exile in Europe and fearing for the fate of Borisovo, his estate in the same borderlands. And because the Red Army at one period in the summer of 1920 had been so successful in its invasion of Poland, many of the exalted but fearful owners had hastened to sell some of their wooded property to timber merchants. Now, in the course of the Russo-Polish peace negotiations, they were vitally interested in seeing these forests remain on the Polish side of the new border.

Strange as it may seem, still another and a very different group was likewise interested in the same problem of the Russo-Polish frontier line. These were some Jewish spiritual leaders, chiefly Orthodox, from many countries. Their appearance, side by side with the aristocrats and the timber merchants, was quite striking.

The Jews feared the Sovietization of the area in question, for they were sincerely convinced that only under Poland would the cultural cradle of Russian Jewry be saved. This was the region known for its little town of Slovuty, where in old tsarist times a celebrated edition of the Talmud was published despite the persecution and physical violence visited upon certain outstanding Jewish leaders for the printing of the tome. And this was the province where another little settlement, Kirets, won renown among the Jews of eastern Europe for its remarkable rabbis. Here also were Pinsk and other centers which, in the eyes of Orthodox Jewry, served as symbols of the utmost flowering of Jewish thought.

I was approached by several influential rabbis, who besought me to help them in this all-important matter. My task was to see to it that the Soviet government did not insist too strenuously on its claims to this territory. They said to me: "Russian Jewry is doomed. It will die either spiritually or physically—perhaps both. The older people are being destroyed as businessmen and other socially undesirable elements. Even when some of them aren't persecuted, they are dying out anyway, because life in Russia is so hard. The young folk marry non-Jews and are fast assimilating—disappearing as Jews. The Polish-Russian borderlands are the only great remaining reservoirs of Orthodox Russian Jewry. These reservoirs can be saved only by enabling Poland to gain this territory."

These men said to me that they spoke on behalf of Russia's Jewry, but, as a matter of fact, they represented no one but themselves. The Polish government, however, tried hard and in every way to make use of their sentiment and activities, and eventually they won. The borderlands became theirs, for Russia's troubles both at home and broad were many, and she had to be conciliatory to give herself a much-needed breathing spell.

Actually, neither the fears of the Jews about Soviet Russia nor the more modern charges in the anti-Jewish press—to the effect that Jews dominate and run Russia—have proved valid. Stark, sober events have made cruel fun of all that. While in German-occupied Poland and western Russia a majority of the Jews succumbed to torture and death at the hands of the Nazis, most of the Jews who succeeded in escaping with the Russians ahead of the German hordes avoided this fate. Though their lot was a hard one, they managed to save life and freedom as much as any other Russian citizens, despite the fear of twenty-odd years ago that they were doomed precisely because they remained on Soviet territory.

The assertion, which we sometimes hear, that the Jews' emancipation usually keeps pace with their assimilation, was certainly borne out in the case of Russian Jewry. The Jews of Soviet Russia have demonstrated their vitality as citizens and their adaptability to the new and difficult condition of life which faced all the numerous nationalities of the Soviet Union.

Early in 1921, I was again sent abroad. The Kremlin decided that another delegation should visit foreign countries to reacquire for Russia's lumber its traditional foreign markets. I was included; as a matter of fact, I was most of the delegation. Berlin was to be my first stop.

My trip to Berlin turned out to be a minor sensation in Germany's business circles, so great was the German interest in Russia, which was then being remolded by Lenin's New Economic Policy, and so novel were business representatives of this new Russia. Foreign troops of the interventionist powers had just been withdrawn from Soviet territory, and peace was dawning at last. In Berlin, no less than in other European capitals, these questions were asked: Will it be feasible for the world at large to work out normal relations with the Soviet land? Is a peaceful collaboration with Red Russia at all possible? My journey to Germany was one of the first experiments along these lines for both the Soviets and the capitalists, an event destined either to prove or disprove the possibility of such collaboration.

On arriving in Berlin I learned that Hugo Stinnes, the uncrowned monarch of German industries, had reserved a sumptuous suite for me in one of the most luxurious hotels of Berlin, the Esplanade. When I moved in I was startled to hear that some thirty-five other rooms in the hotel were occupied by timber-importers, who had come from all over Europe—to meet me! Among them were Englishmen and Belgians and, naturally enough, Germans who wanted to buy Soviet timber. There were Norwegians and Swedes, too, who did not need our timber—who, on the contrary, feared our competition; but they wanted to know to what extent Russia might reappear as a seller of timber.

All these people buzzed around, feeling out the situation. Even those who did not as yet plan to do any business with us tried to find out whether they could obtain better terms from their Scandinavian timber-suppliers by threatening to start dealing with the Soviets, by playing off one side against the other.

The press of western Europe opened quite a discussion of this question of trading with Soviet Russia. We were opposed by that school of political thought in Europe which insisted that there should be no commerce or any other contact with the Soviets. This group was supported, now openly, now secretly, by our Scandinavian rivals, who freely predicted that we would not— could not—fulfil a single contract.

"Testimony by witnesses" appeared in the form of depositions by foreign sea captains who "with their own eyes" had seen the terrible coercion that was used on workers and political convicts to produce logs in the forests and lumber in the sawmills of north Russia. These captains said that there was no free labor in the Russian north. The foreign press printed these stories and remarked that nothing had been changed in Russia by the New Economic Policy

126

and that therefore the attitude of the world at large toward Russia should remain the same—wholly negative. In certain countries a law was suddenly remembered, prohibiting the importation of goods produced with slave or other forced labor. Its application to imports from Soviet Russia was vigorously demanded. A number of individuals wrote and orated that trade with the Soviets was contrary to the very spirit of Christianity. Some newspapers abroad added the allegation that the woodchopping in Soviet Russia was done in a reckless and harmful manner; that the Kremlin gave away great portions of the country's woodlands as gifts to its henchmen and thus squandered and ruined the nation's wealth.

However, a few voices sounded on our behalf, too. These were mainly the representatives of liberal political parties and movements. They were joined by businessmen who needed our Russian wood products of well-known superior quality. These business interests, by seeking our timber, also sought thereby a counterweight to the domination of the markets of Europe by the Scandinavian exporters of timber.

The fact that I was stopping at the luxurious Esplanade was very convenient from the viewpoint of establishing contacts with a great number of persons interested in our timber, and it certainly enhanced the prestige of the Soviet North Timber Trust which I represented. But in time it brought me much trouble, too, for three years later the O.G.P.U. investigators grilled me: "Why did you stop in such an expensive hostelry?"

I could not say it to their faces, but similar expenses never bothered any of the prominent Communists who on their trips to Germany used to stop in the same hotel!

While in Berlin I held many interesting conversations on Russia's political and economic problems, which by far transcended the immediate limits of my timber speciality. Among the persons with whom I had these talks were a number of very intelligent individuals who offered me arguments of no mean level. My counterargument usually consisted of pointing to the entire new system of state capitalism in Russia as a worth-while method of practical economics.

Of particular interest and significance were my meetings with the world-famous German industrialist, Hugo Stinnes himself. No longer young and never progressive, he was nevertheless rather favorably disposed toward Russia and her experiments. Yet even he was most skeptical about Soviet economics and said to me:

"I just can't believe that your state, having expropriated huge woodlands from their private owners, can in a short period of time create a rational economy with governmental forces alone. Red tape and bureaucracy are bound to clog up such a system. You won't be able to produce your timber, either in that quantity which you promise to deliver abroad, or of that remarkable quality about which all of us dream, we no less than you."

"But you are mistaken, my dear Herr Stinnes," I argued back. "We didn't take most of those forests away from their private owners. In Russia many forests used to belong to the state even in tsarist times. Only the sawmills were of private ownership. And the owners of these sawmills had fled before their properties were nationalized. Once such sawmills are taken over by the state, we of the state must of necessity introduce a rational economy in them."

"A rational economy?" Stinnes arched his eyebrows. "I doubt the very possibility of such an economy when fostered by the state. Take our German example of the state-appointed Committee on Socialization, which, first of all, was supposed to concern itself with the nationalization of our coal mines. The committee called in various prominent persons as experts and listened to their opinions. There was among them Walter Rathenau, the king of our German electric industry, so to speak. He is one of our outstanding men, as you know, and well educated and enlightened. In a way he is a leftist democrat. And yet he expressed himself against this project of nationalization, and for the following reasons.

" 'You will,' he said to the committee, 'succeed in securing these coal mines without difficulty, especially if you decide to compensate their owners. And you will further be successful in closing down, as you plan, the less profitable of the mines, concentrating all your work on the most profitable ones. But what you won't manage to do is this: you won't manage to preserve at the head of the German coal industry that remarkable personnel which, by giving the industry all its thoughts and efforts, has brought the coal industry of our country to its present high standard. These are the owners and the directors, who are now so vitally interested in the mines, who are spending all their time in fighting their competitors, and who in the course of this fight have improved the production techniques so brilliantly. But should you try to create a single state-owned and state-controlled coal industry in Germany, all these men will leave for other industries where they will surely find a better and financially more remunerative opportunity for their organizing talents. The state will remain with its mediocre officials and clerks.'

"That is what Rathenau said to our committee. And now, will not the same danger threaten your timber industry in Russia after its nationalization?"

"No, Herr Stinnes," I replied. "It's an altogether different matter in Russia. In our Soviet republic it isn't just one industry that has been nationalized. All our industries are nationalized. Therefore, our talented specialists, our timber experts and other industrialists and managers have no chance of seeking other branches of economy as the arena for their knowledge and ability. Also they are not looking for any other arenas because gradually all of them have become economists in the employ of the state. Until lately, while the system of War Communism prevailed in our economy, these men played the secondary roles of so-called consultants in the various organizations of the Soviets. This, it is true, did not satisfy them completely, did not afford them a wide enough field for the activities of the kind to which they had been accustomed previously and to which they have every natural right.

"But now the Soviet government is attracting them to higher posts in such large trusts as our North Timber Trust, for instance. More and more such trusts are being formed in Soviet Russia, and more and more such specialists are accepting the new posts willingly and gladly. Even now, at this early stage of the new system, they work not because they fear the government but because they are eager to work. Most of them are heart and soul in such work. Under these changed circumstances we confidently expect a high productivity from their personal labors as well as from the entire industry which they now happen to guide, be it the timber industry or what have you."

But Stinnes was adamant. He asked:

"Will this new form of state trust indeed bring such a radical change in the economy of your nation and in the mood, the psychology, of the former industrialists and owner-managers of your works? Don't forget that as before, as under the system of War Communism, they will continue to be the objects of the tremendous pressure of the state—the state which is guided by motives completely alien to the motives of these new employees, the state which runs these enterprises along principles entirely strange to these men's habits. Profits are calculated differently. The very form of the enterprise is so strange, so novel to these men!"

But I would not agree with this either. Again I argued:

"You forget that these industrialists were not complete bosses in their enterprises even in tsarist or private-capitalist times. The banks of Russia, like the banks practically everywhere in the world, were the true and superior owners of those works and plants which were supposed to have been directed by their proprietors. The banks dictated to the nominal owners and directors much that these men often considered bad policies but nevertheless had to carry out. Well, the Soviet state has merely taken over those plants from the banks. The former proprietors and former directors of the factories and plants will not find the state's dictation any more difficult to obey than they used to find the bank's edicts. You must remember that the New Economic Policy brought back to Russia's economy the old system of strict accounting, the profit-and-loss system—the thing which all these new employees of the state consider as the most elementary requisite of rational economics. Lenin fully realizes that the state must handle these outstanding employees in a different way. He orders the entire state machinery to treat them with respect, for they are a valuable human property of the state, an asset in a sense, just as any capital is an asset. Lenin tells his Communists to take lessons from these specialists, to surround them with the attentions they truly deserve."

But I hardly convinced Herr Stinnes. Actually, of course, such problems are solved not in conversations and argument but by years and years of historic experience. I had not really intended to become an apologist for the Russian system of government, but it is in the nature of man to want to defend the structure he is helping to build, when human ideals are the inspiration of these labors.

As I look back upon those years and those talks, I still believe that by and large I was right in my premises and predictions. In the long run, that is, I was right—so I felt then; so I feel now.

And yet I must note here that most of the former timber industrialists who went to work for the Soviet state as its employees eventually came to grief. Within a few years after those talks in Berlin, after the timber industry of Soviet Russia was finally reorganized on its new state-managed foundations, many of those former capitalists were arrested and tried by the Soviet government on all sorts of charges. Some of them were liquidated without the formality of trials. They were charged with the long-forgotten sins of their private capitalistic past—long forgotten perhaps by them and their friends but not by their Communist bosses. They were also accused of allowing their new Soviet apparatus to lapse into certain administrative errors—errors that were perchance inevitable or not of their own making at all.

Even as I spoke to Stinnes, trouble was in the making for me personally, stemming from some deals which I had made for the Soviets with foreign industrialists and businessmen, in good faith and in the sincere conviction that I was achieving much good for the Red republic which I represented abroad. I did not know it yet, however, and proceeded with my trip.

(19)

WINNING OVER THE FRENCH

PARIS WAS NEXT. CERTAIN FRENCH INTERESTS WERE PROPOSING A PURCHASE OF OUR timber, involving about a hundred million francs. I went to France at the suggestion of Comte Jacques de Lubersac, a rightist member of the French senate.

Naturally there was much opposition to any trade with the Soviets in the conservative circles of Paris; and we had to overcome it somehow. Various contacts and influences were brought into play, and the powers that were finally agreed not to stand in the way of a Soviet-French transaction.

One of the main influences was an article that appeared in one of the conservative newspapers of Paris above the signature of a rightist deputy of the French Chamber, who was chairman of the chamber's committee on foreign affairs. In his article the deputy wrote of a letter he had recently received, showing how beneficial it would be for France to make use of Russian timber in the reconstruction work then beginning in the northern departments of France, which had suffered so much destruction in the war of 1914–18. The author of the article concluded: "Although I continue to be opposed to the Soviet system irrevocably, I cannot but support the suggestion contained in this letter, for most of the arguments offered by the writer of the letter are truly sound." Of course, we knew that the author of the article was also the

130

author of the letter he so praised; but this maneuver opened the way to the first French purchase of our Soviet timber.

There were some other interesting sidelights to the establishment of our first contact with the industrial and commercial circles of France. A young Swiss, for instance, played a noteworthy role in achieving this delicate connection for us. In the years immediately preceding World War I, he had been a tutor in the home of a prominent Russian aristocrat. When, in the course of the war this nobleman became active in the work of the Russian Red Cross, the tutor became his secretary in this new activity. The Russian revolution found him abroad, and in the process of his work he met the celebrated Norwegian explorer, Fridtjof Nansen, whom he convinced of the necessity of organizing aid to Russian refugees abroad and especially to the starving population inside Russia. Because of his friendship with Nansen and the humanitarian aspects of his effort, the young man obtained the Soviet government's permission to visit Russia. This and other contacts of his, both abroad and in Russia, gave him the opportunity to act as a go-between in the first business negotiations between the Soviet republic and foreign lands.

When I first met this young Swiss, he told me his views on the possibility of trade between Soviet Russia and France. He said that the problem of the old tsarist debts to France was the greatest handicap; so long as these debts were unrecognized by the Soviet government, the attitude of the French toward the Kremlin would remain hostile. And so long as Russia was not diplomatically recognized by France, she would remain isolated, for France played a dominating role in European diplomacy in the years immediately following the first World War. The leftist groups in France, although sympathetic toward Russia, were of little help in winning such recognition; but the Swiss had an original idea. He was now suggesting to the Kremlin, through me, a complex preliminary game, the result of which, he promised, would be the recognition of Lenin's government by France.

This was where Comte de Lubersac came in. According to what the young Swiss told me, the aristocratic French family of the De Lubersacs was in close business contact with the German interests of Hugo Stinnes—because of certain involved transactions originating in the war reparations which Germany was to pay. There were three De Lubersac brothers, each one of whom occupied an important position in French politics and business. Jacques, the leader of the monarchist group in the French senate, at the time headed a business combine interested in the reconstruction of the war-ravaged northern departments of his country. Odon was the chief owner and manager of a large commercial and banking house of profitable connections with Argentinian banking capital. He was also the mainspring of tremendous imports of English coal into France. The third brother, Jean, was well known for his work with the Second Bureau, or intelligence arm of the French republic, an activity which took him to Russia, where he succeeded in establishing contacts with certain representatives of the Soviet government.

Reparation deliveries in kind, handled for Germany by Hugo Stinnes, were

131

sent to France through the firm of Odon de Lubersac and were addressed to the concern headed by Jacques de Lubersac. My Swiss acquaintance turned out to be a connecting link between Stinnes and the De Lubersac brothers, and this was the plan he brought me:

The northern departments of France needed timber for their reconstruction. It would be easy to convince the French government that the Russian northern pine was really the strongest and most durable kind of wood, that the French market should be open to Soviet lumber, even if there was as yet no trade agreement and no diplomatic intercourse between the two countries. Stinnes would buy this lumber from the Soviets, in his turn selling to us certain sawmill machinery and other equipment, and would then transfer it to the De Lubersac brothers, who, together with Stinnes, were to sign his contract with Soviet Russia, so that there might be some direct settlement of accounts between Russia and France. True, there was some difficulty because of the lack of a Soviet-French agreement, which would raise the duty on Russian timber to four times the ordinary tariff. But, said my friend, even this problem might well be solved by the influence of such people as the De Lubersacs.

The plan interested me. I relayed it to Moscow and soon received word from the Kremlin to go ahead with the negotiations. At the time the French government gave no visas to Soviet citizens, and I doubted if an exception would be made in my case; but I told the young Swiss that I was willing to go to Paris for further discussion if a visa were issued to me. In twenty-four hours, as if by magic and despite all my skepticism, two French visas were ready, one for me, the other for my secretary.

A few days later I took the train for Paris, accompanied by my secretary, the young Swiss, and a Dr. Farman, who was one of the main aides of Herr Stinnes. In Paris I stopped in the Hotel Lutecia on the left bank of the Seine. Two detectives, I noticed, watched every step I took, day and night.

My negotiations, I soon learned, were to be carried on not only with the De Lubersac brothers but also with representatives of the well-known Banque de l'Union parisienne, as well as with a member of the financial group of Louis Lucher. Indeed, all the ensuing conferences included one or another agent of the bank and Lucher's delegate, too—the late Colonel Wayl. Dr. Farman sat in on behalf of Stinnes. It was he, together with one of the De Lubersacs, who made the proposal to secure from the Soviets a timber concession or two in the Murmansk area, where at one time prior to World War I the Lucher interests were building the Murmansk-Petrograd railroad.

Comte Jacques de Lubersac was especially attentive to our party, and clearly wanted to emphasize the importance which he attached to our coming to France. He arranged a grand luncheon in our honor, not in a restaurant, as was customary, but in his own house.

Thus the ground was prepared for the negotiations involving one hundred million francs. This was a transaction for the sale of our Soviet timber to the French Société centrale de Bois. Again the De Lubersac brothers were instrumental in helping me get the contract. In this particular case, Brother Odon found himself in the peculiar position of representing Russia's interests in France!

Altogether, I had a very interesting time. Through my Swiss friend I met Dimitri Navashin, whose name later figured prominently in a number of sensational events. At that point this Russian was still anti-Soviet, although even then he was beginning to show signs of wanting to make his peace with the Soviets. Subsequently, Navashin returned to Russia and was appointed to high posts in the Soviet administration, and came back to western Europe as an important official in the Soviet bank agency in Paris. Eventually, however, he broke with the Soviets. One day his body was discovered in the forest of Boulogne—he had been murdered. There were many rumors, but no one knew for certain why and by whom he had been slain.

It was also in Paris that I once more came across an old friend, Skobelev, a non-Bolshevik socialist of tsarist times and of the Kerensky era, who in time crossed over to the Communists, becoming Soviet Russia's unofficial representative in France. At that point he was not as yet with the Soviets. I was visiting him one day, shortly before my departure for Russia, when the telephone rang, and Skobelev replied: "Yes, he is here now, why don't you come over? The three of us will have some wine together."

Presently a middle-aged Frenchman came limping in, a picturesque heavy person with a beret on his head. It was Anatole de Monzie. He spoke to me warmly of Soviet Russia and chided the Kremlin for its sluggishness with regard to France. He said:

"Your government is trying to bring about a pro-Soviet feeling in France through its connections with the Communists and left socialists. This is a mistake. Tell Lenin that the best way to win France over to doing business with Russia is through the businessmen of France. They are our only realists."

And, in truth, our very first earnest *rapprochement* with France was effected through such people as De Monzie and Navashin. For a number of years, both before and after French recognition of the Soviet government, De Monzie did much for Russia in France. He was Russia's herald, so to speak. As a lawyer, he represented the Soviet government in a number of lawsuits in the courts of France. As a member of the French parliament, he was the spokesman for the idea of collaborating with the Soviet republic and sharply criticized those French rightists who opposed it. Unfortunately, however, his zeal for collaboration proved too great, and he eventually co-operated with the Germans in World War II. The last news of him was that he was being tried for his life by the new resurgent France.

A similar character whom I met during my first visit to Paris was the now ill-famed Fernand de Brinon, Laval's sinister henchman and Hitler's main supporter in France. The lumber broker with whom I was dealing told me that I should try to win the support of the newspaper *L'Information*, then the most influential business journal in France. Preliminary arrangements were duly made, and I was well received by a responsible representative of the paper, on the staff of which he was then beginning his career. This was De Brinon. The day following this interview, *L'Information*, forgetting its previous attitude in the matter of tsarist debts to France, came out with handsome praise for the efforts being made to resume trade relations with Russia; and this, too, helped my work.

Later that year, in London again, Krassin and I had a very interesting visit from the deputy Ernest Lafont, a French socialist leader. Unlike most of those who sought out Krassin, this Frenchman had politics, not business, in mind.

At that juncture the Socialist party of France was in an almost chaotic state. A split had just occurred within its ranks, the left wing forming the Communist party of France, which soon gained a good deal of influence. The Communist party proceeded to fight the Socialist party, and in the course of this struggle the French Communists used any means at their disposal, including some that were not entirely honest. Things were made easy for them by the fact that within the Socialist party there were many different trends and elements at loggerheads with one another.

During World War I, Lafont had been in the right wing of the French Socialist party. As I remember it, he came to Russia in 1917 on a visit, together with Marcel Cachin and the English laborite, Arthur Henderson, to urge the socialists of Russia to continue the war against the Kaiser's Germany, in true alliance with France and England. Now, in 1921, a brief four years later, his friend Cachin was one of the leaders of French Communism. As for Lafont, he combined in his attitude an admiration for the Russian revolution and a revulsion at the political practices of the French Communists. A somewhat naïve idea governed him, an idea which was nevertheless typical of those times: to find a path to an agreement with Moscow over and above the head of the French Communists. This is what brought him to London to see Krassin.

Lafont's wife was with him on this trip. She was of Russian origin, from a rich Odessa family. She was expensively dressed, with diamond rings sparkling on her fingers. The pair spent two days in London, and at Krassin's request I saw much of the Lafonts during their visit. Lafont complained to me:

"We are stifled by the atmosphere in France. We hate our well-fed and triumphant bourgeoisie. But our Communists are doing tremendous damage to our working-class movement, and I want to bridge the chasm between our Socialist party and the revolutionary Russia."

All his efforts availed Lafont precisely nothing, even though Krassin duly communicated to Moscow whatever Lafont wanted Moscow to know about his sentiment and his plans. A truly Jacobin implacability reigned in Moscow in those days, particularly toward the socialist parties of the Western World. The Kremlin kept inciting the Communists of Paris against the French socialists: "Show no mercy to those social-patriots!" As for Lafont personally, Moscow sent these instructions: "If Lafont is stifled in his bourgeois sur-

134

roundings, let him quit the Socialist party and join the Communists of France."

The curious sequel was that Lafont did follow this advice, for a brief period at least. Once a Communist, he journeyed to Moscow, and later became one of the most prominent leaders of the French part of the Third International. But it did not last long; he disagreed with his fellow-Communists on a number of tactical problems, he broke with the party, and returned to his old socialist fold.

(20)

"NOTHING TO FEAR"

FOLLOWING OUR TRADE AGREEMENT WITH ENGLAND IN 1921, OUR COMMERCIAL activities in London developed very well indeed in the course of the next few years, up to 1924. They also led to considerable successes on the other markets of Europe. We carried out in full the contracts we had signed; the quality of the goods we sold improved with each year; deductions from the purchase price, which our customers had the right to make for poorly graded lumber, decreased in a few years from 15–20 per cent of the total to the normal rates of 1–1.5 per cent.

Soon after beginning our work in England, I succeeded in obtaining credits for Russia from Lloyd's Bank. The first credit was to the amount of £500,000, then the maximum set for Soviet deals. Within a year, however, the amount was raised to £1,000,000. The news of our getting credits from the British caused a veritable sensation in the world of commerce, and I felt justly proud when some Londoners, in introducing me to their friends, made a point of adding: "This is the man who got credits for Soviet Russia."

In London I also organized Soviet Russia's first three mixed-stock companies, with one-half of the stock belonging to the Soviet government and the other half distributed among former concessionaries and owners. The capital of these companies was represented by the proceeds from the sale of nationalized lumber previously owned by the concessionaries. Their mills, now taken over by the Russian government, were rented to these mixed companies for the duration of their contracts and for a nominal fee, to permit the sawing of logs annually sold to these companies by the forests on a fixed stumpage basis. A representative of the Communists was always chairman of these companies, and a capitalist was their managing director.

This was the first swallow of the new Russian politicoeconomic spring— the first result of the new policy of concessions to foreign capital then inaugurated by Moscow. The agreements to this end were signed by Krassin as the people's commissar of foreign trade during one of his sojourns in London. I knew that at the time there was no corresponding official sanction from the Political Bureau, the highest organ of the Communist party in Russia. Apparently Krassin had orders to sign these agreements from Lenin himself. While signing the documents, however, Krassin glanced at me slyly and asked: "What do you think, will I be hung for this?"

One of the concessionary contracts was signed by a Norwegian named Prits. This man had for many years been in the timber business in the north of Russia. He was of most conservative convictions and had once said to me, "I will never try to meet Soviet Russia even a quarter of the way, not to speak of halfway." Proudly he had added: "I don't bend before anyone. See my cane? It's ten centimeters longer than the ordinary length for such a cane. I had it made purposely so—to hold myself as erectly as possible." This was before he signed the concession agreement. Having signed it, he began to work with Soviet Russians with a will. In time he had established in Russia a whole series of businesses, all very profitable to himself. However, these businesses of his did not last beyond the general cancellation of concessions to foreigners in Russia.

It was with these first concession contracts that I returned from London to Moscow. In a rather triumphant mood I carried the documents directly to Lenin. They lacked translations into Russian, for Krassin had said to me before bidding me goodbye in London:

"Vladimir Ilyich reads English very well. Just give it to him in the original. If it were available in Russian, the other members of the Political Bureau would pick on this or that feature, and there would be unpleasant discussions of such questions as the workers' control of the plants, the regulations of the inner control of the production, and so on."

Lenin listened to my report of these deals with much approval. He then requested that I compile a brief résumé of the contracts.

"Do you want it in Russian?" I asked.

"No," he replied, "leave it in the original English. I will translate it myself during the Politbureau session. This way there'll be less discussion and things will be speedily dispatched."

The next day Fotieva, the secretary, advised me that the Politbureau had given its prompt approval to the contracts. One more day passed, and I received an official message, on the letterhead of the Council of Labor and Defense, over the signature of Lenin himself. It read:

"A report on our policy of concessions will be heard at an early session of the Council of Labor and Defense. Comrade Liberman is hereby requested to have ready his remarks on the trip abroad from which he has recently returned."

Came the day of the session. The meeting was attended by all the people's commissars who were members of the Council of Labor and Defense. Tomsky, the chief of the Soviet labor unions, was also present. Lenin was in the chair and, as usual, reading a book while running the meeting. He opened the gathering by asking:

136

"How many minutes should we give the speaker of the occasion?" Before anyone could say anything, he gave his own answer: "Two minutes."

Tomsky protested. He suggested ten minutes. It was quickly settled at three minutes.

Lenin then went back to his book and would not listen to either the speaker or the ensuing debate. And yet, when the moment came for him to stir once more into his characteristic action—when he began to dictate the final resolution of the council's session—I was astonished. Into the text of the resolution he proceeded to incorporate all the facts and arguments which I had brought with me from abroad about the new policy of concessions, all the salient points I had used during the debate and, earlier, in a private conversation with the man himself. Thus Lenin's decision to grant concessions to foreign capitalists won out.

I was very surprised to hear, however, that Lenin had to manipulate and maneuver with all sorts of subterfuges when he wanted the Political Bureau to make decisions which he judged essential. I had not thought that that was necessary for Lenin; I had believed that his word was law for all his aides and collaborators.

Sometime later, in London again, I had an occasion to speak of this to Shotman, one of Lenin's closest assistants. Shotman, in his additional capacity as secretary of the Supreme Council of Economy, came to London, and I met him often after office hours as well as during our working day. In a night club, over our glasses of whiskey, our tongues somewhat loosened, I told Shotman how amazed I had been a few months before, in Moscow, while watching Lenin's actions at that meeting of the Council of Labor and Defense. I said to him:

"If I am not mistaken, you and Lenin shared living quarters during his and your Siberian exile before the revolution. Lenin is very fond of you, I understand, and you ought to know him as few men do. Can you explain to me why he had to maneuver his closest aides of the Politbureau and the council the way he did? Why didn't he, for instance, let me translate the concession contracts into the Russian?"

Shotman smiled knowingly:

"Indeed, it's hard to understand Vladimir Ilyich. But he takes stock of everything. He knew there was incipient opposition in the Politbureau to this particular bit of business. Certain members of the Politbureau feared that Krassin might smuggle his anti-Communist heresies into these new agreements with foreign capitalists, especially since Liberman the Menshevik helped to cook it all up. But Lenin is not afraid. He is convinced that with the aid of these agreements, through these new mixed-stock companies, the Soviets will break the steel ring of the capitalist hostility to their own vast advantage. That is why he decided to avoid the discussion of certain points of these agreements that are essentially quite weak from our Soviet viewpoint. That is why he saw fit to leave both the contracts and your digest of them in the original English, without translating them into the Russian."

Shotman thought a little, then added: "Yes, Vladimir Ilyich Lenin always runs true to form. There is only one Lenin."

Two more enterprises were soon created in connection with our export of Soviet timber, and both were expressions and examples of this new state capitalism we had begun to practice. Both proceeded to yield good results in a fairly short time.

One enterprise had to do with transport. We felt a shortage of transport with the growth of the work of the North Timber Trust. Strictly speaking, there was no Russian merchant marine left by that time. In the northern waters it was the Scandinavian fleet that dominated our commerce—mostly small freighters fitted out for the peculiar conditions of shipping in the White Sea. They called for our timber at such tiny ports as Kola, Onega, and Mezen. But a majority of the owners of these Scandinavian ships were somehow connected with the timber industries of their own countries. In other words, we depended for our timber transport on the ships of our competitors. It was bad business.

We decided to counteract this situation by creating mixed-stock companies in which we would have at least one-half of the outstanding shares. The first experiment was the establishment of a company in which 50 per cent of the stock belonged to certain Norwegian interests owning the Bergen Steamship Company, and the remaining 50 per cent was in our own possession.

We set as our goal the construction of fifteen new steamers specially fitted to carry small timber cargoes. We gave this new company of ours the exclusive right to transport Soviet timber, but the entire technical side of the company's work was left in the hands of foreign experts. Presently, according to our program, we received a number of excellent freighters built in France, Germany, and Norway. The company developed its activities satisfactorily.

The second problem facing us was a better organization of the sales of our timber abroad and, above all, in England, the country that remained the chief buyer of Russian wood. The way the British handled their timber purchases was unique. By stages, over a period of many years, several large firms had arisen in England to play the role of brokers in this tremendous business of buying and distributing foreign lumber. They were mighty concerns, with numerous staffs and with superior banking and other credit connections. Not a single major operation involving the import of timber into Britain could possibly be completed without the approval of these powerful brokers. Their place in the life and business of England was so solid, so much of a tradition, that in the first World War it was the custom of the British government to set aside a certain sum out of each appropriation in the purchase of timber for the war needs of the Empire as commission due one or another of these firms. This was done even though the government could have managed without resorting to the assistance of the brokers.

In these circumstances there was nothing else for us to do but deal with the long-established firms of London.

138

On my first trip to London I approached one of these agents. I had known him well before the Russian revolution, during my work on behalf of the Balashov forest interests. In those years, on his frequent journeys to Russia, the Englishman had spent many hours wining, dining, and chatting with me. Now he was genuinely glad to see me, and invited me to spend a week end with him. As we relaxed, he told me that his affairs were in fine shape and that he was one of the chief agents then buying and distributing Scandinavian timber in England. Because of this connection he was, rather naturally, extremely skeptical when he heard of my plans to bring Russian timber back to the British market. At times during our conversation he even displayed an unpleasant sharpness. When, for instance, I suggested that he take upon himself a broker's function in this matter of staging a Russian comeback, he declared:

"I like you very much personally, Mr. Liberman, but I cannot deal in stolen merchandise. That wood you are trying to sell is stolen from its rightful owners."

Within a year, after we had won our first considerable successes, however, this same man came to me with a rather humble and insistent request that we add him to the list of our British brokers! But the other Englishmen would not hear of it, not wishing to accept a new partner in their virtual monopoly on the sale of Soviet timber. "He held himself aloof when it was risky," they said. "But now, when it's safe and profitable, he wants to join us!"

I sided with the man, nonetheless. After long arguments I managed to win the other brokers' consent and gave him an agency for the timber from one of our smaller wooded areas near Mezen; but the others remained stubborn in their refusal to accept him as a member of their own group. By this time, I must note, the general attitude toward us—the representatives of the Soviet timber industry—was quite different from the earlier atmosphere of risk and fear. These staid London brokers learned not to spare the expense of resplendent dinners, abundant with caviar and champagne, as they courted in us the Soviet government and its cornucopia of contracts.

There was one old London firm of timber brokers of my acquaintance whose members used to froth at the mouth as they spoke to me of the "stolen timber" offered by the Soviets on the British market. Within a year and a half these same gentlemen were energetically bidding to be among our agents. I was even more astonished when I heard from Moscow that the Cheka headquarters insisted on satisfying a request from these Englishmen—that the Cheka chiefs were voicing their surprise at the omission of this London firm from our list of agencies!

Otherwise, the general feeling in the higher circles of Moscow was one of disapproval of the very idea of using any agencies whatsoever abroad. The Kremlin maintained that we could sell our timber to foreigners without the aid of brokers; but this was the ignorance of men unacquainted with the customs and traditions of foreign markets, especially those of the City in London. Nevertheless, to please all concerned, we once more resorted to the medium of a mixed-stock company. Again, as in other instances, the Soviet government took 50 per cent of the stock, allowing the foreigners to buy the other half. Our co-owners in this case were the three largest British brokers in timber. This was a practical solution, as the events soon proved. On the one hand, it gave fine publicity to our timber; on the other, the creation of the new company opened our way to Britain's banks and generally facilitated our transactions.

There was, for instance, the time—early in our foreign work—when we sold a shipment of timber to "Alsius," a Dutch firm. This was one of the first export cargos of the Soviet government since the close of the Russian civil war. When the ships brought their cargos from Archangel to the ports of Holland, a most embarrassing circumstance came to light: the shipment to the "Alsius" people included some of the lumber we had nationalized in the yards formerly belonging to that very firm in Archangel! We never did find out whether there was anyone's ill-will and purposeful selection behind the occurrence or whether it was indeed a coincidence.

At any rate, the "Alsius" people used one of the steamship captains as their witness to bring a suit against us. They were successful in proving that the timber was originally theirs, and the court issued an injunction against the Soviets, forbidding us either to collect the money we claimed from the Dutch firm or to sell the lumber to some other concern. This was bad news to us. Holland was an active buyer of Russian timber; the injunction, together with the whole story leading up to it, could not but create a bad impression of our activities abroad. The news at once reached England. Our new British clients began to hesitate, fearing that the Dutch trouble might find its replica in British courts, too.

But we managed to come to an agreement with the "Alsius" owners. These sensible Dutchmen followed the British example, after all—they signed with us a document establishing a mixed-stock company, with themselves as half-owners of the stock. The timber in question was counted by us as part of these Hollanders' investment in the new company. Everybody was happy. Lenin himself felt that such a solution was most advantageous to our interests.

And yet, much later, toward the end of 1925, when Lenin was no longer among the living, the O.G.P.U. used this incident, too, as one of the charges in their "case" against me.

Speaking of our experience with the "Alsius" owners reminds me of the fact that our other beginnings on the Dutch market were also pretty difficult, yet they, too, in time blossomed forth as profitable business ventures. Beginning with 1921, we were gradually succeeding in making a breach in one commercial fortress after another. The Van Geldern pulpwood mills at first would not hear of buying some of their raw material in Soviet Russia. They were frankly afraid that we would not live up to the promise of our contracts, and what would their Dutch mills do then, left high and dry without any of the stuff they needed for their operations? With much difficulty we finally persuaded them to purchase a small shipment. A fabulously low price was the main inducement. Within a few years they bought in Russia up to 80 per cent of their requirements, this despite the fact that by that time our Soviet timber was more expensive than the Scandinavian product, for the Dutch knew by then of the immeasurably superior quality of the Soviet timber.

The North Timber Trust formed, besides, a few other auxiliary companies abroad. Among these was a concern which handled our purchases of Spitzbergen coal, needed by the steamers that freighted our timber in the north.

All these companies were established before Russia gained diplomatic recognition, and actually they helped to pave the way for such recognition. Thus the formation of our Soviet-Norwegian steamship company predated the first diplomatic exchange between Soviet Russia and Norway. Similarly, a mixed-stock company which we organized to deal with the Dutch hastened the introduction of better political relations with Holland, although no definite diplomatic recognition came to Moscow from the Hague for a long time. The initial large order of Soviet timber from the French led to a diplomatic agreement between the two countries.

In this way did our North Timber Trust, a fundamentally business-like organization, play in a number of countries the role of a political vanguard, of a battering-ram breaking the very first holes in the wall of the blockade, of a trail-blazer preparing the ground for better, more normal relations between the Soviet republic and the rest of Europe.

My feeling of satisfaction was by no means the only personal consequence of all this activity. There were consequences of a far less pleasant nature as well. One chain of events in particular brought me much grief. To tell the story from its beginning:

When Lloyd's Bank first agreed to give us credit, its officials requested the right to send an observer to Archangel to watch shipments of our timber to England, against which shipments the credit was originally opened. This was a logical, legitimate request. I relayed it to Moscow and received a quick reply by wire that the request was granted. Incidentally, the same message contained an expression of thanks to me for the successes won in the reopening of Russia's foreign trade. Lloyd's Bank soon named its representative for Archangel: a certain Yates, an Englishman who had lived in Russia for some thirty years and had at one time owned a paper mill there. A sister of his was married to a Russian named Kolotilov, formerly a rich timber industrialist and now one of the directors of our own North Timber Trust—a Soviet state employee, in short.

For its correspondence with Yates, Lloyd's Bank used a commercial code, to notify him, in a brief manner, of such matters as, let us say, "Such-and-such steamer will leave on such-and-such date." This was the usual custom for banks and other firms. The bank worked out the code with the code specialists of the Soviet embassy in London (this was after the diplomatic recognition of the Kremlin by His Majesty's government), and our envoy at the time, Christian Rakovsky, gave his consent. To mark our first deal with the bank with due solemnity, we arranged a gala luncheon for the Englishmen responsible for the transaction. Our Soviet officials rose to the occasion with speeches testifying to their gratification at this new step bringing the two countries, Russia and England, closer together.

Yates left for Soviet Russia, and our work progressed smoothly. For several years he labored at his post in Archangel without any apparent interference, but some three years after the first transaction with Lloyd's Bank, the O.G.P.U. began to even up accounts with me. It was then that I was charged with the "crime" of responsibility for the code used by Mr. Yates! The O.G.P.U. investigators declared that Yates was an agent of the British Intelligence Service and that the code was being used to relay secret information about Soviet Russia. In vain did I protest that I had taken no part in the preparation of this "secret" code and that the Soviet embassy itself had approved this code, the "mysteries" of which were well known to its officials in London as well as to the Foreign Commissariat in Moscow. In this trouble no one could help me, for by that time the prominent Communists who had once telegraphed me their thanks for bringing about the agreement with Lloyd's Bank were no longer at their posts: Lenin was dead, and Krassin was living his last days on earth, bedridden in London.

Unaided and unprotected, I was grilled by a certain Katsenelson, the chief of the Economic Division of the O.G.P.U., who had by then gained a sinister reputation as an expert in such cases as mine. In a pseudo-friendly tone, he asked me:

"And why did you spend the week end with that British broker in London?" He mentioned the name, the time, the place. He knew everything. He even asked this question: "Why do you change your suits so often?"

Others who were questioned at about the same time were startled by this query: "Your wife uses a great deal of perfume. Why so?"

In general, the O.G.P.U. officials realized, of course, that those employees of the Soviet state who had to be in contact with the foreign world could not do otherwise than dress and behave somewhat like foreigners—that is, differently from other Soviet citizens. We were even allowed tuxedos. But this "permission" was fraught with danger to us, the recipients of such privileges. All of us, including the most prominent Communists in our midst, uneasily foresaw the day when we would be charged with the exercise of these privileges as with a terrible sin. We would be made to answer for such sins, that was clear.

An outstanding and rather amusing case in point was the one which concerned one of my Communist chiefs, Karl Danishevsky. He was an old Bolshevik with a record of considerable merit. As such he was singled out by Trotsky, at whose suggestion Lenin appointed him to head our North Timber Trust. When I met him, I found him a man tested and tempered in the fire of the civil war—a strong and daring man. But even he, on his trips abroad to do business for the Soviet state, never ceased to feel the eye of the O.G.P.U. close upon him—upon the one-time president of the Supreme Revolutionary War Tribunal!

Once, while shopping with me for clothes at a foreign tailor's, he noticed that I was choosing suits of different colors. He said to me:

"Why do you order suits of all these colors? They will make people in Moscow remark at once that you have a tremendous new wardrobe. It's much safer to order a number of suits of one and the same color. Then no one will find fault with you. No one will know that you have so many new suits but will think it is just one new suit."

I accepted his advice gratefully. Both of us bought a number of suits, of varying quality and thickness of cloth, but all of the same dark-blue color. If not for Danishevsky and his wise counsel, I would have lived to see one more charge added to my eventual indictment by the O.G.P.U.

Of course, when I complained to high Soviet officials of the annoyances to which I was submitted, they invariably stated that the Soviet regime was an honest regime and that if my conscience was clear I had nothing to fear!

(21)

CAPITALISTS ARRIVE IN MOSCOW

FOR ABOUT TEN YEARS—FROM 1918 TO 1927—THE PROBLEM OF FOREIGN CONCESSIONS in Russia was a subject of much discussion within Soviet Russia and abroad, both in Europe and in America. It claimed considerable attention because it was so intimately connected with the whole crucial question of Europe's economic and political stabilization. Long articles in the press were devoted to concessions; weighty reports both pro and con were delivered in scholarly societies. And practically all statesmen of the time, from Lenin to Lloyd George, made detailed declarations of policy on the subject.

But if we compare all this turmoil with the results achieved, we have a curious picture. The results were practically nil; the mountain labored and brought forth a mouse. Between 1921 and 1928 the Soviet government received from abroad some twenty-four hundred applications for foreign concessions but signed a mere 178 contracts. And these contracts included 3 which were not exactly concessionary, since they involved technical or engineering services to the Soviet state by foreign concerns. By October 1, 1928, only 68 concessionary enterprises survived in Russia, with an aggregate capital of 61,000,000 rubles and a personnel of twenty thousand.

The concession plan was something of a favorite with Lenin. Unlike most of his closest aides, Lenin was a well-educated and thoughtful economist. In the 1890's he had participated in the struggle between the Russian Marxists and the Russian Populists. The intelligentsia of Russia was at that time divided by passionate arguments as to the country's economic destiny. The Marxists insisted that, like other countries, Russia would inevitably follow the path of capitalistic development. The Populists (*Narodniki*) maintained that, because of the unique organization of the village commune, the Russian people would skip the capitalistic phase and at once proceed to build a socialist way of life.

In this debate Lenin took the side of the Marxists, soon becoming one of their leaders. He did not believe in the socialistic mission of the Russian peasantry; instead he expected that the proletariat would become the spearhead of a socialistic triumph. And according to his views in those days, the rise and growth of the proletariat in Russia would be dependent upon the development of industry and capitalism there. To prove the historical inevitability of Russian capitalism, he wrote in his earlier years a number of articles for the press, in addition to his book entitled *The Development of Capitalism in Russia*.

A quarter-century later, Lenin found himself leading the revolution, and in a rather paradoxical situation: the tumultuous elements of that revolution were plainly striving to effect a lightning-like liquidation of capitalism, despite all his theories about its historical inevitability. Since he was now, in the era of the revolution, more a politician than a scholar, Lenin himself was demolishing capitalism at a pace and by methods that a decade or two earlier he would have considered sheer madness. True, he was heading the revolution; yet, at the same time, he obeyed its stormy impulses.

In practical affairs, nonetheless, he could not forget all that he had known and understood before. And so now he envisaged for Russia and its Communist regime a kind of advanced capitalist economy to be brought about by giving concessions to foreigners. He called it "State Capitalism" and was ready to create opportunities for its rise and growth. Some of his followers were puzzled and voiced protests. To combat this opposition in his own ranks, Lenin came back to this question time and again in his speeches and articles of 1920–22, in which he tried to prove that Russia was sure to derive benefit from this unorthodox use of foreign capital. As he said, the workers' state needed the foreign bourgeoisie to teach it how to run large industries, and this, to his mind, fully justified the price paid. He added that ever since the Swedish invasion in the early eighteenth century, Russia had always learned something useful from foreigners.

Still, the prime factor with Lenin was always the political one. These concessions to foreigners, even the preliminary negotiations with businessmen from abroad, were the bait which would help him to overcome the political hostility of foreign capitalists toward Soviet Russia. By handing out concessions he would sow disunity among these capitalist powers, which as yet presented a united front of enmity toward the Soviets. He would create, in one foreign country after another, influential groups of capitalists vitally interested in preserving peaceful relations with Moscow. A war against the Soviets would mean a loss of these capitalists' new investments in Russia's concessions. In Lenin's entire scheme one could see the craftiness of a good strategist. He himself held that such craftiness was absolutely necessary if the workers' state wished to do business with capitalistic states.

While Anglo-French intervention in Russia was at its height and while the era of War Communism was in its darkest hours, Lenin wrote his famous letter "To the American Workers" (September 23, 1919). In it, for the first time, he publicly and clearly announced his willingness to offer concessions to foreign capitalists—"if they stop this war against us." When the intervention was terminated and the Soviets' relation with western Europe and America still remained strained, Lenin boldly led the Council of People's Commissars in shaping and issuing the decree regarding the granting of concessions to foreigners. It was even decided to prepare a list of possible concessions—a sort of catalogue of goods for the world's bourgeoisie interested in doing business with the Red republic.

Abroad, special representatives of the Kremlin carried on concession negotiations, endeavoring to assure prospective clients that it would indeed be quite feasible for them to work peacefully in the Soviet state. These agents in Europe's capitals promised huge profits to foreign businessmen who would risk their capital in the young Soviet republic.

Nevertheless, political aims remained paramount with Lenin even in this campaign. There were cases when carefully drawn-up contracts for concessions were suddenly thrown into the wastebasket just because the government of the country whence the would-be concessionary hailed was inimical to the Soviet government.

When the news spread that foreign capital could be invested in Russia again, various representatives of the European capitalistic nations began to arrive in Moscow. As usual in such situations, businessmen with adventurous inclinations were in the vanguard. Presently they filled the two large hotels of Moscow—the Metropole and the National. Among such guests were men who had made a great deal of money during World War I as "merchants of death" but in the early 1920's no longer could depend upon their munitions factories as sources of income. Others were men who had lost their fortunes because of the war and hoped to recoup them somehow. In the latter group were a few owners of steamship companies which had been practically wiped out in 1914–18.

All these visitors had energy and ingenuity if not capital. When they lacked capital, they at least had connections which they hoped could bring them money, if need be. This new Russia seemed like a good place to start their renewed climb up the ladder of wealth and position.

Among these arrivals we also found politicians and artists. One individual turned out to be the proprietor of a big night club, who had journeyed to Moscow as an agent for a group of several important foreign firms. These firms had in mind a gold- or platinum-mining concession but were willing to settle on any deal that would give them a chunk of Russia's fabulous native resources.

Some of our visitors came to Moscow with letters of recommendation from outstanding Communists in Europe. Others had letters from non-Communist political leaders in foreign lands who had done the Bolsheviks favors of one kind or another long before the Russian revolution, little dreaming that these long-haired, poverty-stricken exiles would some day go home from their Paris mansards and London basements to rule one-sixth of the earth.

The would-be concessionaries were often in a very delicate position because their own governments were sternly boycotting Soviet Russia and were turning jaundiced eyes on all bankers, industrialists, and other businessmen who sought collaboration with Moscow. They begged us to make a deep secret of their presence and business in Moscow. However, should the requested concessions be granted to them, they indicated that they would not be afraid to announce the news to the entire world, even at the risk of being ostracized by their fellow-capitalists abroad.

Some of the arrivals from foreign countries at once managed to find a few handy assistants among the native Russians—lawyers, economists, and other members of the local intelligentsia. They promised these "former men" (as upper-middle-class individuals were sometimes called by their fellow-Russians) jobs in the future concessions. Meantime, the Russians served the foreigners as solicitors, helping them in their efforts to obtain concessions.

The Cheka, as a general rule, kept a disapproving eye on any Russian who had dealings with visiting foreigners; but in the case of would-be concessionaries it made a singular exception. Its officials not only failed to see anything subversive in the relations between Russians and these new foreign friends but even encouraged such contacts; for, in full agreement with Lenin's dictum, the Cheka believed that the appearance of each new concession-seeker from abroad made one more breach in the capitalistic blockade of the Soviet republic. Moreover, many of the "former men" used by the foreigners were also in the Cheka's pay. Thus the Cheka kept open convenient channels of information from the outside world.

This does not mean, of course, that adventurers and schemers were the only ones interested in the concession policy of the Soviet government. The hotels of Moscow sheltered a motley crew of foreigners who were often a poor excuse for their name of businessmen, but in the cities of western Europe we met men who proved to be far more substantial in both their capital and their interest in the possibilities unfolding for them in Russia. I personally witnessed some of this earnestness when, in the early days of the Soviet concession policy (1920–21), I traveled abroad for Lenin's government.

One day in 1921, for example, while both Krassin and I were in London, a certain gentleman called on me with a very ambitious project. He wanted to see Krassin, he said. He had means—and a unique background—for his plans to do business with the Red republic. His connections were in the electrical industry of Holland, of which he was one of the founders and leaders. When he finally saw Krassin, he said:

"I don't need money, I have more than enough of it. Frankly, I don't want to be involved in new enterprises. But this is different. You see, I am a grandson of Karl Marx—the man who inspired you and all the other leaders of the Russian revolution. That is why I want to build the first great electrical works in Russia. Let me establish a large factory to make electric bulbs. I am acquainted with Lenin's plan for electrifying Russia. I am convinced that a country which realizes so well the importance of electricity in man's destiny will not perish. On the contrary, it will expand and flourish."

Krassin, as already noted, was himself an electrical engineer. He shared Lenin's idea that Russia's electrification would solve all the problems of mankind. What the Hollander had to say and offer made a tremendous impression on him. An exchange of telegrams with Lenin began forthwith. Lenin, too, was overjoyed. All other leading Communists in Moscow were bursting with pride: Here was Holland refusing to recognize the Soviet government, and yet one of Holland's best-known sons, one of her outstanding capitalists, wanted a concession from the Soviets to build electrical works in Russia!

For some reason or other, however, nothing came of this interesting proposal. As I remember it, certain German firms, although claiming no kinship to Karl Marx, eventually obtained this particular concession from the Kremlin by submitting a higher bid.

In my capacity as chief of the timber industry of Soviet Russia, I was thrown more and more into contact with the would-be concessionaries and their Russian aides. Timber concessions topped the list of new possibilities for foreign capital in the Red republic and served as the magnet attracting outsiders. In fact, almost every concession was, somehow or other, connected with timber exploitation. In view of my experience with foreigners, too, Lenin often wanted to know my opinion of the business propositions made by outsiders to the Soviet government. Thus most of these concession cases passed through my office.

Of special interest to me were the feelings and ideas of Russian intellectuals who served the foreigners as solicitors and other assistants. In pre-Bolshevik days they had been great lawyers and civic leaders, and, as I was not a Bolshevik, they did not fear me but spoke freely. Some expressed the hope that, by way of these concessions to foreign capital, Russia would eventually escape the clutches of Communism. Concessions, they said, would help Russia to relax the Soviet regime. Others felt that concessions were necessary in order to afford Russia contact with the world at large—to save the fatherland from strangulation. Economic patriotism mainly governed these men when they strove to assist the foreigners in gaining concessions.

For that matter, the idea of concessions to foreigners was supported not only by the Communists, but by all other political parties as well, from the extreme right to the extreme left. (Of course, the Communist dictatorship outlawed all other parties; but, somehow, political divergence was apparent in Russia at all times, however faintly.) Most of the doubts about the policy of concessions were voiced not by any Communist or socialist circles but by groups of nonpartisan intellectuals: economists, professors, specialists in all fields, members of scientific committees, and so on.

Such men were afraid, above all, that the concession policy would eventually enslave Russia to foreign capital. And such enslavement, they pointed out, would be even more humiliating than anything that had already happened to our ill-starred land. These intellectuals charged that the Communists and their Lenin were showing a woeful lack of patriotism in thinking up and carrying out this concession policy. "It's all the same to the Communists," they said. "Russia's fate is immaterial to them, but it's we who will some day have to pay for their madness."

The Communists, who had a patriotism of their own, answered the whispered accusations of their opponents:

"We don't care how much or how little we are now conceding to the foreign capitalists. We don't care—because in the long run we'll outsmart them. Right now we need their brains and their money, and so we are paying a price for both. But later all this will be ours for nothing, for the world revolution is just around the corner!"

Then there were other and stronger voices of protest against concessions, voices more important than the nonpartisan intellectuals. They were heard in labor-union circles, and some of those who protested in that group were Communists. They asserted quite openly:

"What were we fighting for? We have just finished chasing our own capitalists out of Russia, and now, behold, we have to accept those foreign capitalists! Why, safeguarded as they are by their foreign diplomats, they will exploit us even more mercilessly than our old native bosses!"

The pro-concession Communists argued back. One of their economists, V. P. Miliutin, said:

"Lenin has told us that we must pay for our schooling. Now, it's preferable to pay foreigners, for later, by paying a small additional price, we will be able to free ourselves of them easily—just as soon as we grow strong enough. We can afford to give them all they ask for, because a social revolution in the rest of Europe is bound to come within a few years. Then whatever these capitalists are now investing in Soviet Russia will be ours without any payment, really."

The foreigners coming to us knew perfectly well that this was what Lenin and his followers hoped would happen, but they were not worried. They paraphrased the argument in their own way, thus: "The Soviet regime won't last long anyway. And when capitalism returns to Russia, we, thanks to our concessions and investments, will be in on the ground floor."

In general, the majority of the Communists were rather cautious and dubious about the novel idea of inviting foreign capital into Soviet Russia. But their doubts were conquered by the prospect of their country's rapid industrialization. Many of them envisaged Russia's transformation, at a pace truly American, into a highly industrialized state. If the peasants of Russia were to be the chief sufferers in the process, well, the Soviet regime found its best support among the workers, not the peasants. Let the peasants suffer, if need be, for the good of changing this Russia of the muzhiks into a brand-new mechanized Soviet land.

148

When it was decided that our government would participate in the Genoa conference, in its attempt to make peace between revolutionary Russia and the capitalistic world, Lenin stressed the point that the meeting in Italy was, for the Reds, "a demonstration." According to him, Genoa was to provide the stage whence the Soviets would, over the heads of the capitalists, address the still hesitant workers of the world. At the same time, Lenin felt that the bourgeoisie of the world could be won over and outsmarted, not by any propaganda, but by some definite bait. The bait was simple yet effective: concessions. Lenin was positive that the trap would work at least along enough to give him a breathing spell. By winning over a part of the capitalistic world through these concessions, he was going to hammer a wedge into the unity of the capitalistic countries' hostility toward Soviet Russia.

And since timber concessions were the best bait of all, I was summoned by Lenin on the eve of the Genoa conference to prepare a map of the forests of Russia. Lenin told me that in marking the wooded areas as available for concessions, I should be guided by three main principles: First, only those forests should be open to exploitation by foreign capital which were situated away from populated centers. Second, forests subject to concessions should be in a checkboard arrangement vis-à-vis Soviet state farms. Lenin felt that by creating better labor conditions in our Soviet state farms, we could eventually "demoralize" the capitalistic organization of the concessions. In the meantime, the efficiency of certain capitalistic methods of the concessionaries and their managers would, in their turn, be a model for a better organization for production on those Soviet farms. Third, the areas subject to concession should be as far away as possible from railroads and good water transportation. The foreign capitalists would thus be forced to improve the latter somehow—at their own expense. Such improvements would benefit us in our plans for exploiting adjacent woods and subsequently introducing other Soviet industries into these areas.

When my map was ready, Lenin intrusted to Miliutin the writing of an explanatory report which was to accompany it. In addition, a slim, attractive book was published in several languages to acquaint foreign capitalists with all the opportunities which the Soviet government was willing to open to them in Russia—on certain terms.

Although the capitalistic world thought at first that the concession policy was the initial step in a series of Soviet surrenders and some quarters went so far as to believe and assert that it meant a decisive change from Communism back to capitalism, in about two years it became clear to the entire world that the concession policy was nothing but a lure.

To be sure, the manganese concession at Chiaturi, in Transcaucasia, flourished for a time. The concessionaries were a group of Americans headed by W. Averell Harriman, later American ambassador in Moscow. This concession made history in Europe because of Mr. Harriman's high-mindedness. He refused to profit through what he considered the spoliation of the legitimate owners; and, before proceeding to Russia to seek the concession, he stopped in Berlin to meet all the former owners and obtain their approval of his plans. He volunteered to pay them a royalty on the proceeds of the concession and thereby earned not only their blessing but their admiration. His concession became known as one of the soundest and was, of course, morally unassailable, even from a purely bourgeois point of view.

In Siberia, too, the Lena goldfields were exploited by a British company. Neither of the two concessions was destined to last longer than the Soviets really wanted it to last, but fortunately neither was terminated by the heralded world revolution. Both concessionaries were able to turn their businesses over to the Soviets on the basis of amicable settlement.

(22)

VANDERLIP AND OTHER ILLUSIONS

Sometimes a foreign capitalist, no less than the Soviet government, indulged in political or semipolitcal maneuvers as he engaged in bargaining with the Kremlin for a concession or two. Sometimes he merely sought publicity. And while the Kremlin was not always sure how much weight a foreigner carried in his own country, it kept up the negotiations for the sake of its aims in international politics.

W. B. Vanderlip's visit to Moscow in 1920 was a case in point. This American businessman came to Russia to seek a concession that would have given him practically all of Kamchatka to exploit. Lenin himself was much interested in this plan.

Kamchatka was then still occupied by the Japanese interventionists. Lenin, by giving this concession to Vanderlip, expected that American diplomacy and American troops would be brought in to push the Nipponese off the peninsula. He considered an armed conflict between Japan and the United States inevitable, and in March, 1920, he declared: "Japan and the United States are on the eve of a war. Some ten million killed and twenty million maimed—such will be the cost of this war to the two opponents. There is no way of preventing this war."

Lenin wanted to make use of the Japanese-American rivalry even before it should become a clash of arms. In one of his speeches on his concessionary policy, he said: "We will only gain if we grant to the Americans a concession for the peninsula of Kamchatka, which legally belongs to us, but actually, at present, is in Japanese hands."

Moreover, Lenin considered a sharp economic conflict between America and the rest of the capitalistic world unavoidable—"because America is richer." He felt Russia would profit in this contest by doing business with the United States.

150

Vanderlip did nothing to dispel Lenin's illusions. He promised that the news of the grant of the Kamchatka concession to an American would arouse the approval, even the enthusiasm, of American public opinion and would lead to a speedy recognition of the Soviet government by the new Republican administration, which, he correctly predicted, would move into Washington in March, 1921.

Lenin regarded Vanderlip as one of the most outstanding leaders of American business. His proposal therefore seemed sound, and the visitor was treated by the Kremlin with much respect. A contract was finally drawn up, and the Kamchatka concession was solemnly signed by the authorities in Moscow. But when it was Vanderlip's turn to sign the historic document, it developed that he could not pledge the financial and political guaranties which the Kremlin had from the beginning expected of him. He soon left Russia.

In the meanwhile, the press of Europe and America carried long and sensational stories about the presence of the great Vanderlip in Moscow and his promises to the Soviets. But when the Republicans won the election, President-elect Warren G. Harding officially announced that he knew nothing of Vanderlip's affairs and promises; that neither he nor his Republican party had entered into any negotiations with either Vanderlip or the Bolsheviks. And Vanderlip himself proved to be a much slighter figure in the financial world than his name had caused the Kremlin to believe. It was discovered, in fact, that this W. B. Vanderlip was only a namesake of the millionaire Vanderlip; he was an engineer full of initiative, whom the Russians failed to identify properly because they were taken in by the excitement in the press that accompanied his visit to Russia.

Kamchatka, though soon returned to the Russians (not without the pressure of American diplomacy, among other factors), was not given to any American as a concession. In fact, it was the sly Japanese who received concessions in that region after it had been regained by the Soviets.

Other concessions which for one reason or another failed to come off successfully included the much-talked-of project of certain Norwegians to create a Great Northern Route through Russian possessions. Certainly, it proved to be among the most grandiose and interesting plans discussed between the Soviets and foreigners in the early 1920's. This was the project: With the aid of foreign capital, water transportation was to be improved and important railroads were to be laid across some of the least populated wooded areas of northern Russia. A strip twenty versts wide on each side of the new railroads was to be handed over to the concessionaries for the exploitation of the surrounding forests, the erection of sawmills, and for other industrial development. Timber, eventually to be exported from this region to foreign markets, was to pay the foreigners back in part for the capital to be invested. A sort of "inner autonomy" was to be granted to the latter's undertakings. It was under-

151

stood that these foreigners needed such autonomy because they were to work on capitalistic principles.

The protagonists in this instance were two brothers, Norwegian shipowners who had grown immensely rich in the course of the first World War, when their shipping interests had increased to six times their original worth. The war over, the two brothers felt the need of a new field for their capital and their energy. When they arrived in Moscow, they announced that, as their capital was Norwegian, it was "neutral." By that they meant that they were not aggressive and that their funds were not tied to the politics of the Entente. In short, they claimed to be fearless in spirit and independent in politics. They felt and said that they should really be acceptable to the Soviets.

Moreover, they proudly pointed to the workers' party of Norway, which had left the Second International shortly before this and was inclined to join the Third International. This party, the two brothers asserted, was favorably inclined toward Communist Russia. And, further, they declared, Fridtjof Nansen himself was in favor of their plan and would in the near future become its honorary patron. Nansen's name was then very popular among the Russians, for he was at the zenith of his fame as a polar explorer, the indefatigable searcher for the Great Northern Route.

A Russian engineer by the name of Voblyi was appointed by the two Norwegians to act as their representative in Moscow. He was a brother of the well-known economist, Professor Voblyi, and the son-in-law of the notorious reactionary deputy of the Duma (the parliament of tsarist times), V. Shulghin. He brought their project to V. Groman, a well-known Menshevik and learned statistician. One morning I was invited by Groman to his apartment.

There I found Voblyi, who proceeded to unfold to me the Norse proposal in all its alluring detail. Both he and Groman maintained that here was Russia's chance to end her isolation and find a true path to the rest of Europe; that Norway, having done Great Britain so many favors and services during the war, would surely use her influence upon the English to straighten out their diplomatic relations with the Soviet republic. Groman added: "And the most important thing is that Norwegian capital is not at all aggressive!"

Presently the Kremlin began earnest negotiations with the two Norwegians. The negotiations proved to be long and tiresome, but they led to nothing. There was a sudden crash of prices, valuations, and rates in the shipping world, and the Norwegian capitalists ceased to be capitalists. They still had the spirit to carry on with their proposal, but that was not enough for the Soviets.

No less piquant was the story of a blueprint for a concession involving shipping on the Volga and Kama rivers. One day, without any appointment, a certain G walked into my office. He was one of the G brothers, famous during World War I for their tremendous operations at the head of a whole group of industrial and insurance companies in Russia, one of which had been a Volga steamship company. All these enterprises, of course, had been liquidated by the revolution.

I was surprised to see him because I knew that, following the Bolshevik coup d'état, G had fled abroad, with the aid of a fraudulent Polish passport. Now G said to me:

"How do you do, Comrade Liberman? I come to you at the behest of Comrade Krassin and Comrade Lezhava. I am sick and tired of licking the boots of that corrupt and rotten Europe. I want to help build our new Russia. I want to create conditions thanks to which the Volga and the Kama would become true Soviet rivers."

And yet, my visitor admitted, the aid of foreign capital and foreign engineers was essential. His plan was to attract foreigners to the gigantic task of restoring and expanding the shipping on the two great Russian rivers. Freight shipments would be important, naturally. Timber would top the list, and that is why he had come to me.

His vision consisted of brand-new, or at least highly modernized, steamers plying up and down the Volga and the Kama. He exclaimed: "They will be floating skyscrapers, with stores, libraries, fine dining-rooms, and what not!"

He used the name of Lezhava because, until the revolution, that Communist commissar had indeed served as manager and a member of the board of directors of one of the insurance companies controlled by the brothers G. My visitor assured me that in this vast project he had the wholehearted support of his former employee. He also told me that Lenin's brother-in-law, M. T. Yelizarov, was no less favorably inclined toward his project. Yelizarov had, in prerevolutionary times, also worked in the G brothers' insurance company, having, in fact, secured his position through Lezhava's protection. Remembering and valuing the organizing abilities of his former employers, Yelizarov had now convinced Lenin that G's project was both useful and plausible.

An engineer named Malchenko was engaged by G to be the "wirepuller." Malchenko was an old friend of Lenin's. Together with Lenin and other pioneer revolutionaries, he had worked in the Union for the Liberation of the Working Class when this organization was founded in St. Petersburg in 1895. On opening their concession-seeking office in Soviet Moscow, G and his friends placed Malchenko in charge, with a monthly salary of five hundred rubles—which in the deflation period of the 1920's was considered quite a boon.

G felt that he was on his way to success. He was back in Russia to stay, or so he believed. He even prevailed upon the Communist government to issue to him, as a personal favor, a Soviet passport in lieu of his fake Polish document.

There was generally much discussion about this concession. When talking to other concessionaries, Lenin boasted of the river-shipping plan, even before it was fully worked out and officially approved. But here the labor-union circles again raised their indignant voices. Leaders of the water-transport workers reminded Lenin of Meshkov, the celebrated Volga shipping tycoon of tsarist times, about whom Maxim Gorky used to write such amazing stories. The union leaders said, "We did not chase Meshkov out in order to clear room for a German or French exploiter."

Leon Trotsky once remarked: "The Volga must become an honest Soviet river." He said this in the heat of the civil conflict, when, as the war-lord of the revolution, he was endeavoring to push the White armies off the strategic Volga banks. But now the transport workers used this proverbial phrase, too, in order to indicate their displeasure with G's plans for bringing foreign capitalists into the "purged" shipping of the great Russian stream.

Long negotiations began, and the transport workers won out. G's scheme ended most tragically for him: he was executed by the Cheka for sins that were only whispered about. If I am not mistaken, his agent Malchenko was also shot.

The attitude of Soviet labor was generally no mean handicap to be overcome by the concessionaries.

Eventually, most of the concessionary enterprises created in Russia at the time of the New Economic Policy were broken on the rocks of complex and awkward problems connected with the labor question. The chief trouble lay in the paradox of the foreign capitalists' employing Soviet workers.

From the very start the concessionaries strove to secure for themselves maximum rights at a minimum cost of Soviet intervention in their affairs. In their turn, the Soviet governmental organizations attempted to stake out as wide a field of control as possible. Safeguarding the rights of the Soviet workers in the employ of foreigners was a foremost task of the Red authorities. Throughout the preliminary negotiations, this problem was the cause of much contention between the Kremlin and the foreign concessionaries.

There were also other arguments revolving about the concession problem. One of them concerned the Soviet principle never to hand anything that was once nationalized back to its former owners. The decree of nationalization remained irrevocably in force, with no exceptions and no reservations. Thus the entire property of an old company now involved in a new concession was considered as part of the basic capital of the freshly created mixed-stock corporation, in which the old capitalists (alias new concessionaries) held shares equal to those owned by the Soviet government. Both co-owners were equally interested in the further development and success of these new companies. As Lenin defined it, a concession was a contract between the state and the capitalist. The latter contracted to organize or improve the production in a given industry—the chopping and rafting of timber; the mining of coal; the producing of ore, oil, or what have you. For the right to do this the capitalist paid the state a share of the yield he got out of the Soviet natural resources and kept an equal share as his profit.

In the course of our negotiations with Prits, another Norwegian capitalist, it became known that one of his old partners had categorically declined to join with him in his new business with the Soviets. The former partner felt that the Soviets owed him money for some nationalized goods. We finally decided to set aside, from the future sales proceeds of the new company, the sum of £40,000 sterling to be paid to this man if he would agree to participate in the concession, since without his participation Prits could not go on with the deal.

As Krassin signed this singular contract, he believed that the Kremlin would follow its previous practice in approving concessions; that is, Lenin would confirm the agreement in its general outlines, leaving the details to Krassin's personal discretion. However, the new Concessionary Committee had just begun to operate in Moscow. From that point on, all the concessions, in all their details, had to pass the scrutiny of the committee.

By ill-luck the eagle eyes of the committee members spotted the £40,000 in this particular agreement, and the committee ruled that paying this sum would amount to a thinly disguised denationalization. While approving the concession as a whole, it refused to honor that clause. Leo Kamenev, Trotsky's brother-in-law, signed this ruling in his capacity as the chairman of the Concessionary Committee.

I happened to be the one in Krassin's entourage to receive this document. At once I got in touch with Krassin: "What shall we do?"

Lenin by this time was so ill that he handled hardly any affairs of the state. It was useless to appeal to him—or to anyone else, for that matter, when Lenin himself was unavailable; for only Lenin could understand and allow such a "violation of the law." Any other leader would either suspect a personal interest in this case on my or Krassin's part or would fear that he himself would be suspected of personal involvement, were he to permit this unheard-of exception to the general rule of nationalization.

When I came to Krassin with the problem, my friend thought a little, then slowly and significantly he took the paper from my hands, tore it, and burned the pieces with a match, saying: "You received no letter from Kamenev....."

Then he added: "This is the first tangible deal after so many empty talks with our foreign customers. If we now declare that we want to change some of the already agreed-upon terms, we will disrupt all further negotiations with foreigners. As for the £40,000, you can easily make that sum while selling them their own timber. Thus the wolf will get a full belly, and the sheep will remain intact."

I, too, had a great desire to accomplish things for Soviet trade at any price, so I agreed with Krassin in this plan. During this period the welfare of the republic was our highest moral law, and reopening Russia's trade with the rest of the world was a gigantic stride in the direction of such welfare.

But within a few years, when the O.G.P.U. began to persecute me, through long sleepless nights I often asked myself this question: "What will happen if the O.G.P.U. starts to grill me in earnest and recalls this incident of the 'lawless' payment?"

Fortunately, in all their grilling of me the O.G.P.U. men somehow overlooked this particular episode of my activities.

The Soviet government at times not only granted concessions but sought them. There were, to my knowledge, at least two such cases. The first bid was made in Persia. Sometime before World War I and the revolution, a wealthy Georgian industrialist, K, obtained tremendous timber concessions from the

155

shah. These included great stretches of oak growing on the slopes of a plateau bordering on the Caucasus and the Caspian Sea. But from the fall of 1914 on, these routes were clogged by Russian war traffic, so no exploitation of the timber concessions could be started by their Georgian possessor. The revolution of 1917–18 further delayed his plans.

It was early in my work for Soviet Russia that Krassin summoned me and introduced me to K. Together we worked out a new project. The Georgian's concessions were to be taken over by the Soviets. They would use his privileges in Persia to build in the latter country special plants for the production of ties for the railroads of the Caucasus. The better grades of that Persian timber would be exported abroad, of course.

To this end I formed an expedition, which I forthwith dispatched to Persia. Members of the group spent several months there, studying all the facets of this problem. The prime minister of Persia liked the idea of transforming the concessions into a Soviet enterprise. In Russia the Politbureau approved the project; here the concessions in Persia were regarded not in their commercial sense alone but as a political weapon to boot. It was felt that they would aid the growth of Soviet influence in the Middle East. The Kremlin realized, of course, that these novel concessions in Persia would have to be operated on a strictly capitalistic basis, but in this case no protest arose from the faithful of Moscow.

The second concession sought by Russia had to do with the coal of Spitzbergen. The Soviet North Timber Trust decided to buy some of the mines belonging to an Anglo-Norwegian company on that island. In this instance, too, the exploitation of the works, though not of the workers, was going to be purely capitalistic. We needed this coal for our steamers carrying White Sea timber to foreign ports. But there was another reason for our purchase of the mines: we had certain air-transport projects in mind, because of which we had to establish contact with the island of Spitzbergen.

As far as I personally was concerned, one of the most interesting of all our efforts to attract foreign capital to Soviet Russia was the negotiations with Ivar Kreuger, the Swedish match-king, who later committed suicide.

We met in Paris. Krassin, who was with me, said one day that he was going to lunch the next day with Kreuger and a Russian banker-*émigré*, who was a friend of Kreuger's. He asked me to join them. The third Soviet official to be present was Christian Rakovsky, who had just been appointed to Krassin's post as the Russian envoy in London while Krassin was being transferred to Paris.

We knew some of Kreuger's plans. He aimed to obtain a monopoly on match-making in Soviet Russia, in turn securing for the Soviet government a foreign loan of $50,000,000. Krassin needed me at the luncheon conference to answer questions about timber production and the problem of exporting Soviet matchwood to the factories of other lands. But I was also flattered to learn that Kreuger's friends in the Swedish timber syndicate had mentioned my name to him and that he wanted to meet me. In fact, he asked me to visit him a half-hour before the luncheon.

I came to his office at the appointed time. His secretary warned me to watch Kreuger's hands during our conversation: "Should he take a bunch of keys out of his pocket and begin to play with them, this will be the sign for you to leave. When the keys are brought out the interview is completed, and you are not to try to prolong it under any circumstances."

This sounded familiar to me—Krassin had a similar habit, taking his ring off his finger and playing with it when the conversation no longer interested him. Anyone who knew him well usually left at this point.

When I entered Kreuger's inner sanctum, I saw a tall, round-faced, rosy-cheeked Scandinavian. His blue eyes were deep set and seemed to search my face minutely. His forehead was high, perhaps because of incipient baldness. His manner was soft and polite; his voice was low and quiet. He began by saying that the Russian peasant lacked matches and that this was one reason for the peasants' hatred of the Soviet regime. Should we, the Soviets, intrust Kreuger with the organization of our match industry, he would improve it tremendously—and the Soviet government would become popular!

Kreuger stopped talking to offer me a cigarette. I accepted and reached for my lighter. As I struck the light, he smiled: "You should be ashamed of yourself—using a lighter in my presence, even though it's undoubtedly of the best make possible!"

He opened a box of Swedish matches, struck one, and said: "Don't you think this is more pleasant, and far more personal and individual?" Then he added: "I tell you, every time a Russian peasant strikes one of my matches, he will bless the Soviet regime!"

Returning to his main object, Kreuger spoke of those Russian match factories which before the revolution had belonged to him. He declared that even now, under the Soviets, these factories performed much better than other factories of non-Kreuger origin. "It is because the old employees have remained at their posts," he said, and then expressed his conviction that his old engineers and workers would be glad to see him back as their boss if he should receive the concession he sought.

After a while I attempted to change the topic of our conversation, but then I saw the keys make their appearance. As he began to play with them I rose, and together we left for the restaurant and the general conference.

At the luncheon, conversation was at first about the match concession but soon turned into an entirely different channel. Kreuger and his Russian adviser suddenly proposed to us a breath-taking plan: The Soviet government should create a special financial organization abroad, to be composed of only a few persons, to be managed by this Russian émigré and to be controlled by no one else than Kreuger. This group of financiers would proceed to liquidate amicably all the claims then still pending abroad against the Soviet government for all the foreign investments nationalized by the revolution. The liquidation would be through a series of commercial agreements.

Kreuger and his friend were ready and willing to place at the disposal of this new organization a capital of several million dollars. With this fund the group could buy up all the old Russian stocks and bonds still being quoted on western European exchanges. Part of the fund was to be used for a skilful job of bribing the European press. The newspapers, under Kreuger's guidance, were to print stories which would alternately depress and raise the quotations on those old securities. As the prices fell, Kreuger's group would buy up the stocks and bonds; as they rose, the group would sell them.

Having got their hands on all these securities, and thus most of the claims against the Soviets, the group would naturally settle the claims with the Soviets, to the mutual advantage of the Kremlin and the capitalists composing the new organization. The money with which the stocks and bonds would finally be bought up would, in the long run, have come not from the fund of the group but from the profits made in the stock-exchange gamble directed by Kreuger.

The idea of such speculation, I knew, would be totally unacceptable to the Soviet government. However, in order not to offend Kreuger and his Russian friend, Krassin and Rakovsky pretended that they were interested. They listened attentively, and when they finally spoke they avoided the moral issue and merely said that such a gamble was extremely dangerous. In a few days Kreuger sent us a written résumé of his plan. Krassin and Rakovsky relayed it to Moscow, but, of course, nothing was done about it by the Soviets.

A few years later I happened to see Kreuger again, but in entirely different circumstances. It was toward the end of the 1920's, after I had quit Russia and was living abroad as a private individual. Since the match concession had not been granted to Kreuger and no other plan of his had been accepted by the Kremlin, he was, by the end of the decade, one of the most furious enemies of the Soviet government. I was approached by a baron who turned out to be one of Kreuger's contact men and who said that Kreuger wished to see me. I went, out of curiosity. To my astonishment, the Swede spoke to me as follows:

"I know that you have left the Soviet employ. Undoubtedly you feel the same disgust for the Soviet government that I do. I am now organizing an international group to combat the Soviet government—to discredit the economic policies and acts of the Soviets. You know Soviet economics. I want you to assume certain functions in this work. I will give you an annual fee in English pounds sterling. We will agree on the amount, I am sure. You won't have to do any other work. This agreement will be personally between you and me. It will not be cumbersome for you in any sense, I assure you."

Naturally I turned down this offer. I merely said that I was not fit for such work.

In 1932, along with the rest of the world, I read in the newspapers of Kreuger's suicide and of the criminal involvements which had led to this final act.

158

(23)

IMPASSE WITH URQUHART

LENIN, INTELLIGENT AND EDUCATED AS HE WAS, COULD NOT DIFFERENTIATE BETWEEN two such contrasting characters as Urquhart and Kreuger. For him they were two branches of the same capitalistic tree, as a cross and an ax-handle are made of the same wood.

In its time the affair of Leslie Urquhart's concession received much publicity. Not only was Urquhart a rich man, he was also prominent in the City of London and exerted considerable influence in the governing circles of his country. The Soviets knew this and were attracted by the far-reaching possibilities which Urquhart's connections might open up in the course of the negotiations. Krassin, in London, was in charge of the negotiations, and I was kept informed of their progress.

Urquhart was middle aged and of medium height. His shoulders were broad, his face was round. As a matter of fact, everything about him was rotund: his chin as well as his face; his stomach no less than his head. He did not at all resemble the typical Britisher of our imagination—the lanky, tall, sinewy one.

Urquhart spoke very good Russian. That, as well as his physical appearance, made him seem the reincarnation of an old-time Russian landowner, an enlightened nobleman of tsarist times. He hardly looked the part of a British businessman seeking concessions in the Soviet republic; and, actually, he was not seeking new concessions but was merely trying to obtain recognition of the copper-mine concessions that he had owned for many years in the Siberian Urals before the revolution.

His own fellow-Englishmen regarded Urquhart as one of the best-informed British businessmen and valued highly his knowledge of Russia and things Russian and his ability to adapt himself to the changing Russian scene. He often repeated the old Russian saying, "If you live with the wolves, you howl like a wolf"—the Slav peasant's equivalent of "In Rome do as the Romans do." Urquhart was proud of his allegedly intimate acquaintance with the way of life and thinking of the Russian muzhik and the Russian worker. He was convinced that he knew perfectly well just how one must treat the Russian masses in order to get along with them.

To the old Russian regime Urquhart always referred scornfully. Yet it was clear to us that he liked its memory much better than he liked the revolution and its results. He did not believe in the future of the Communist government and spoke with open disgust of the new regime. He reminisced continually about the vast stretches of land and the tremendous enterprises which he had once exploited in tsarist Russia; and the gist of his remarks was: "Let the comrades try to bring such enterprises back to life. In the course of their effort, the whole world will see for itself that without the help of foreign capital the

159

Russian workers and engineers will continue to blunder and bungle for a long, long time."

Urquhart simply could not stand the thought of the Soviet state's participating in any real, worth-while scheme of production. This failing was the main stumbling block in the way of the eventual success of his negotiations with the Kremlin.

Thousands of individuals in both England and France were vitally interested in the outcome of these negotiations. Mostly small holders of old Russian bonds, they were especially numerous in France. The English holders of unpaid tsarist obligations were fewer, but some of their holdings were larger. Urquhart was the most prominent one, and as such he headed the British committee which united all the claimants in England—all those who had suffered from the Soviet repudiation of tsarist debts and the expropriation of foreign capital in Russia.

That is why his negotiations with the Soviets, although seemingly concerned with economic problems only, were also of a definitely political nature. Indeed, government circles in London made it clear to Krassin that a concession, if granted by the Soviets to Urquhart, might prove a great stride forward in the matter of improving Anglo-Soviet relations. The London stock exchange, too, was sensitive to all the ups and downs in Urquhart's *pourparlers* with the Kremlin: the stocks of Urquhart's old Russian companies now rose, now fell, depending on the good or bad news from Moscow about his negotiations for the concession.

At one point the negotiations seemed to be going quite well and appeared to have approached a final understanding. To be sure, there were a few bad spots, but these could be eliminated through a personal visit by Urquhart to Moscow. And so he was invited to come to Soviet Russia—his very first visit to the country after it had gone Red.

In London the common gossip of the City was that the Soviet government wanted to give Urquhart the requested concession but that the problem of his treatment of Soviet labor stood in the way and that Krassin had not been empowered to settle this and other thorny questions in his capacity as merely the Russian ambassador in England. Since Urquhart spoke Russian, it was natural for him to be asked to Moscow to settle the outstanding points in man-to-man talks with Lenin and other Soviet leaders. The trip was thus considered to be a favorable omen, and the concession contract almost as good as signed.

On his arrival in Moscow, Urquhart was received with the utmost civility. He had interviews with a number of high-ranking Soviet officials, among them Lenin himself. In turn, the Englishman was brimming with politeness and flattery. On the surface it looked as if the matter were happily settled.

Both sides fully realized that signing a document was not all, however. The promises of the Soviet government, given to this foreigner, could remain a dead letter if at any future time the government were to choose a nonco-operative course. The authority on Soviet territory was Soviet. It could at any point turn the entire affair of the concession whatever way it wanted. Any work at all by the concessionary might be made impossible. Were Urquhart and other foreigners to risk going in anyway, the development and fate of their concessions depended not on the letter of their contracts with the Kremlin but on the general political atmosphere in Russia and abroad. Nevertheless, both sides attached much importance to the contract itself, of course.

Lenin knew that the contents of this contract, when published abroad, would play a definite role in the fortunes of Communism in foreign lands. The effect would be either positive or negative, depending on the extent to which the document safeguarded the rights of the Russian worker and the Soviet state in their contract with Urquhart.

As for Urquhart, he felt that the wage rates and other compensations of a western European worker had nothing to do with the needs of the Russian worker, especially in that God-forsaken Ural province where his prerevolutionary properties were and where he had been accustomed to a strictly colonial treatment of the working "cattle." The demands of the Soviet government in this connection seemed utterly ridiculous to him. He was all for an old-fashioned, "patriarchal" kind of labor-capital relations.

As we have seen, Urquhart was also one of the most active leaders in the British organization of persons having complaints and claims against the Soviet government. This doubtless colored his deportment in the course of his negotiations with the Kremlin. It tended to make him present his case not merely as an individual claim but also as a collective affair—the affair of all Englishmen who had lost their investments in old Russia. On the other hand, the fact that he represented so many claims on behalf of other people and firms might have made the Kremlin more conciliatory toward him in his personal seeking of this concession.

To Lenin, Urquhart was an English millionaire, the personification of all foreign capitalism, the force that at one time waxed fat on exploitation of the Russian worker and was now striving to regain its former rights and privileges. This prompted Lenin to play a cat-and-mouse game with Urquhart. He would now lure the Englishman on with promises, now repulse him with stern implacability. Lenin in his public speeches to Russian workers liked to refer to Urquhart and his enterprises and plans, always connecting this strictly economic topic with his discussion of the politics of the British government.

At length Urquhart returned to London, the contract still in abeyance. He had the Soviet terms with him, but somehow he let the whole matter slide into temporary oblivion. He could have continued his negotiations with Krassin in London, but he would not do this in earnest. He clearly shunned any further serious discussion and would not accept the Soviet conditions already offered to him.

By that time I was back in Moscow and had attended one session of the Council of Labor and Defense, the agenda of which included the problem in which I was then so interested—that of mixed-stock companies. Before the starting time the room buzzed with private conversations. Lenin, as usual, surrounded by a number of books, most of them open, now and then exchanged remarks with Ryckov, Tomsky, Sheinman, and others. At times he addressed a sentence or two to all of us together and to no one in particular. The room became still when among such remarks we suddenly heard Lenin's question:

"Whatever has become of 'our comrade' Urquhart? We don't hear of him or about him any more. And yet he was so polite and obliging when he was here on his visit. He was so full of flattery that we thought any minute now he might file an application for a membership in the Communist party!"

After a moment's silence a laughing voice answered: "If we have time before the session begins, Vladimir Ilyich, let me tell you a Jewish story."

This was Moisei Frumkin, Krassin's vice-commissar in the Commissariat of Foreign Trade and one of the oldest party members. His eyes were small but sharp and quick, and a sly smile was on his face. He was a striking figure, in his youthful blouse, with his black hair and a tiny well-groomed beard. This was the story he told us:

"A Jewish woman was very sad because her husband had gone away and showed no sign of returning to her. Her friends finally advised her to go to a wise rabbi with the question, 'When will my husband come back?' But, as was usual in such minor cases, the rabbi's assistants would not let her in for a personal interview with the sage. She had to submit the question in writing, inclosing the customary fee of fifty kopecks. An asssistant brought back the rabbi's answer: 'Your husband will return in two weeks.' Two weeks passed, and two more, and still there was no husband. The woman went to the rabbi again, sent in the question and fifty kopecks for the second time, but received the same written reply: 'Your husband will come back in two weeks.' But when a month had elapsed after that, with no result whatsoever, and then a third month, the indignant woman demanded a personal meeting with the rabbi. It was granted. The rabbi listened to the woman, then said: 'Your husband won't return at all.' Heartbroken, crushed, the woman left the rabbi's study. On her way out she encountered the assistant and she halted to berate him for deceiving her with the two previous answers, allegedly given by the rabbi. But the assistant said: 'I didn't deceive you. Those first two replies were from the rabbi.' 'But why,' wailed the poor woman, 'why did he say on those first two occasions that my husband would come back to me?' 'Because the first two times he didn't see you in person!' was the assistant's explanation.

"Well, Vladimir Ilyich," Frumkin summed up, "we should all understand why Urquhart will never return. He hadn't seen us before he came here."

There was a burst of laughter in the room. Lenin laughed together with everybody else but soon returned to one of his books and said nothing. It was clear to us, however, that the anecdote made him think. The joke, it seemed, made a stronger impression upon him than was Frumkin's intention.

When Urquhart first left Moscow, it had been decided that he would continue his negotiations with the Soviets through Krassin in London. And Krassin's relations with Urquhart were quite different from those Lenin had maintained in Moscow. Krassin would meet Urquhart not solely on business grounds. The Soviet envoy in London and his family became close to Urquhart and his family in a friendly, social way. Krassin's family was frequently invited to Urquhart's country place for the week end, and Urquhart was extraordinarily tender to Krassin's children, whom he seemed to like genuinely. This friendship was not appreciated by Krassin's foes in Moscow, where the envoy's every step was known, where every fact was filed away by the Commissariat of Foreign Affairs and the Cheka for future reference.

Because of the ups and downs of Urquhart's old Russian stocks on the London exchange and because of this personal friendship between Krassin and Urquhart, rumors soon circulated in London that the Bolsheviks were enriching themselves on these fluctuations of the old stocks. As for Krassin, I can say categorically that the rumors were absolutely baseless.

Finally, on September 9, 1922, after all the interruptions and complications, the concession contract was signed in London. But as Krassin was affixing his signature, he told Urquhart that the last word of confirmation was still to come from Moscow, mainly on account of the Soviet labor problem. The problem was whether or not the Soviet laws protecting Russian workers were to be applied to the native personnel to be hired by Urquhart for his concession; and undoubtedly this qualification was no last-minute thought on Krassin's part. He must have had corresponding instructions beforehand from Lenin himself—to insert the reservation into his understanding with Urquhart.

The chances are that this last remaining handicap would have been solved in Moscow somehow or other, but just then important political events invaded the economic sphere under discussion. In the fall of 1922, at Lausanne, an international conference was called to settle sundry problems connected with Turkey's postwar status. The age-old questions involving Turkey, the Black Sea, and the Dardanelles had always interested Russia mightily .... but the Soviet government was not invited to the Lausanne conference!

London was plainly responsible for the cutting omission, and, as a result, relations between Russia and England took an immediate turn for the worse. Consequently, on October 5 of that year, the Council of People's Commissars resolved: In view of this hostile act of the British government, the Soviet government is to refuse its final approval of the concession contract signed by Krassin and Urquhart.

Thus the Urquhart concession, which had aroused such high hopes, came to an irrevocable end. From its very beginning, Lenin had considered this whole affair in the light of prospects for a world revolution, or at least a European upheaval. The question of the leeway he would give to the forces unleashed by his own New Economic Policy and of the extent to which concessions could be granted to foreign capital was decided by Lenin wholly in conformity with his own appraisal of revolutionary fevers abroad. When such fevers appeared to be rising, when they seemed to signal the approach of a great mass movement against the owning classes abroad, generous Soviet concessions to capitalism at home and especially abroad were regarded as unnecessary and

163

even harmful. When, on the contrary, the revolutionary fevers in foreign lands were low or were being checked by the capitalists, Lenin was willing to make some compromise or other with the bourgeois world. The feeble status of his revolution abroad for the moment usually convinced Lenin that he and the Soviet republic would have, for a long period yet, to suffer this "capitalistic encirclement." Some form of coexistence with the capitalistic world had to be found by the Soviets.

(24)

THE LAST OF KRASSIN

WHILE HE WAS THE SOVIET ENVOY IN LONDON IN 1921 AND 1922, LEONID KRASSIN established himself very solidly indeed in that capital. His range of acquaintances and contacts widened constantly; he won the esteem of many British industrialists. He was suited to his role, for, being of a practical turn of mind, he easily found a common language with the "most practical people on earth," as the English were sometimes called in Russia. It was not long before he was in the good graces of David Lloyd George, whom he saw often. In his private talks with the British premier, Krassin could permit himself the liberty of complaining about the difficulties besetting his work in the field of Russian-British *rapprochement*. Some of Lloyd George's aides were frequent visitors in Krassin's house; the Russian's family had in the meantime come to London, and Miss Brady, one of Lloyd George's secretaries, became a friend of Mrs. Krassin and the girls.

The house soon became a center where Krassin met his staff members, various businessmen, and a number of Russian *émigrés*. His wife, Liubov Vasilievna, was a wonderful hostess. She knew how to make people feel at ease, what persons to bring together, and whom to invite for Krassin's own use or interest. The house was full of young people: Krassin was Liubov Vasilievna's third husband, and she had six children, three of them by Krassin. By this time my boy lived in London, and whenever I had to leave for Moscow he moved to the Krassins'. I, too, became almost a permanent member of Krassin's household, so often did I visit the family circle. I thus had increasingly frequent occasion to discuss with Leonid Borisovich matters not just of my department but of general political import as well.

If anyone wished to meet Krassin informally or to know him better, his best chance was in an invitation to tea from the Russian's wife. When the family and the guests were seated at the table, Krassin would appear from an adjoining room, a smile on his lips, and his hands busy with the wide gestures so characteristic of him. He made his customary round of the table, tapping one of his daughters on the shoulder, pulling another by her pigtail, teasing a third one for her "bourgeois tendencies"; and only then would he take his place and begin some amusing story—such as the one I once heard him tell about a prim Englishwoman of high society who had wished to pay him a compliment by saying: "You don't seem like a Bolshevik at all—you haven't a knife between your teeth!"

Among the Russian *émigrés* who came as guests to Krassin's house there were some who hated the Soviet government and did not conceal their views—but they nevertheless felt that business was business. They came because they dearly wished to restore their lost or reduced fortunes by sharing in the newly resumed trade between Britain and Russia. To Krassin they, in turn, were most useful—well-nigh indispensable in the first period of his work in London. So Liubov Vasilievna invited them to her teas.

While most visitors were businessmen, there also were men who had strictly political motives in coming to Krassin's house. At that time London was the only western European center where the Soviet government had a true diplomat as its representative. And so they came to London, to Krassin, these men of all lands in both hemispheres who wished to talk about economic and political problems of the world with an official and sober-minded agent of a state which was otherwise isolated. In Krassin's London house I met all sorts of visitors, from members of the French Chamber of Deputies to industrialists from the nations of both North and South America. They all agreed that Krassin was one Bolshevik with whom it was possible to reach an understanding.

Nevertheless, Krassin's position grew increasingly difficult. He had an onerous task. He was to represent a country which was potentially rich with raw materials and foodstuffs and ready to do business with the outside world. In the process he was to observe all the traditional forms of diplomatic prudence, refraining from interference in England's domestic affairs, and never resorting to the aid of her radicals. He was a trade envoy, not a full-fledged ambassador, since in that initial phase the British government did not recognize the Soviet government. Nonetheless, in direct contradiction to his trade status, Krassin was to secure this political recognition first of all. Along with the recognition, he was to obtain from the British a number of other purely political concessions. Such was Moscow's view of the job in London. Men close to Lloyd George used to say to Krassin:

"The Prime Minister knows that you and 'they' [that is, Moscow] are not one and the same thing. He will be very glad if you suggest to us just what we should do to strengthen your standing in Moscow."

This ambiguous situation created opposition to Krassin both in London and in Moscow. He was not at all liked by the British Communists or by many radically inclined British trade-union leaders. In their opinion, "commercialism" in his London office ranked above all other considerations. With their complaints they reached the party in Moscow, particularly the Commissariat of Foreign Affairs, where Maxim Litvinov was then gaining an ever greater influence and where—as in the Council of People's Commissars—political

165

considerations outweighed commercial ones. Beginning with 1922, events and trends were less and less favorable for Krassin.

In every European capital, men in the know closely watched each step made by our envoy in London. The consensus in the various governments and the leading political circles was that trading with Russia should be carried on while shunning the nation politically. None of the great powers would recognize the Soviet government, and thus Lenin's main goal remained unachieved. The Commissariat of Foreign Affairs was dissatisfied with, and even hostile to, Krassin. This tended to make him more and more of a representative of the Commissariat of Foreign Trade.

Meanwhile Lenin's illness took a decisive turn for the worse, and hope for his recovery waned. This further aggravated the situation for Krassin, whose weight in Soviet Russia was based chiefly on Lenin's personal confidence in him. Now, rather freely, the bitter quip was heard in Communist circles that the Commissariat of Foreign Trade was "Krassin's own little store," allegedly wholly superfluous in the circumstances of the latest Soviet practice, which, on the one hand, had established a nationalization of industries and, on the other, had introduced the New Economic Policy. Krassin's opponents argued that each industrial enterprise of Soviet Russia would know better than Krassin and his Commissariat of Foreign Trade how to handle the problem of purchases and sales abroad in its own field; that any intermediaries were unnecessary and even pernicious. In time they declared openly that Krassin's commissariat was a parasitic organization, existing at the expense of other economic units of the Soviet nation, and should be abolished.

The campaign was also directed against Krassin personally. "Deficiencies" in his work and the mode of his life abroad were held against him. His children studied in "bourgeois schools" and associated with the British upper class; his daughters seemed to be after "good husbands." Too, there was gossip about his private affairs—the weakness he constantly betrayed toward the fair sex. Through some women close to him, a few dubious and greedy men reached him at times. They frankly strove to make money through this connection; Krassin understood their aims very well, and his explanation of his own attitude sounded convincing:

"Soviet Russia won't perish from an occasional profiteer's unclean gain in this business deal or that. On the contrary, Soviet Russia will gain the services of certain specialists who can be bought by this method."

At last Moscow decided that Krassin had been abroad too long, that it might be good for his soul if he breathed his homeland's pure air for a while. And so he found himself compelled to spend a winter in Moscow. His wife and one of his daughters were with him. I came to Moscow from one of my foreign trips that winter, and the daughter asked me point-blank: "Do you think they will ever let us out?"

I showed my astonishment at such a question, and the girl, lowering her voice, added: "Avel Yenukidze tells us that Stalin pathologically can't stand Daddy, and Stalin is the boss."

166

Yenukidze remained Krassin's only supporter. In those days Yenukidze had Stalin's entire confidence (although later, in the middle 1930's, he was among those who perished in the purges), and he advised Krassin not to be in any unseemly hurry about leaving for foreign parts again. He also suggested that Krassin edge closer to the high-ranking Communists in Moscow, excepting Trotsky, whose friendship was already—in the early 1920's—considered unwelcome and even dangerous. Shortly before that time Krassin had become rather friendly with Trotsky, for the two had discovered a common view of foreign-trade problems.

In the meantime, relations between the Soviet government and Downing Street grew strained. The climax was the famous note of the British government, the so-called "Curzon Ultimatum" of May 9, 1923. In it the British demanded cessation of Communist propaganda outside Russia, particularly in the Near East. The men of Moscow felt that the ultimatum was a result of the failure of Soviet-British negotiations for the industrial concessions originally proposed by Leslie Urquart.

Krassin was still in Moscow when the Curzon Ultimatum reached the Kremlin, and he was ordered to return to London at once. That beautiful spring evening I, too, received a telephone call from the Kremlin and was told to be at the airdrome at seven o'clock the next morning. At the appointed hour, at the airdrome, I met Krassin with his two faithful secretaries, Grozhan and Greenfield. It turned out that all four of us were to fly to London. A small plane was taxied forth, and we boarded it behind a pilot who, I think, was a German. By evening we reached Berlin, where we stayed overnight, and the following morning flew on to London.

On the way to London, Krassin explained to me the behind-the-scenes reasons for my part in the proceedings. The Kremlin, it seemed, was worried that if the British persisted in their new hostility they might order all the Russian Communists out of England. This was where I came in—a non-Communist. Surely the British would allow me to remain in London as the new head of the Soviet trade delegation.

The flight to London via Berlin was a bumpy one, and I admired the ease with which Krassin, alone of all the passengers, bore the air pockets. He sipped out of a bottle of red wine until he finished it, the while dictating to one of his secretaries a long newspaper article on the future role of aviation in fighting forest fires. All this time I was thoroughly air-sick.

The negotiations which Krassin began on his arrival came to a favorable conclusion, and I did not have to take up a new function in London. The minute we landed, Krassin's friends, as well as various persons who were close to the British government, came to us with good news. They said that the incident should and would be settled amicably and that Krassin would certainly be helped by the British to settle it. And if he were successful in this new mission, it would certainly strengthen his position in Moscow, notwithstanding the Commissariat of Foreign Affairs and that group of Communists who had of late opposed him.

The main British demand was cessation of Communist propaganda by Soviet Russia in foreign countries, and here Krassin was glad to make concessions, for personally he was against such propaganda. But one had to remember Moscow's self-chosen role as the leader of the world-wide revolutionary movement; she could not so lightly give up this advantageous position. On the other hand, the revolutionary fever was rising in Germany at the time, and, expecting a full-scale revolution in the Reich at any moment, Moscow would be inclined to regard whatever propaganda concessions Krassin made in England as mere scraps of paper.

When this crisis had passed, however, Moscow's dissatisfaction with Krassin and sundry personal intrigues against him resumed their course. The boiling-point was reached late in 1924, when he was finally demoted to the envoy's post in Paris. This was a sad blow for him, as London was the center of the commercial and other negotiations in which he was interested. In France the chief occupation of the envoy proved to be the petty problem of old tsarist debts and French creditors, who clamored for payment. Krassin's whole task was to find a formula of compromise between those creditors and the Soviet government. But no one in Moscow ever seriously thought of being truly conciliatory to the Frenchmen, and Krassin knew beforehand how small and futile his work would be.

Christian Rakovsky was appointed as the Soviet representative in London. By this time a Communist opposition to Stalin had begun to crystallize in Moscow, and it was Stalin's way of combating it to remove the leading oppositionists from their domestic posts and scatter them abroad as envoys. One of the first to be shipped off was Rakovsky, Trotsky's closest friend.

On the other hand, the more insecure Krassin's position became in the party, the more time he was compelled to spend in Russia. During one of my own trips to Russia, in 1925, I was greatly alarmed to hear that Krassin was ill with leukemia. The story was that the Political Bureau of the Communist party had placed him under medical observation in the famous private hospital of the Council of People's Commissars. This was the hospital in which, in that same year, People's Commissar of War Michael Frunze was operated on in accordance with a decision made by the Political Bureau—the operation ending in Frunze's death and Klimenti Voroshilov's elevation to his post. And in the Moscow trials of 1937 testimony was heard that in the same hospital, pursuant to the orders of Secret Police Chief Yagoda, Maxim Gorky himself had been poisoned. (On these and other charges Yagoda was convicted and executed.)

When I telephoned Krassin in the hospital, he was overjoyed to hear a friend's voice and asked me to visit him. I went at once.

As I entered the small private ward, I was shocked to see a doomed man. Krassin had grown much thinner, his features were sharper. He tried to jest, but the humor was bitter. It was clear that he had not come to this hospital of his own desire. He would have preferred western European physicians. He wanted to be closer to his family, who were still abroad. For the first time I found, instead of his once never failing gay smile, a bilious sneer and acrid sarcasm, which were aimed at others and at himself, at the Moscow government and at that "bourgeois world" which used to surround him abroad and to which he used to take like a duck to water.

A few weeks later he was allowed to leave the hospital. He journeyed to Paris, but resumed almost none of his old activities. And yet at this time, in 1925, Paris was after all becoming an important center for Soviet diplomacy. In October, 1925, when Rakovsky was shifted to Paris, Krassin was sent back to London.

In November, 1926, I was in Paris when a telegram reached me from Krassin's wife—a request to come to London at once. I went immediately. When I entered Krassin's room he was on his deathbed, but he recognized me. I will never forget his last words to me, which might have been said in a delirium, or which might have had a deep meaning to him:

"The whole world is a mass of little match-boxes, and all humans are matches. Each one lives with his own little thoughts in his own little world. How I pity them all! All of them struggle, they fight one another, but actually it's just a game in order to forget one's self. Time to go!"

There was a faint smile lighting up his face—as well as a shadow of death. He died on November 24.

At eleven in the morning we gathered in the main building of the Soviet embassy. In the center of the great salon, with its dark-red furnishings, stood the open oak casket. Krassin's body looked alive, but calmer and younger, as if the man had at last been freed from his physical sufferings. An almost imperceptible smile on his lips seemed to emphasize the last words I had heard from him.

At one side of the casket stood the family; at the other, the entire personnel of the embassy. Chopin's funeral march was being softly played in an adjoining room. A door opened, and a woman stepped in, gracefully and lightly. She was about thirty-five or forty. Her dress was black, as was her large hat. A dark veil covered her face. Slowly, quietly, she stepped to the casket, placed an armful of red roses upon it, remained for a few minutes, then, without taking her eyes off Krassin's face, backed her way to where his family kept vigil. She joined the widow and the daughters. There was a slight stir in the group, but no one appeared surprised, as though the family accepted the woman as a friend. I looked at the widow questioningly, and Liubov Vasilievna moved her lips silently, forming the words, "It is she."

So this was the woman whose husband—the White officer—had once been rescued by Krassin—she who had lived with Krassin in Moscow for years. In 1921 she could have left Russia safely, for after the Treaty of Riga she could have been repatriated to Poland, in view of her Polish origin. But she stayed in Russia with Krassin.

Years later, when Krassin was appointed Soviet envoy in Paris, she likewise appeared in France, where, she claimed, she had property and investments. During Krassin's last illness she won over his family by showing much concern over his health and trying to find better doctors. She even began to tell the Krassins that she would like to make their daughters her heiresses. She assured the family that she was rich but all alone and lonesome and simply adored the girls! Presently she was practically a member of the family.

After Krassin's death and funeral she begged the widow to give her a power of attorney to open Krassin's safety deposit vault in a Stockholm bank. According to her, the vault harbored great riches, but no one else should go to Sweden to open it, lest the press notice it and print undesirable rumors. The new widow finally agreed and signed the necessary papers but, by way of precaution, sent one of her older daughters along.

When opened, the vault yielded only thirty thousand Swedish crowns, which, it appeared, had been put away by Krassin in 1917 on the eve of his return to Russia. He had always conceived of this money as belonging to his family, and under no circumstances had he felt it within his right to touch it. Small as the sum was, it was in reality his family's last safeguard against a rainy day.

In the presence of the daughter, the woman took the money and a few family heirlooms out of the vault, then astonished the girl by declaring that years back she had lent some of her pearls to Krassin. She had been looking for them in the vault, and since they were not there she was going to take the money and the family heirlooms in payment for them. That was her story. And she took the currency and the jewels and walked out. The Krassins found themselves almost destitute.

In time it became known that the stories occasionally appearing in the European press of the 1920's about "Krassin's immense riches" had originated with this adventuress. She had spread such tales in the hope of improving her own credit in certain circles. Out of Krassin's riches, she had said, she would soon get another and yet another sizable gift. Since Krassin had never made any secret of his relationship with her, her boasts had been believed abroad, if not in Moscow. Although such stories were not taken at face value in Russia, they did now and again cause doubt as to Krassin's integrity. At one point a rather plausible theory had it that Krassin's enemies at home had first sent this woman to win his sympathy—that she had all along been an agent of a Soviet governmental organization hostile to him. At any rate, her success with Krassin in the 1920's cost his family dearly by the end of that decade.

Years ago I insisted to Krassin's friends that this tragic episode should not be made public. But many of the personages involved are gone by now, and it seems only proper to reveal the truth about a matter which once gave rise to so many rumors. I do not believe it casts shadow on Krassin's memory. He was human and therefore fallible. But in this episode he was guileless and unselfish

—from the time he first helped the woman's husband to the year when, dying, he, together with his wife, accepted the woman's devotion as sincere.

In Krassin's person a remarkable and fascinating figure passed from the scene. When asked for my impression of him, I have usually replied that from the conventional point of view he should be regarded as an "amoral" human being. For he never knew any difference between the good and the evil; he evaluated them as of equal worth. Essentially he had no faith in anything. While the dogmatism, the intolerance, and the narrow-mindedness of his Communist party mates were alien to him, he tended to justify the cruelty of the Soviet regime, if only because to him it was inevitable in the fight against Russia's inertia and backwardness. He used to remark to me that, beginning with the times of Tsar Ivan the Terrible in the sixteenth century, each of Russia's forward steps had been accompanied by the murder or similar sacrifice of thousands and millions of people. To him this was painful, hard, but historically necessary.

Krassin was undoubtedly a Russian patriot, according to his own lights. He sincerely loved Russia and was always ready to serve her, to help her progress. The interests of his country were above everything else with him; and in his work he was unswervingly guided by certain higher considerations which, somehow, managed to survive in him side by side with his mocking, negative attitude toward the high-sounding phrases and popular slogans of the day. He once wrote me, for example (when my wife was having trouble with the O.G.P.U.):

"I do hope that you will not be grieved or disheartened by the difficulties encountered by your wife. You are performing a great task. If some persons do not appreciate this enough, remember that you are working not for individuals but for a greater Russia. Therefore—calmly continue your work."

In my own work, and partly even in my personal life, Krassin played an important role. For many years many things bound us together. Especially after Lenin's death, he was one of the few Soviet leaders to bolster me up in my worst moments. In turn, he valued my work, and repeatedly showed his esteem in practical ways. He knew of all the handicaps placed on my path by some Moscow officials and not only condemned them for such conduct but suffered because of it himself.

It may be rightly said that, while Lenin was first a revolutionary and then a statesman, Krassin always acted as statesman only.

171

OTHER BOSSES, OTHER EXPERTS

BESIDES KRASSIN AS COMMISSAR OF FOREIGN TRADE, THERE WERE TWO SUCCESSIVE appointees of the Communist party whose task it was to see that the North Timber Trust hewed close to the party line. In this capacity they were my bosses. George Lomov and Karl Danishevsky were the two mentors who were charged with supervising the production of the lumber industry, while Krassin was in charge of the export. Neither of the pair was an outstanding leader at this time; on the other hand, they were no mere soldiers in the Communist ranks. They were officers of the political army of the party, and, as a group, such men are often more indicative of the spirit of a great political and social movement than its foremost leaders.

Lomov was born into the family of a prominent tsarist official. On joining the Bolsheviks in his youth, he found himself among that "second growth" of the party which counted Nicholas Bukharin as one of its most remarkable figures. This young group seemed to be destined to inherit the traditions and the power of Lenin and his older associates, the founders of the party.

It was as a high-school boy of sixteen that Lomov had become acquainted with Ryckov and had entered the Bolshevik party. When I met him, he was still quite youthful, and was desperately trying to grow a beard so as to look older. Actually, at the time of the revolution, he turned out to be the youngest member of the party on record.

He looked every inch an intellectual nihilist out of Turgenev's pages. He was an idealist, and with fire and passion he would argue in defense of any theory that was questioned by anyone in sight. He was tall; his features were fine; his forehead was high beneath his unruly hair. His gestures and movements were clumsy, possibly because of his natural shyness.

He loved a good book, good theater, and especially ballet. In party affairs he was an ardent follower of Bukharin, whom he considered to be the most valuable of the Communist group. He referred to Bukharin with love, as well as reverence. Together with his idol, he voted against the Treaty of Brest Litovsk, regarding it as a shameful document.

Theoretically Lomov hated the old capitalistic regime of Russia, and yet at the same time there was no mistaking the deep respect which he felt for some of its leaders, particularly those who had risen to their prerevolutionary positions from the liberal professions. On many occasions he would, for instance, send to me former Russian industrialists, each of whom brought a note from Lomov, reading something like this: "The bearer was well known in his industry in tsarist times, and, although a bourgeois, he is really an honest man, and we must give him a chance to survive." At the end of each such message there were Lomov's postscription apologies and further explanations of why he felt he had to intercede for these men.

On other and frequent occasions, Lomov stressed his disapproval of Communist snobs of proletarian origin, who loved to show off their importance in the party and their new high posts in the government of Soviet Russia.

Lomov lived in the Kremlin, but very modestly, in two small rooms, despite the fact that he had a wife and several young children. This was where I sometimes visited him, bringing his children a half-pound of butter or sugar, which they sorely needed. Lomov himself always dressed skimpily and shabbily. Once, however, on his return from a trip to the Urals, I found him practically lost in an oversized fur greatcoat. I could not help asking, with awe in my voice: "George, where on earth did you get this coat?"

He was visibly embarrassed as he replied: "Terribly cold in the Urals, you know. So the Cheka sent this over for me. Most likely it belonged to some liquidated bourgeois or other."

Generally speaking, he was on bad terms with the Cheka, but, during the sessions of the Council of Labor and Defense, he deferred to Dzerzhinsky with much respect. On its part, the Cheka did not take Lomov too seriously. The highest Communist leaders shared this attitude, not regarding Lomov as a person of deep thought or great promise; yet most of them genuinely loved this strange young man. A slight, semifond smile played on many a face during the important meetings of the inner councils of the party if Lomov happened to take the floor and hold forth. Still, when it was imperative to head some government department with a 100 per cent Communist or to send a trustworthy man as a liaison officer to deal with the bourgeois world, Lomov was the choice of these same leaders.

For this reason he was detailed to be the chairman, first, of the Central Timber Committee, and later of the Central Oil Committee. In the latter capacity he had to meet representatives of foreign companies—men sent over by the Standard Oil management, also Sir Henry Deterding, and the like. Lomov would converse with them politely, and they went away greatly pleased with the way he treated them. Yet, on leaving their company, he would fume and rage and spit in disgust.

He was an honest, direct man, with old-fashioned ideas about the comradeship of the revolutionary circles and about the morals of the revolution itself. I distinctly remember one occasion when, on the telephone, he blasted no less a personage than Michael Kalinin himself, the "president" of the Soviet republic. The outburst concerned one of Lomov's personal friends, a rising figure in the Communist party. The wife of a prominent government official had been paying too much attention to Lomov's friend, and Kalinin intervened by ordering the woman to cease and desist. Should she disobey the order, the recipient of her attentions would be barred from admission to the Kremlin. It was on learning of this order that Lomov telephoned Kalinin, shaking in his ire and shouting:

"You may be Russia's 'president' but you certainly stuck your nose in where it doesn't belong! Since when do we Bolsheviks interfere with one another's personal affairs? That's like the old regime, that's reaction! You, Michael Ivanovich, should know your place and not be a busybody bothering such outstanding comrades!"

For at least a quarter-hour afterward no one could approach Lomov with any routine matter, he was so excited and indignant.

In 1922 Lomov was replaced in the North Timber Trust by Danishevsky—at the insistence of Trotsky, who wanted to place his former military assistants in Russia's economic orbit. Karl Danishevsky was a singular and most interesting man. He was a Lett, the son of a prosperous peasant family. As a youth he had had to flee Russia because he had been involved in the Lettish revolutionary movement of 1904–5, and the punitive expedition of the tsarist General Meller-Zakomelsky was on his and many others' trails. He was already a member of the extreme radical wing in Latvia, which, almost without exception, belonged to the Bolshevik faction in the Russian Social Democratic party of the time. His Bolshevik underground *nom de guerre* was "Herman."

In 1907, during the London convention of the Russian Social Democratic party, he was elected as the Latvian representative on the party's central committee. Later, over a period of years, he worked in the secret Moscow organization of the Social Democrats and belonged to the group of so-called "Compromisers." Although from time to time he supported the Bolsheviks in their theories and actions, on the whole he was inclined to be more with the Mensheviks. Since the Bolsheviks needed aid and comfort from the Latvian movement in their struggle against the Mensheviks, they courted Danishevsky intensively.

After 1917, he climbed the ladder of revolutionary rank with ease and speed. He participated in the many campaigns of the Russian civil war as a member of the Supreme Revolutionary and Military Council of the republic. He was, besides, the chairman of the Revolutionary Military Tribunal, which judged and punished the guilty and the innocent.

Danishevsky was one of those Communists whose job it was to accustom former tsarist army officers to the new Red Army service. It was a complex task. These officers were, deep down in their hearts, bitterly anti-Soviet, but for a variety of reasons many of them joined the Red Army—had to join. Danishevsky's assignment was to treat them with such finesse that they would feel really wanted and trusted by the Soviets. Danishevsky had to convince them that they truly enjoyed all the rights and privileges promised to them when they first joined. But, at the same time, he had to be constantly on guard, remembering that some of them might be in the secret service of the enemies of Soviet Russia. And so in his relations with these men he was now affable, now ruthless. I recall his stories of how sometimes he would entertain an officer in his house, knowing full well that in a day or two he would have to arrest, try, and execute the luckless man, already suspected but as yet being watched in the hope of finding more evidence and new accomplices.

This conduct was not only part of his business but also part of his nature. At one and the same time Danishevsky was both cruel and sentimental. Sipping his tea, he would calmly tell me how many death sentences he had signed in his revolutionary career and then suddenly become upset because his dog had its paw caught in a door.

Upon the termination of the Russian civil war he was, like many other Red Army leaders, transferred to the field of Soviet economy. That was how, in 1922, he came to take Lomov's place as my superior in the North Timber Trust.

I was not entirely free of worry as I awaited his first appearance in our office. When he came, I beheld an athletically built man, cleanly shaved, with his hair combed smoothly back, his eyes azure-blue beneath his high forehead, his lips thin, small, and determined. He wore a military uniform and high soldier's boots. His opening speech to me was this:

"I know all about you, but I am taking you under my wing. I am acquainted with the Cheka's attitude toward you. The Cheka was too tough on you, but that was because Lomov proved himself a softie and couldn't stand up for you properly. I am no softie, I am no Lomov. I am a walking Cheka myself. In the Army I had the same duties and rights as the Cheka has in civilian life."

He did take me under his protection, and we enjoyed good relations from the very start. Throughout the whole period of our work together he really took my side. Without any hesitation whatever he supported me in the most difficult phases of my service.

But later, when I quit my Soviet post and settled abroad as a private individual, Danishevsky changed his attitude toward me radically. I heard about this from a British friend, a lumberman who wanted to give me a position with his firm when I needed a livelihood. Before I could start on my new job, the Englishman chanced to tell Danishevsky of my prospective employment. He remarked to Danishevsky that he, the Englishman, hoped this would not alter Danishevsky's attitude in his business dealings with him. "You and Liberman used to be such good friends," the Englishman said.

"Yes, I was his friend," Danishevsky blew up, "but now I'd hang him if I could!"

My former friend believed in the sacredness of the Bolshevik principle, "Who is not with us, is against us."

While the Bolsheviks were most intolerant toward Mensheviks and other moderate socialists, they did at times show their kindlier side to representatives of the nonpartisan intelligentsia. Now and then they eagerly sought out such intellectuals and drew them into Soviet work. But here, too, were frequent cases of distrust, suspicion, and grave errors on the part of the Communists.

One of the many cases in point was the episode involving Alexis Mesh-chersky, the former director of the railroad-car building works at Kolomna-Sormovo. He was a gifted engineer, organizer, and industrialist. Well educated, with experience which had taken him through a number of European countries, brimming with energy and far-reaching plans, he strove to create in Russia an industrial concern after the latest German models, with which he had been well acquainted in the years before World War I. His plans for such an enterprise dated back to the eve of the revolution: he had wanted to unite into one great company, not only a whole series of plants which by their nature complemented one another, but also all sorts of auxiliary mines and factories which would have assured the main mills of the company raw materials, labor reserves, and so on. Before the revolution disrupted his further dreams and blueprints, Meshchersky did manage to add the timber undertakings of Perm to the main structure of the Kolomna-Sormovo plants. Incidentally, this is how I first met the man—through this tie between the machine-works and the Perm timber lands, with which I was closely concerned at one time before the revolution.

In April, 1918, Meshchersky suggested his plan to the Soviet government: all the metalworks of Russia were to be brought together into one giant unit, with its stock divided evenly between the state and the industrialists. But the Council of People's Commissars rejected the project, deciding, instead, to nationalize all the metal and machine-building factories. From that moment on, Meshchersky was considered by the Soviets as one of the foremost agents of capitalism. He was suspected and put under constant surveillance. His life in Russia became more and more impossible, and he used to complain to me:

"I am willing and ready to continue my work, to collaborate with the government and the labor unions, but I simply cannot work with the local factory workers' committees. It's all the same to me, really, whether a company or the state owns these factories. If anything, I rather prefer the state to those banks that used to have such a deadly grip upon us industrialists. Besides, by owning everything, the state can give us as our additional tools those auxiliary plants which we need so badly. It can also liquidate the harmful competition between large mills—the competition between, say, the Briansk plant and the Kolomna one."

Throughout 1918 the Supreme Council of Economy was quite puzzled about Meshchersky and what to do with him, with his plants and plans. One faction in the Council demanded that all engineers of tsarist times be fired and that an entirely new personnel be organized, instead, as "our genuine revolutionary management" for those factories. This faction was headed by a certain Tamarin, an individual with a rather unclear past, who had recently returned to Russia from foreign exile and who had never had any industrial or business experience. He was opposed by a group in the council advocating the inclusion of the old management in the new Soviet administration of the mills. This group, of course, also spoke of the necessity of bringing members of the

176

Communist party and labor-union representatives into the new management, as fellow-directors of the old administrators. At last the council voted to give Larin and Lomov the job of drawing up the necessary scheme for such a new board. They were to use their judgment as to whether or not to invite any members of the old management into the new board.

Knowing of my friendship with Meshchersky, Lomov asked me to find out if he would be willing to stay on the board once it was sovietized. Having already had a number of conversations with Meshchersky, I was able to assure Lomov that he would be only too glad to stay. I was assigned to take this offer to Meshchersky formally; he accepted immediately, and within twenty-four hours the Larin-Lomov project was ready.

Little did we reckon with Tamarin's hostility! On learning of the preliminary exploration and agreement between Meshchersky and us, Tamarin and his men got in touch with the local factory workers' committee—the organization with which Meshchersky felt he could not get along. The committee, in its provincial Volga town of Sormovo, rushed over to the regional Cheka. The very same night Meshchersky was arrested.

Ryckov, the chief of the Supreme Council of Economy, was indignant. He called upon Lenin to do something about it, and Meshchersky was released. When the new board met, Meshchersky was on hand as one of its members.

But Tamarin was also appointed to the new board, as were a few representatives of labor unions. An old Bolshevik worker, Chubar, who had worked as a mill hand in Meshchersky's plants, was appointed to the chairmanship of the board. When the roster was complete, all the board members were summoned to Ryckov's office. Addressing the men with a few words of greeting, Ryckov made a point of showing especial deference to Meshchersky, saying how much he trusted him. Then he said:

"Before the revolution your boss was that banker Shaikevich. I am sure you feel much better now that Russia is your boss! We revolutionaries will use a revolutionary method as we create a great industrial combine which will be the pride of the Volga region!"

Not long after this meeting, however, news reached us that the old personnel at Sormovo—the tsarist engineers still working there—were not yet reassured. They did not seem to know how seriously to take the new Soviet decision to spare and use them and apparently were planning to quit and flee. Meshchersky begged me to go to Sormovo and tell them that he, Meshchersky, was not being taken into the new management as a hostage of the Soviets, that he was remaining at his post of his own free will and that they should do the same.

I took the first train for Nizhni-Novgorod, the nearest large city to Sormovo. The train was late, arriving not in the morning, as the timetable promised, but at eleven o'clock at night. The Sormovo plant was some distance out of town, so there was no chance of my getting there the same night. I decided to seek shelter in Nizhni-Novgorod.

But all the town's hotels had been requisitioned by the Soviets and converted into government offices. Where to go? The streets were ankle-deep in mud, as I soon found out when I began slogging along the dark pavements. A man was coming my way. I stopped him: "Do you know of any place where I may be taken in overnight?"

He turned and pointed at a faint light in the distance: "Go there. They'll tell you."

The road was difficult, the light was far, but I finally reached it. As I ascended the stairs to the second floor I suddenly realized that I was in the regional offices of the Cheka! But it was too late to retrace my steps. I faced a worker who seemed to be a Cheka official.

Trying to hide my uneasiness, I declared to him that I had just come from Moscow on the business of the Central Timber Committee, by which I was employed, and that my errand to the plant of Sormovo was to ascertain how much fuel the plant had in reserve. The worker said: "We have no place for you to stay overnight. The best you can do is find a seat in our waiting-room, and wait for the morning."

Meekly, I followed his suggestion. A slow, horrible night began for me. As I sat there, in a corner of the waiting-room, groups of men and women were brought from the outside and taken into the inner quarters of the Cheka. I could hardly distinguish the faces; all I saw was human figures in their overcoats and sheepskins. Others were taken out of the inner quarters, through the same waiting-room, and a few minutes after each group had passed I thought I heard shots. It might have been only my imagination—but at any rate, I lived through not a night but a nightmare.

At about four o'clock in the morning a man came in. He looked like an official, with his holstered revolver and assured manner. He crossed the room toward me—much to my horror. He stopped and said: "I am a member of the Cheka collegium. What can I do for you?"

Recovering my presence of mind somewhat, I stated my name and errand. He listened closely, then turned away and soon returned to my corner with a glass of hot tea. I accepted it in great surprise, but without any appreciable reassurance. I was more than glad when the sun finally rose and I could resume my journey to Sormovo.

But the grim impressions of that night would not leave me for a long time afterward. I began to understand why Meshchersky feared Sormovo and its workers' committee and their close ties with the Cheka. No wonder he accepted the place on the new board: it meant he could stay away from Sormovo, in the comparative safety of Moscow, where I could help him and where Ryckov and Lenin could save him in case of need.

The workers of Sormovo and Tamarin's faction in Moscow, however, did not give up the fight so easily. Within a few months Meshchersky found their opposition so strong and effective that he could not continue at his post. The board was soon to be reorganized, anyway, and this was the signal for him to quit.

Meshchersky fled abroad. I saw him in London on my first visit to England, in 1920. Once more he wistfully talked of his desire to work with the Soviet regime somehow or other. He criticized bitterly the way our delegation had, a short time before, spent the last reserves of our gold in purchasing locomotives in Sweden.

"Damn it," he stormed, "if the Soviets had used that gold to buy a little essential equipment for my old plants at Kolomna and Sormovo, if the entire organization and production of those plants were revamped, you wouldn't have to buy any foreign locomotives! My plants could have built those locomotives for Russia!"

When in the same year I returned from London to Moscow, I told Lenin about this conversation. As I talked I noticed that Lenin did not betray any enmity toward Meshchersky but, on the contrary, seemed to sympathize with some of his words as I quoted them. But all this was of no practical consequence: Meshchersky never returned to his homeland. Even Lenin himself could not or would not always overcome the spirit created by his own revolutionary slogans, placing much of the power of the revolution in the hands of local authorities.

Other intellectuals and specialists gradually got used to their status and work in the new regime, but in the first years their status was uncertain, to say the least. They were always threatened with poisoned dossiers. The awful specter of purge, with its usual sequel of imprisonment and shooting, consequently hung over them. Such a situation was not conducive to good results in their work, of course, and within a few years the Bolsheviks themselves had to take measures toward improving the conditions in which these men worked. This new phase, in which nonparty specialists were allowed a peace of mind, an assurance of an unclouded tomorrow, began toward the end of the 1920's, in the era of the first Five-Year Plan.

(26)

A STORM GATHERS

It was early in 1925 that clouds began to gather over me. For the previous seven years the official attitude toward men in my position had been markedly uneven, as I have pointed out: at times the *spetsy* were arrested by the score and quite a number of them shot; and at other times a fairly liberal policy prevailed, and the government attempted to find common ground for real collaboration with us. Something or other always seemed to happen, at home or abroad, to bring about the replacement of liberalism with terrorism.

Until 1925 the Cheka spared me. Lenin's personal favor toward me, Krassin's influence, also my own achievements in the timber industry and lumber trade of Russia—all these made me an exception to the general rule of mercurial ups and downs in the treatment accorded the experts. But I, too, like all other non-Communist specialists in Soviet employ, was listed in the secret archives of the Cheka. A dossier on Simon Liberman was being steadily put together by the Red inquisition; the data expanded; the charges grew—against a day when the Cheka would deem it possible to tackle me in earnest.

This powerful bureau had for years been irritated by the immunity which I enjoyed because of Lenin's friendliness toward me. There was one incident in particular that Dzerzhinsky and his successors remembered well.

Early in the 1920's my four-room apartment was adjudged by the authorities to be too large for my family and me. In view of the shortage of living space in the overcrowded Moscow of the time, I was told to accept as my coresidents two more families, both of the working class. This was a general practice in Soviet Russia; no one, except the highest members of the government, were exempt from it. And so, while my family and I kept two of the four rooms, each of the two others was given to a worker's family.

One of the new tenants turned out to be a Communist with a wife and a small child. Evenings he would get drunk and beat his wife mercilessly. My little boy, then five or six, saw these performances, as the Communist would chase his wife all over the apartment, our rooms included. Obviously it was not a suitable environment for my son, so I decided to take him on my very next trip abroad and place him in an English school.

But this was not easy. The Soviet authorities preferred to keep an official's family in Russia while he himself was on a foreign mission. It was a guaranty that the man would came back; in crude reality, it amounted to a system of hostages. I thought I would try for a passport for my son, anyway. First, I consulted my chief and friend, Alexis Ryckov. He said:

"Of course, I understand that you want to have your son somewhere near by in England while you work in our London offices. That is natural, but I doubt the wisdom of your plan on general principles. You should really sacrifice your personal feelings, and give your son his precious opportunity to grow up not in the bourgeois milieu of England but in the free surroundings of Russia, with the young Soviet generation."

Nevertheless, Ryckov promised to help me.

Next I went to Lenin—not specifically to discuss this matter, but to mention it casually while reporting on an important economic problem. As Lenin seemed willing to listen, I explained the situation at home in detail. He did not argue and gave his consent the minute I finished.

But there was Dzerzhinsky's agency to be reckoned with. The Cheka protested Lenin's decision. Viacheslav Menzhinsky, chief aide to Dzerzhinsky, categorically refused to permit my son's departure from Russia. When I came to see him, Menzhinsky said:

"We have enough schools in Soviet Russia. You don't have to look for any in England. Anyway, the less you parents interfere with the problem of your children's education, the healthier it'll be for the young ones, especially in our era of transition."

He thought a little, then continued: "I am against your own trip to England, too. Krassin has enough Mensheviks surrounding him without adding you to his entourage."

Once again I approached Lenin. He listened closely, nodding from time to time as if in agreement with me, and saying: "Yes, we know, we know." He then picked up his telephone and called the Cheka. After a brief talk with Dzerzhinsky, he turned to me: "Well then, we'll have to discuss this at the next meeting of the Politbureau." As he rose to say goodbye, he added: "Get ready to leave for London. Can't waste time now, you know." Apparently he was quite sure that the question was to be decided in my favor.

Indeed, within about a week, Ryckov handed me an excerpt from the minutes of the Politbureau, reading:

Subject of discussion: Proposal by Ryckov and Lenin to grant a passport to Liberman and his son Alexander for a trip abroad.
Resolution: To instruct the Cheka to issue the passport.
Division of the vote: Against—Dzerzhinsky and Zinoviev. For—Lenin, Ryckov, and Kamenev.

This whole episode was completely characteristic of Lenin. Actually, he did not have to present the question to the Politbureau: he could have decided it himself by an executive order, which, coming from him, would have been instantly obeyed by the Cheka. But his method, as always, was to act through the Communist party and its supreme organs, this time the Politbureau—to make a decision not in his own name but in the name of the party and its authority. Despite his extraordinary weight in the affairs of the party, Lenin always avoided giving the impression of making personal decisions which might have relegated the party to a secondary position, and might have lowered the party's influence.

The passport was issued to me. But before discharging his duty, Menzhinsky had another talk with me. Menzhinsky was not only Dzerzhinsky's first deputy but later, after his chief's death, also the successor of "Comrade Felix." But he did not last long in the new post, dying soon after his ascendancy. When I dealt with him in the matter of my son's passport, Menzhinsky was already seriously ill. He spoke slowly, with an effort.

But as he questioned me, he appeared to be well versed in my life and work. He might have known of my personal affairs not only through his agents but also through his sisters, who were actresses and often met my wife in her capacity as founder of the first Soviet children's theater.

"Are you a Menshevik?" he asked me.

"By my personal views, yes," I replied. "However, I do not participate in any Menshevik party work, for I am now a nonparty expert in Soviet employ."

"Let me remind you," the Chekist went on, "that not too long ago you were elected by the employees of the Central Timber Committee to the Moscow Soviet of Workers' Deputies as a Menshevik. You defeated your own boss, George Lomov, who was a candidate from the Bolsheviks."

I argued back politely that at the time this election had not been disputed by Lomov or my other superiors, that I had been allowed to take my seat in the Soviet for at least a few months.

"If so," Menzhinsky raised his voice impatiently, "if you now are not a member of the Menshevik party, why don't you make a public declaration that you are no longer a Menshevik?"

At that time such letters did appear frequently in the press of both Moscow and provincial cities. But their authors were guided mainly by an opportunistic desire to make a career. Their declarations, "breaking with Menshevism," made repulsive reading, and I said to Menzhinsky: "I cannot make such a declaration. No one would believe in its sincerity."

He insisted, he argued, he sneered at me. But he had no choice. The Politbureau had instructed him to issue the passport. He had to do it, and I took my son to England. But the Cheka never forgave me for it.

And now, in 1925, after Lenin's death, other things were remembered, too. The Cheka leaders had always seen in me a man who "disrupted" the Communist front of the people's economy by bringing back old private lumber dealers as his helpers. In addition to this, I was the one who had organized the sale of Soviet timber abroad via foreign brokers, who, according to the Communist definition, were nothing but parasites. At that time a get-rich-quick promoter, connected with a British labor union operating building co-operatives, had tried to induce me to sell Soviet lumber directly to his building co-operatives without using the British brokers. In other words, he allegedly wanted us to by-pass the "parasites" by selling through him. But he had no other contacts with the British lumber market. It all looked fine on paper, but if I had switched from the experienced brokers to people like him, I could have placed only the quantity of lumber that the co-operatives themselves consumed; my direct sales to them would have violated the unwritten code of the British lumber market, where tradition commanded that sales from foreign shippers to British importers be made through accredited brokers and not directly to consumers. The quantity that I could have sold to the co-operatives would have represented only a fraction of what Soviet Russia wanted to sell to the British market. Of course, the by-passing of the brokers would have greatly pleased the trade-unions and harmonized with the main current of Soviet thought—although the British labor organizations were anything but Communistic. Of course, I had to decline all these eager plans and offers, and the Cheka remembered every complaint that had consequently been made about me.

Then there was the old charge that by causing the establishment of mixed-stock companies I not only handed back to the bourgeois elements part of their property despite its nationalization but also gave them an opportunity to re-enter Russia in order to continue their exploitation of the people.

My explanation was that, in whatever I had done, my motives were of the best: I had worked for Russia's welfare. But what is "welfare"? The concept is a subjective one, and the Communist leaders often changed their own understanding or explanation of the principle called "Russia's welfare."

The year of 1925 brought about the Cheka's reckoning with me, partly because by then Lenin was gone and partly because Krassin was hovering between life and death. Also the entire program of the Soviet government was drifting away from the New Economic Policy, leftward ho! Serious onslaughts upon experts of all kinds were the order of the day. Trials were held one after another, of "plotters," of "counterrevolutionaries," of economists, and so on.

At this juncture both the Soviet Union and the Communist party were laboring through a serious crisis. The political status of the government was strong; but the economics of the country were in a woeful state and getting worse with every month.

The crux of the matter was in the collaboration of Russia's peasants and workers, under the workers' leadership, which had been the slogan and the last will and testament of Lenin. The workers had to become more powerful economically as well as politically. The socialist sector of heavy industry had to be widened, and this called for new capital investments.

Yet the concessionary policy had by then failed to acquit itself. There was no hope of attracting fresh funds from abroad. To find loans abroad? This did not work out either. The only way to get new money was to squeeze it out of the peasantry. But this would have endangered the very idea of a peaceful bloc of peasants and workers, as envisaged by Lenin.

Had Lenin been alive, he would have asserted his authority and perhaps suggested some solution or other. But he was dead, and the field was open for a ferocious political struggle among his inheritors.

It was against this fluid and uncertain background that the Soviet government tried to show itself a strong government. Hence all the ruthless measures against us specialists as borderline elements. The specialists, being by virtue of their jobs close to the upper Communist stratum, were among the first outsiders to learn of the hesitations and deviations of their bosses. This made them doubt the very stability of the Soviet regime. And this doubt at once drew the attention of "the eye of the revolution"—the Cheka.

The government began to ponder the general problem: To what extent did the specialists really recognize the Soviet regime? Would it not be fitting and proper, in accordance with Lenin's own tactics, to punish some of the topmost specialists as a lesson to all other non-Communist experts? Thus began the witch-hunt and the exemplary trials. Just the same, it must be said that some fire did smolder beneath this smoke; not all the charges were trumped up.

This was the epoch of the first important clashes between Stalin and Trotsky, resulting in the latter's defeat. In this period some Communists seriously thought that cardinal changes in the Soviet regime were inevitable, and various rival groupings within the Communist party took shape because of this feeling. And not a few non-Communist experts were in contact and sympathy with the oppositionists—a detail too juicy not to be brought up by the Cheka during the trials of the time.

In October, 1925, while in London, I received a telegram from Moscow—an official message from my superiors. The text, in no uncertain terms, demanded my immediate return to Moscow, "in the line of duty."

The nature of the business I was to attend to in Moscow was not specified. The whole thing looked bad for me; of that there could be no doubt. I remembered only too well that during my most recent stay in Moscow I had been shadowed thoroughly. My new clerks had obviously been the Cheka's men and women, intrusted with the task of completing the dossier against me. As the director of the North Timber Trust, I had met a new member of my board, a man named Breslav. He had once served as chairman of the Moscow regional Cheka, and his cruelty in that capacity was proverbial. He knew nothing about timber, his prerevolutionary trade having been shoemaking. As an exile from the tsarist police he had lived in Paris, where he worked at the cobbler's last and learned a few French words. Another member of my board, also freshly appointed, was Por, a Hungarian Communist and former secretary of Bela Kun. Por was no less notoriously ruthless than Kun.

When I had left Russia to come to London, on the Trust's business, Breslav had accompanied me. It was plain that his assignment was to spy on me. Before we reached London, we had to visit other European capitals, and Breslav hugely enjoyed all this traveling. Rather clumsily he tried to lull my suspicions: he assured me that he loved "comfort and a beautiful life," he boasted that his young wife was the daughter of a tsarist general who had served as the governor of a large province. The man's appearance was far from impressive; blind in one eye, he never looked at you with the other eye either. He never smiled. It was a chore to talk to him.

Por, the Hungarian Communist, remained in Moscow—to be my deputy in charge of the Trust while I was abroad. He was a Hungarian by his former residence, not by origin; he had been born in Galicia. And he brought with him to Russia the worst features of both those lands: the craftiness of the lowest of the Galicians and the cruelty of the most repulsive of the Hungarians. He was small of stature, quick of movement, red-haired and with large freckles on his face—not a pleasant chap to look at or deal with.

It soon became clear to me that Breslav and Por had a mutual understanding—to alternate in spying upon me. Next time it would be Breslav who would remain in Moscow to run my organization, and it would be Por's turn to gad about Europe as my guard.

I also learned that they hated each other. Even before I left Moscow, each one of them had told me in secret that, because of the general distrust of non-Communist experts, it behooved me to have a true friend in the Communist party. Each one recommended himself, naturally. Now Breslav, now Por, warned me to beware of the other.

Both told me officiously that the government trusted me implicitly; but I knew that each had orders to trace my every step. Their special instructions were to watch me in my negotiations with the foreign buyers of Soviet timber and in all my contacts with the bourgeois world.

Nevertheless, I soon noticed that both Breslav and Por gave in to foreign traders in their demands for better terms far more quickly and easily than I ever did. And all the while they filed reports to the Cheka on the "suspicious attitude of this specialist toward the foreign capitalists." They wove their intrigue against me busily and, on the whole, successfully. No matter what the true facts were, the two could and would prevaricate. This was only one example:

Our custom was to begin the sales of Soviet timber early in the spring. We worked hard to get the best prices possible, but we were not the only sellers on the London market; there were also our Scandinavian rivals. Throughout the spring and often all summer long, too, we sold one shipment after another, frequently obtaining advantageous prices but occasionally taking it on the chin.

Toward the end of each year we had the most trying job of all on our hands: to sell the remnants of our stock. The best timber had gone by then, and we had to accept lower quotations and, at that, be thankful for them. By that time the purchasers were buying not for immediate resale or their own consumption but on speculation—they would store the purchased timber against an emergency call in the winter or in the hope of a higher market the next spring.

No one saw anything illegal or untoward in the risk on their part or the acceptance of lower prices on ours. Experienced men in the field felt this was quite legitimate and normal—but not so Breslav and Por, together with their Chekist superiors. They accused me of collusion with certain British firms and of a deliberate postponement of my selling operations until the end of each year, in order to let these Britishers have our Soviet timber at lower prices!

Collusion, eh? The Cheka said, "That reminds us," and dragged out some of my transactions of 1920. These were the deals involving my reservation, for the railroads of England, of 200,000 Soviet ties formerly belonging to a Dutch firm. I had telegraphed at that time from London, making the reasons for the

185

deal very plain, and the Cheka now, in 1925, could easily find all the documents in the case establishing my innocence. But they did not bother with documents but, instead, charged me with a secret pact which I had allegedly concluded with the Dutch firm to safeguard its ties until such time as these railroad ties could be returned to its warehouses in Holland! Other charges were of the same stamp.

By 1925, the Economic Division of the Cheka had enough of a dossier against me to appoint a special commission, headed by the division's chairman, Safronov, "to investigate Specialist Liberman." All my work of the preceding seven or eight years, whatever had been regarded as my good service to the cause of the Soviets, was now branded as sheer sabotage.

At about the same time that I received the summons to return to Moscow, alarming news from various sources began to reach me. Friends and acquaintances, the latest arrivals from Russia, warned me that I would be arrested immediately upon my return. Some of these people were indeed my friends, others were not. In either case they were actually repeating, whether or not they knew it, what my enemies in Moscow wanted them to tell me. These foes, aware of some vestiges of sympathy and support I still enjoyed at the top of the Communist party, were attempting to knife me thoroughly. On the one hand, they assured what Communist supporters I still had that I was guilty and that in acknowledgment of my guilt I would not dare to return to Moscow. On the other hand, they took steps to make sure that I would not return. Thus they spread the sinister rumor, through these travelers bound for western Europe, that I was to be arrested in Russia and therefore should not return.

One of the unsuspecting messengers was Professor Tal, an outstanding authority in international law. He was the legal adviser of the North Timber Trust and had just arrived in London from Moscow. With tears in his eyes he pleaded with me not to obey the summons. He said that I would at once be arrested and tried in Moscow—and perhaps not tried at all but summarily executed, just as so-and-so had recently been seized and shot. He named several non-Communist experts in Moscow who had been "liquidated" in recent weeks or months.

I felt that perhaps he was right. My wife, then staying in Paris, was also besieged by our friends, who implored her to stop me from answering the summons. After a number of sleepless nights, I made my decision. It was to go to Moscow, as ordered.

(27)

THE STORM BREAKS

I DECIDED TO RETURN TO RUSSIA BECAUSE, COME WHAT MIGHT, I DID NOT WANT those nonsensical charges to triumph against me. By refusing to return I would only prove to many that I was really guilty as charged. The accusations would then pursue me the rest of my life. My name would remain disgraced until the end of my days and beyond. It was my duty to my family, to my son, to go back to the Soviet Union and defend myself against slander.

When the arrangements were made, my departure was set for half-past ten one morning. By nine o'clock my apartment was full of men and women, friends who had come to bid me goodbye—forever, some of them thought. Almost all of them tried with last-minute arguments to dissuade me from the trip. What they said was earnest and perhaps true, but nothing new to me. I had made up my mind and would not change the decision.

Among the first callers was the owner of a large British timber firm, a close friend of mine. For a long time he shook my hand, then said:

"It's difficult for me to speak of this, but I must ask you one thing. What is to happen to your son in England if something irreparable happens to you in Russia? Do you want him to continue his education? Or should I give him a place in my office and teach him the timber business? Say the word, and I will try my best to be like a father to him!"

Another British lumberman, a rich and powerful individual, came to say:

"Too bad I am not a brother of yours. I would have made you stay in England and not go back to a sure death in that Russia of yours. But since I cannot *force* you to stay here, let me beg you, implore you once more. Stay, won't you? So long as I am making a living, you will have food and shelter too..... Well, if you are determined to go, I'll take care of your family."

One after another they spoke practically the same words. They were burying and consoling me at one and the same time. Their sympathy was sincere, their arguments sounded convincing, and I did want to believe their offers and promises.

In that gush of sympathy, as a matter of fact, there was much that was of the moment's mood only. Later, when I had quit the service of the Soviets and was a jobless resident of western Europe, I called upon the man who had once regretted not being my brother. "Oh yes, of course," he said. "I would be only too glad to give you a job with my firm, but—you know how it is! Your former employers, the Soviets, are sore at you, and I cannot offend them and endanger my trade with them by engaging you. So sorry, old man!"

I went from London to Moscow by way of Berlin. There I called on some of my old friends, the Menshevik exiles. They, too, argued against my return to Russia. "The Communists feel they no longer need you non-Communist specialists," they said. "They are certain they have by now gained enough experience of their own. They think they know everything and are beginning to hate the experts. The experts have done their duty and should go, else they will be removed forcibly."

Another argument was: "You won't be able to defend yourself in Moscow. You won't be able to prove that whatever you did was done in the interests of the nation. For actions that were considered correct and legal in the era of War Communism became criminal in the succeeding period of the New Economic Policy, but now are once again held to be fine and noble, because there is a shift to the left in Russia these days, definitely. The government wants to demonstrate to its own people and to the world at large that only naïve and stupid individuals could believe that Russia was really moving toward a moderate state capitalism. If, in order to prove this conclusively, the Communists feel it necessary to chop off a few non-Communist heads like your own, be sure they'd do it. And doubtless you will be among those to go, once the decision to do this is made. Your name is well enough known in Europe, and by shooting you, they will gain the publicity they may want for their new policy."

While saying this, one of my Menshevik friends showed me a report which had just arrived by underground channels from Soviet Russia. Citing the names of certain former Mensheviks and other moderate socialists who had held responsible posts in Moscow as economic experts, the report pointed out that they were "no longer at their posts." My friends said:

"See? It certainly is naïve of you to think that you will be an exception, that you will have a chance to defend yourself and prove your innocence. You are taking an absolutely senseless step."

But I would not listen to them.

I arrived in Moscow late in October, 1925. The day was frosty but not snowy, and the sun shone brightly but without much warmth. The train reached the capital at three o'clock in the afternoon. On my previous trips I had been met by a number of friends and associates; this time only my secretary was at the station. Pressing my hand with feeling, he said: "I am seeing you perhaps for the last time. An extraordinary commission of investigation has been eagerly awaiting your return."

The next morning I went to my office. Formerly, most of the staff had made it a point of coming into my office or stopping me in the halls to greet me. But this time they all shied away from me, were afraid even to say "Hello." I felt lonely, forsaken by everybody. Only the closest of my old friends sneaked in to shake my hand and at once scurried off.

Thus began an experience that lasted two months. I forgot my pride, and, without expecting any of my friends to rush to my rescue, I called on them. Doggedly I went from one superior to another, from one old friend to another.

They shook hands with me sympathetically, but it was clear that they saw in me a doomed man.

I had been away from Moscow one whole year and now found great changes. Ryckov was no longer my immediate chief; he was now in the Council of the People's Commissars. To my astonishment, all my efforts to see him were of no avail. At last I was told that it was the fault of a former friend of mine: he had lied to Ryckov about me, convincing him that I had never believed in the Soviet regime and had on one occasion confessed that my friendship for Ryckov was insincere and selfish. Ryckov was embittered and resolved to do nothing to save me now that I was on the spot.

And this was the same Ryckov who had been among my closest friends for so many years! But life was like that in Soviet Russia, and in the end Ryckov's fate was far worse than mine. We were to meet and become friendly again, a few years later when he went abroad for a cure. We often got together in some little foreign restaurant, and I listened as he, with tears in his eyes and terrible sarcasm in his words, spoke of the degeneration of the Soviet regime. By that time Dzerzhinsky and a number of his aides from the O.G.P.U. had replaced Ryckov and his men in all important work, particularly in the Supreme Council of Economy. A few more years passed—and Ryckov was tried and executed together with many others.

My troubles merely came earlier than Ryckov's. At home, as in the office, no one would visit me, and in the evening I stayed all alone as if quarantined. All my friends—those that could still be regarded as friends—feared to call on me no matter how much they might have wished to do so. They were certain that the O.G.P.U. watched my home, too, taking careful note of all comers and goers.

I was not completely alone, in that my parents, both in their seventies, lived next to my room. I could not tell them of my trouble, however, and they could not understand my depression, which, of course, they saw plainly. My mother was very puzzled by it all. For years, ever since 1918, she had convinced herself that Russia was governed by just three persons: Lenin, Trotsky, and her son. Why, then, was I so worried?

The most sinister and tormenting aspect of the whole thing was the continued absence of any formal charges against me. The chairman of the extraordinary commission and the O.G.P.U. investigator, who had the run of the North Timber Trust while fishing for evidence, dug into the office files and called now one of my subordinates or associates and now another to be grilled about my past activities. They locked the doors of those office-rooms of the Trust where they examined the files. They enjoined the men and women whom they questioned to keep the details of the questioning completely secret. All this was done while I was somewhere in the offing—in my lonely office, perhaps next door. When the investigators met me in the halls or in the general office, they were studiedly correct and polite with me. They asked me how I felt and for how long I had come back to Russia and whether I had brought my family with me.

I walked away bitter, hating everything. Then I perked up. "Fight back!" I cried to myself.

I decided to present a report covering my entire service with the Soviets since 1918. With the help of two secretaries and working at top speed one whole month, I wrote one hundred and fifty pages of facts and figures. By then I knew more or less what accusations to expect from my foes, so I answered every one of the probable charges. When it was ready, I handed the report in several copies to several high officials in the Kremlin to whom I still had access. But the only result was further nerve-racking procrastination on the part of the O.G.P.U. They intended to prolong the investigation, without bringing it to a head, so long as I had any fight left in me and any possible supporters or defenders in the Kremlin.

My life became more and more difficult and unbearable with every day. I was beginning to wish for any end to the mental torture, even if it were arrest. Each knock on my door seemed at last to announce the O.G.P.U. agents. I wondered if suicide might not be the best way out. I said to myself: "Once I am arrested, my nerve may break. I may begin to confess things I have never done. I may sign any documents prepared by the O.G.P.U."

This prospect frightened me more than anything else. And so, expecting that the arrest would occur in the middle of the night, I placed a sharp razor under my pillow each evening before retiring.

And yet I wanted to live, to be free. In my growing despair I was clutching at straws. Once, amid my gloom, I was visited by Prits, the Norwegian concession-seeker, whom I have mentioned before. Long ago I had done much to create the mixed-stock company which he now headed, and on this dark day before his departure from Russia he was coming to see me about something or other, without realizing that I no longer had any power. A wild thought crossed my mind. I rose to my feet, spoke frankly to him of my predicament, and besought him:

"You will be in London in a few days. It may not be too late to save me. Please see my friends in London, and tell them of the danger threatening me. Ask them to do whatever they can to rescue me."

The Norwegian looked at me steadily and replied: "Mr. Liberman, you in your time defended the interests of Soviet Russia against mine so persistently and firmly that I have no reason to help you now."

Among those who accepted my report of self-defense was Roiseman, a prominent member of the Central Control Commission. In 1923 and 1924 he had toured western Europe, inspecting and purging the various Soviet trade offices abroad. He had been very stern in dismissing some of the personnel and bringing to trial those who could be induced to return to Russia. While in London he had examined the work of my timber-sales office and, on one occasion, had heard from both the high Soviet officials and certain British friends of the Soviets much praise of my activities in England. (The praise, incidentally, had to do with that very episode of the railroad ties which was now one of the criminal charges against me!)

Whether because of this firsthand knowledge of my work abroad or because of other circumstances, Roiseman, despite his reputation as a ruthless purger, now seemed to me more humane than many other less stern officials. He read my report and appeared to be agreeable when I asked him to rescue me. I had hope, at last.

Others who read my report seemed also impressed. Ryckov sent this message through Lomov: "I prefer not to see Liberman, but I will do for him all I can."

But the report had other consequences, too. The investigators now decided to counterattack. They would grill me! My real tortures began.

One evening, close to midnight, my telephone rang. An official but rather courteous voice said: "This is the O.G.P.U. If you are not too busy tonight, will you be good enough to pay us a call and have a talk? We will send a car for you."

I immediately got in touch with my sister, then living in Moscow, and told her this latest news. "If I don't come back," I said, "don't tell the old folks the truth, but invent something to reassure them....."

But I came back, and the same invitation was repeated again and again, practically every night. My "talks" with O.G.P.U. officials usually took place in a small, poorly lighted room, which I reached after a long walk through dim and seemingly endless corridors, under the escort of a soldier with a rifle. On entering the building I was given a special pass, which I was to hand over to the man in the little room, before he and I began our "talk."

The man had a copy of my 150-page report before him. He would say: "Well, tell me, Comrade Liberman, on page so-and-so you say so-and-so, yet we picture this particular episode quite differently. We picture it as....." Then, suddenly, apropos of nothing under discussion, he would ask: "Are you very friendly with so-and-so? You have spent a lot of your leisure time with him, haven't you?" Or: "And where is your son studying now? Isn't that a very expensive and bourgeois school?"

Outside reigned a complete and terrifying stillness, from time to time interrupted by soldiers' steps in the halls and the distant chimes marking the passage of hours. The monotonous way the O.G.P.U. man asked most of his questions had an enervating effect amid this stillness of the night. After my day of worry and fatigue, the man's voice in this queer nightly conversation piece would begin to blend with the sounds of the far-off steps and chimes. My thoughts were slow, drugged: "When will this end? Will it end?" At last, by four o'clock in the morning or thereabouts, the man would rise. In a tired, listless tone he would say: "You must forgive our disturbing you like this."

He would call out to a soldier in the corridor and issue him a pass for me.

And still I would not know whether I was to be free that morning or not. But, yes, the soldier was taking me to an outside gate. I was to be free for one more day.

And the very same evening, the telephone would ring again. The war of nerves went on.

Throughout all these tortures I felt with a special sharpness the very essence of the so-called "revolutionary dictatorship." This revolutionary dictatorship, based on a singular type of class justice, was responsible for a way of life in which you could breathe and live so long as the government was good to you or at least was not interested in you. But the moment this favor or indifference became ire or even suspicion, you found yourself isolated as if stricken with a plague. The staunchest of your friends risked meeting you in secret only. Your subordinates dreaded their contact with you. Your superiors scorned you or, at best, felt sorry for you.

All feared to discuss your case openly with you—feared to mention your political affliction, again as if it were a deadly plague. Under such circumstances a man would rather be confined in a solitary cell than see these scornful or pitying glances, than feel himself an inmate of a moral prison.

To appeal to the public opinion of the nation? There was no such thing. There was only the opinion formed at the top or in the punitive organizations of the state. Your superiors, regardless of their sympathies, had to act on that and nothing else. Down the vertical line, from the Politbureau to the lowest Communist cells, all opinions and orders were chuted. If you were not a member of the Communist party, you could not really defend yourself personally. Everywhere an attitude was formed toward you in your absence, so to speak, and you were powerless to change it.

Those Soviet employees who had happened to spend some time in western Europe were particularly hard hit when the decision went against them. Only in their circumstances could one really fathom the entire meaning and value of the concept and practice of civil liberties—a phenomenon which, according to the creators of the Russian revolution, was nothing but a "bourgeois invention."

Nevertheless, I want to stress one further feature of the Soviet regime—a factor that must be taken into consideration if one is to understand fully the situation in Russia in that period. This is the role played by various subordinate organs of the government in the important business of the Politbureau. These subordinate organs did influence the deliberations and directives of the Politbureau. This was true despite the fact that the entire nation was under the strict control of the centralized revolutionary dictatorship, that everything was subject to orders from the Politbureau sitting in the Kremlin.

And another thing must be remembered: Around each punitive organization of the Soviets gathered many honest but narrow-minded men who saw a potential enemy of the regime in every non-Communist, especially if the

192

latter had once been a member of either the middle or the upper class or of a non-Communist political party. Therefore, no matter how strongly you yourself were convinced of your own innocence and no matter how much you may have believed that the supreme Soviet power was above personal intrigues and would not surrender you to the mob, there was no safeguarding you against such petty suspicions and personal revenge. Because the subordinate organs had this influence upon the upper authority, there was no safety for you. And for men who had in the past fought for the revolution and had completely accepted it when it came, this fact was especially hard to take.

Soviet Russia is a land of democracy in the sense that everyone has the right to work, is secure against need and hunger, and enjoys his national and racial equality. But all that has its limit. And the limit is where the interests of the individual clash with those of the state. In Soviet Russia the state is above everything else. But since the question of what is good and what is bad for the state is decided by mere mortals—the one and only political party being made up of mortals—any Soviet citizen my find himself the victim of outright lawlessness. He may be faced by an absolutely baseless indictment. Only through superhuman efforts can he reach the very top of the government with his protest and complaint, and only then—provided the indictment is not of a political nature—can he faintly hope for a miracle of mercy.

There is a great deal of virtue in the celebrated Sanskrit saying: "You must sacrifice your own self for the sake of your family; and your family for the sake of your community; and your community for the sake of your country; and all the world for the sake of your soul." In the Soviet Union they seem to believe in this saying, except that the crucial word "soul" is replaced with the words "the new regime." And this replacement has been made despite Lenin's basic idea that all state authority is something transitory, a mere temporary phase of the all-important journey toward social justice.

(28)

FINAL DECISION

ON NEW YEAR'S EVE I WAS ALONE. EVEN MY PARENTS HAD LEFT THEIR ROOM NEXT door for a quiet celebration with friends. I sat in my chair, absorbed in my gloomy thoughts. A feeling of complete hopelessness gripped me. Only a miracle could save me.

On the second day of January I went mechanically to my office. There was a knock on the door. I raised my head and said "Come in." The office manager of the North Timber Trust stepped in. He was a Communist. He stood stiffly and said: "Comrade Dzerzhinsky instructs you to leave the Soviet Union within the next twenty-four hours." I thought I was dreaming. Then I decided that this must be a cruel joke. But no, there was nothing unreal or jesting about the news.

A telegram had come to the Soviet government from a Swedish timber syndicate, expressing readiness to begin negotiations with the Soviets about adopting uniform prices for the British and other customers. But the telegram clearly stated the Swedes' preference for me as a member of the Soviet delegation for such negotiations! The Soviet trade mission in London was vitally interested in the establishment of a common price scale with the Swedes, so it insisted before the Kremlin that I be sent back to western Europe. This was the cause of Dzerzhinsky's sudden decision to spare my life and send me back to foreign lands.

I immediately telephoned Dzerzhinsky and requested an interview. He told me to come in two hours.

By 1926, Dzerzhinsky was not only the dreaded chief of the O.G.P.U. but also the head of the Supreme Council of Economy, in which capacity he was my immediate superior, having replaced Ryckov.

As I opened the door leading into Dzerzhinsky's private office, I beheld, behind a large desk, the already familiar figure of the Russian Torquemada. The desk was placed so that everyone entering the room came face to face with Dzerzhinsky. On seeing me, he rose and took a few steps forward to meet me, although the room was really too small for this courtesy. He stretched out his hand, and I shook it. As on my first meeting with him in his apartment years back, I was again impressed by his nervous yet soft movements. But his face seemed duller now, and the eyes were more deeply sunk. His forehead looked higher, his hair unkempt and perhaps scantier than before. He was dressed in a khaki suit of a semimilitary cut. His boots were high, of a kind worn by Russian army officers.

"Do you remember me, Felix Edmundovich?" I began. "I didn't deceive you, did I, when you trusted me despite the suggestions you heard from some of your advisers? The only difference is that on that first occasion I came to you with Lenin's support, and now I am practically alone in this fight. How can I prove that whatever I did four or five years ago, now charged against me as an offense and a crime, was done for the good of the Soviet republic? How can I show that my only thought has always been Soviet welfare? I worked as a Red merchant and on occasion I may have erred, but if those deeds of mine be errors, should I be punished for them four or five years later?"

Dzerzhinsky's piercing eyes were on me for a few seconds. He said: "It is because I believe you that I am instructing you to leave the Soviet Union within twenty-four hours."

It was a fact that, since the Supreme Council of Economy had taken Dzerzhinsky as its new chief, the O.G.P.U. had somewhat changed its attitude toward the non-Communists working under that council. Even those experts who had earlier been listed as suspicious characters were now given clean bills

194

of health—so long as Dzerzhinsky himself considered them indispensable to the council.

"I know," I replied to Dzerzhinsky, "that I am needed now, that someone, somewhere, somehow deems it imperative to use my services abroad. But if there is still suspicion of me, frankly, I won't be able to work well in such an atmosphere."

Hardly had I completed this sentence when I noticed an expression of irritation on Dzerzhinsky's face. He quickly shot back at me: "There are no indispensable ones to the Soviets. Not individuals, but masses, are creating our revolution. We stride forward even if Lenin is no longer with us. I suggest that you leave tomorrow evening."

"But please understand," I argued stubbornly, "that unless I am reassured I cannot, I will not be able to, work abroad for the Soviet Union with all the peace of mind I need. I want a reassurance that these serious charges are no longer pending against me."

Before Dzerzhinsky could say anything to this, I added in a low voice, with considerable embarrassment: "I fear for myself, for my own decision. I may not return to Soviet Russia after all the sufferings I have recently undergone here."

Dzerzhinsky sat back, stared at me, and delivered a little speech.

"Comrade Liberman," he said, "you don't really mean it. If you had meant it, you wouldn't have said it to me the way you did. Not to me! You forget that our state, our power, is one of workers and peasants. As such, the regime has the right to control its specialists. This government of workers and peasants will not harm you so long as you honestly serve it. Mistakes do happen, of course. Don't forget that this is the epoch of a great revolution! Your work has for its arena a Soviet outpost abroad, surrounded on all sides by the capitalists of Europe! Now, don't forget, you are leaving on the very first train tomorrow evening. In the meantime, the Workers and Peasants Inspection will consider your case—the charges against you, whatever they are. This will be done in two or three days, and you will hear the decision even before you reach your destination."

"But suppose the decision goes against me?" I asked.

"That would mean that I have made an error!" Dzerzhinsky replied. "Bon voyage!"

Next I visited Roiseman, to tell him exactly the same thing. Roiseman listened carefully, and said: "I must get in touch with the O.G.P.U. and with Dzerzhinsky."

A few hours later he gave me the same answer that Dzerzhinsky had: "Your case will be considered, but you must not wait here in Moscow for the final decision. Too much depends on your trip—we have this problem of timber markets and prices on our hands. You must go at once."

I was to leave the next day, at eight o'clock in the evening. I spent that day in a feverish state of mind. At times the idea crossed my mind that the O.G.P.U. was like a gigantic malicious cat playing with a mouse—that it was all a cruel game on its part and that I would be arrested at the very last moment, at the station or at the border. I thought of this even as I was handed my Soviet passport, visaed properly for a trip abroad.

But nothing at all happened to me. I was allowed to board the train, and although I continually expected the hand of fate to reach out and clutch me, we sped onward—and across the border!

I arrived in Berlin safely and stopped at the Esplanade. A few days later a telegram was handed me. It was from Moscow:

"Having considered Comrade Roiseman's report of the results obtained in an investigation of Comrade Liberman's activities, the Central Control Commission resolved: (1) To express complete confidence in Comrade Liberman. (2) To request his continued services."

(Signed) Chairman of the Central Control Commission
Solts

I was overwhelmed. The complete reversal of the situation left me dazed. And suddenly something snapped in me—something went dead inside me. Then and there I felt for the first time that I would never again return to Russia as a civil servant.

This feeling did not force me to cease my work for the Soviets at once. I had carried on this work for too many years to drop it abruptly. Besides, there was the particular mission I had accepted before leaving Moscow. My task was to go to Copenhagen, there to join a large Soviet delegation and begin the negotiations with the Scandinavians. I journeyed to Denmark.

The Angleterre, one of Copenhagen's best hotels, was the headquarters of the Russian delegates. Most of them were simple workers representing the Soviet Wood Workers Union, and not a single one knew a single foreign tongue. It was one of my duties to guide them safely around the Danish capital and interpret everything during the negotiations with the Swedes. Once, when I left them for a while, they did get into trouble, and it was obvious that I was essential to the mission.

The conference finally turned out to be a success. The Russian and Swedish delegates agreed on a program of timber quotas and prices to be used on the British and other markets. It was clearly a triumph.

From Copenhagen I went to Paris, to visit my family, then living in the French capital. I was glad I had carried out my duty as if nothing had happened.

It was in Paris that I felt a sharp psychological reaction. For the first time in months I had a chance to relax. Now all the tribulations of my two months' stay in Moscow came back to me in my relaxed and weakened condition, to plague me as a memory—as a series of nightmares. Finally, irrevocably, I felt that never again would I be able to serve the Soviets. I decided for good and all to quit. The decision itself upset me completely.

I was nervous. I was afraid that agents of the O.G.P.U. were shadowing me. I was on the verge of succumbing to a persecution mania. I went to see several doctors; they packed me off to a sanatorium in Switzerland.

For about six weeks I remained there, in very bad shape, at first. Even the sound of the postman's steps on the gravel path leading to the sanatorium made my heart thump wildly. Then the physician in charge transferred me to a room away from all outside sounds. I was totally isolated, except for those who brought me food and medicine or took me out for brief walks in the quiet of the garden. I was improving. Soon my mail was brought to me again.

Among others, there were letters from Russia. They urged me to return to the service of the Soviets, not necessarily in the timber industry if I no longer wished to be in that field. It was suggested that I accept the post of a Soviet bank director in Paris. If that was not tempting enough, I was to name my own field and position in the Soviet service abroad. The only condition was that each year I was to spend at least three months in Russia.

One such letter was from Moisei Frumkin, deputy commissar of foreign trade. It read:

"All your friends, among them I, cannot even imagine that you may not want to continue your work in the construction of the Soviet Union. I am writing this letter with the knowledge of our leaders. We are all awaiting your early return."

The leaders of whom he spoke were three at that time: Stalin, Zinoviev, and Kamenev.

Later, a somewhat similar letter came from Yakovlev, the chairman of the Central Timber Committee and in the past a notorious Chekist who boasted that during the days of terror in Odessa he had sentenced his own father to death and that the sentence was duly carried out. Yakovlev's letter was brought to me by Por, who by this time was occupying my old post, in charge of foreign sales of Soviet timber.

Each such letter tended to upset me but did not change my decision. I knew that I could not, should not, be tempted by these persuasive words from Moscow. I knew that never again would I be able to serve the Soviets with all the zeal of which I had been capable prior to my last and awful experience in Moscow. If I should yield to these sweet messages and return to their service, it would be with a lie in my heart and on my lips. I could not do it. And so I quit the Soviets and remained abroad.

Before taking this final step, I resolved to see my old friend Christian Rakovsky. By the end of six weeks in the Swiss sanatorium I had recovered

197

enough to be dismissed. I returned to Paris, and there I sought out Rakovsky, who was then the Soviet ambassador in France.

In part my troubles were already known to him. Now, sympathetically, he listened to my detailed story. When I finished, he said:

"Of course, it's a pity we have to lose such people as you. But I don't see how you can possibly make any other decision. Until Lenin's death, his support was your main prop—your fortune's smile. Now it's difficult for you to fight on, all alone as you are, practically speaking. No, I don't blame you for not wanting to return."

At last I was ready to write my official answer. I addressed it to Frumkin, with copies to the Central Committee of the Communist party and the Supreme Council of Economy. This is approximately what I wrote:

"I have never been a member of the Communist party. I worked all those years for the Soviets as a nonparty specialist. I believed in my work; I put into it all my abilities and strength. I gave the Soviet government eight years of my life as one of the 2,000,000 Soviet employees who were, so to speak, called to the colors to do the job. Permit me from now on to be one of the nonprivileged 170,000,000 Soviet citizens.

"The timber industry of the nation is in good order now and can work well. The capitalist countries have the custom of pinning orders and other medals upon the lapels of those citizens who serve them ably. My only reward is the satisfaction of not having been seized by the Cheka.

"I assure you that, though quitting you, I will never fight against you. And I still hope that some day new conditions may allow me to return to work for the Soviets."

Thus ended my active work in reconstructing the Soviet economy. My head was still high when I reflected that, after eight years of service, I was leaving the lumber exports of a reduced Russian national territory as great as they had been in prerevolutionary times.

To my great satisfaction the organization which I planned and helped create was not scrapped after I left, but, on the contrary, expanded and further improved. Thus the opposition of the Cheka was not due to disapproval of my work but was directed against me personally, as an outsider, a non-Communist. A dictatorship, alas! does not really accept such outsiders, though it may use them; and, as the top party leaders could never regard me as one of them, they had to drop me when my use was ended and one of theirs could replace me.

EPILOGUE

THEN AND NOW

WHEN FROM A DISTANCE OF TWO DECADES I LOOK BACK ON WHAT I SAW DURING my eight years of living and working with the Soviets, I think I see clearly those underlying principles of the revolutionary regime which foretold the further development of the U.S.S.R. and brought that country to its present status.

This question is often asked: How is it possible that, despite the iron dictatorship of the Soviet government, the people of the Soviet Union have not only regained their former status as a great nation but have become stronger and more unified, both materially and morally, than ever before—so unified, in fact, that they were able to defend their homeland brilliantly through the cruelest ordeal in all its history?

In order to understand the Russia of today, one must recall certain aspects of her revolution which continue to play an important role to this day. The Bolsheviks came to power, and have kept that power, for a number of historical reasons. One was the absence, at the time, of other organized forces in the land daring enough to let the revolution loose, to carry its drives to their logical conclusion. As Trotsky on one occasion said, when a people, suffering under the yoke of a dying regime and wishing to get rid of that yoke by means of a revolution, meets a revolutionary party which deeply believes in such a revolution, why, there you have all the conditions necessary to bring about a revolution!

Long before 1917 the decomposition of the old tsarist regime had gone so far, the hatred and scorn for that regime among all classes of the populace had grown so strong and bitter, that with the overthrow of the Romanovs the entire sociopolitical structure of the tsarist state went to pieces. When the Bolsheviks nationalized the land, the numerically small nobility lost its only source of political power. The industrial bourgeoisie was also small in numbers and weak in influence and, as a group, lacked that governmental experience and habit of political self-confidence which were the distinguishing marks of its counterpart in the West, the industrial bourgeoisie of the rest of Europe. During the upheavals of 1917–18, these native tycoons proved to be weaklings, totally unprepared to face the revolution in any way whatsoever. It is true that somewhat later, in 1919–21, the bourgeoisie, together with a part of the nobility and certain elements of the intelligentsia, did try to rally against the Soviet revolution and did start a civil war. But in the process of this struggle these groups suffered from a lack of clarity in their ideology, the feeble state of their will to fight, and the total absence of roots in the masses of people—the masses ripe for revolution. The civil war only caused an intensification of the class

199

hatred. As a result, there was a wholesale physical annihilation of the men and women of the old regime. By 1921 the nobility and the upper bourgeoisie—also, in part, the middle bourgeoisie—were liquidated as a class.

But what of the radical and liberal intellectuals? They favored the revolution, of course. Yet in their tactical approach they held fast to the mistaken premise that the revolution should be headed and guided by the bourgeoisie. The fallacy of such a belief had already been amply proved by history. They should have known, but they did not, that by insisting stubbornly on such a flimsy theory they were actually dooming themselves to a most thorough defeat.

Besides, the camp of the intellectuals was badly divided, which further enfeebled and puzzled this group. Russia's socialists of the non-Bolshevik variety feared to take over. They wished to be revolutionary leaders without staining their impeccable gloves. They dreamed idealistic dreams. In short, they failed to place themselves at the head of the popular forces, which, at this juncture of history, longed above all for a firm leadership to take them onward to well-defined ends.

However, certain of these intellectuals soon entered the service of the Bolsheviks. They realized that the new government, no matter how bad, was nevertheless a government of the people and for the people. Others declared themselves neutral and decided to wait—"to sit this one out." Still others discarded their white collars and donned shabby clothes, to become a part of the people. But they did not do this in the idealistic, self-sacrificing way of the penitent nobles and other Russian intellectuals of the 1870's. No, in spirit these men of 1918 and succeeding years were not at all populists. Theirs was a protective coloration. They wanted to survive, to escape famine and death. Losing themselves among the workers and the peasants of the new Russia, dressing and working and living as the masses did, was one of the surest methods of survival. Many of them, while dressing and living like the masses, avoided physical labor; they found petty clerical jobs in the new Bolshevik administration, they accepted positions in the new libraries and schools and theater organizations. By 1924-25 these intellectuals had become flesh and blood of the new life, had made their peace with the Soviet government.

The Bolsheviks, seizing power in the fall of 1917, argued that the workers and the peasants—the majority of the Russian people—constituted the main driving force of the revolution. The Bolsheviks proclaimed themselves to be the leaders of this majority. In truth, they demonstrated their own daring and decisiveness. Having now assigned definite tasks to the revolution, they were firmly and unswervingly leading the people toward the realization of these aims.

The foundation of the new regime was strengthened through a political education of the masses. All toilers were made into class-conscious and active builders of the Soviet nation. Such was the policy of the Soviet government from the very beginning. You can see it as the most distinct thread in the entire fabric of the Soviet revolution, at all stages of its momentous weaving.

To reinforce the dictatorship of the proletariat, to draw the masses of the people into this work of creating new forms of life, Lenin wanted the workers and the peasants to participate in the stern business of controlling the state apparatus itself. One of the aims of such control by the masses was to improve the administration of the new state—to combat its growing bureaucratization.

The first important steps in this direction were made in 1919 when Lenin and Stalin pondered the main principles and practices of such workers' and peasants' control—ways to compensate for the lack of democratic parliamentary representation. In January, 1920, writing to Stalin on this subject, Lenin stressed among other things the necessity of attracting into the controlling bodies non-Communist workers and peasants, as well as those belonging to the party. In 1923, shortly before his death, Lenin wrote and published two articles in which he emphasized the role to be allotted to the peasants, as well as to the workers, in the actual construction and control of the administrative apparatus of the country.

The economists and engineers and other experts in the service of the Soviets were extremely irritated by this persistent effort on the part of the Communist bosses to bring into the state apparatus "all those plowmen and cooks." The specialists said: "This is not meant in earnest. It's only a bone being thrown to the mob by the Soviet government—an alibi for its dictatorship."

But, in reality, this method of bringing the masses into the business of the state led eventually to that "social participation" which permitted such true democrats as Sydney and Beatrice Webb to regard Soviet Russia as a democracy despite the dictatorial system of the political administration.

In one of his articles published in 1923, during the era of the New Economic Policy, Lenin, discussing the reorganization of the Workers and Peasants Inspection, wrote:

"The social structure of our Soviet Republic is based on the collaboration of two classes: the workers and the peasants. To this we now add, on certain limited terms, the *Nepmen*—that is the bourgeoisie of the New Economic Policy. Should there arise serious class antagonisms between our two main classes, a split is inevitable. However, our social structure does not have in its foundation any fissures leading inevitably to such antagonisms. Our main task is to watch carefully the circumstances that may lead to such fissures. We must prevent them. For, in the final analysis, the fate of our republic will depend on whether the mass of our peasantry continues its collaboration with the working class, preserving its fealty to the union with the workers, or allows the Nepmen, the new bourgeoisie, a chance to split it from the workers."

Lenin never recognized coequal rights for the workers and the peasants of Soviet Russia. He held that the workers, being more class conscious, had to be the guardians of the peasants; in their turn, the workers had the Communist party as their guardian; and the Communist party was to be guided by its central organ—the Politbureau. It was within this singular framework that the masses of Russia's populace were to be drawn into the job of administering the country, that their political consciousness was to be further developed.

The complexity of the situation in Russia, according to Lenin, was caused by the numerical predominance of the peasantry, with their typical petty-bourgeois psychology, over the workers, who were the active element of the revolution. Still and all, the Soviet government was to be one of the peasants, as well as of the workers. Lenin said and wrote that the working class, having assumed leadership in the country, should always bear in mind 'the peculiar social position of the peasantry and should not allow it to be unjustly exploited, even for the sake of strengthening the socialist (or workers') sector of the population. On the contrary, Lenin urged, the peasantry must be made aware of the positive features of the new regime. One way to do this was to bring its members, even those not belonging to the Communist party, even those markedly inert and indifferent, into the field of controls which the Soviets established over their own business of governing.

All these facts help to clarify the essential difference between the Soviet dictatorship and any other political dictatorship. Although as stern as any other, the Soviet dictatorship is different because it is not an end in itself but only a means of reaching the true goal—the greatest good of the greatest number of people, provided they were not opposed to the revolution. Lenin set certain theoretical limits to the Soviet dictatorship. When those limits were exceeded in the very process of the state's administration, the transgression was scored as "an inefficiency and a defect in the state apparatus itself."

I recall the silhouettes, the figures of the makers of the Russian revolution as I knew them in everyday contact with them, against the background of their tense work—and inevitably I compare them with the leaders of the great French Revolution of the eighteenth century. Robespierre's personality comes to mind—the man who gave the world the theory of liberty, equality, and fraternity while his practice often violated those basic principles of democracy.

It is not my purpose to discuss here the role of an individual in history. Suffice it to say that I do not believe that the march of events of this or that period is governed by the skill or failures of the era's leaders. We, in particular, live at a time when human masses are far more important and effective than human individuals, no matter how significant in themselves certain individuals happen to be. Not in vain, following World War I, were monuments erected to "unknown soldiers" rather than to outstanding commanders. And yet, even while we recognize the premise of the inevitability of certain historical trends, while we rightly view the masses as the decisive factor behind each event, there is one additional element that we cannot negate.

This element is the alternative that is always available at any juncture—or junction, crossroads—of history. When there is a leader on the spot, with a wisdom and a will all his own, these precious qualities inevitably prevail over a lack of will, over indecisiveness. Such a leader or leaders can appraise the political moment correctly and act quickly, giving to a spontaneous movement of the masses the direction it sorely needs. The historic significance of the Bolsheviks was precisely in their presence of mind and will, in the daring with which they seized the power and the destiny of the nation, outrode the storm, and guided the revolution to its logical conclusion. Nevertheless, while leading the Russian nation to these goals, the Communists considered themselves no more than spokesmen of the people's will (the only possible spokesmen) and acted accordingly—this despite the all-too-evident dictatorial nature of their government.

I remember the spring months of 1918 in Moscow. The situation was paradoxical. The opposition to Bolshevism on the right, from the liberal and democratic parties, was becoming less and less active. The population of Moscow, particularly the intelligentsia, showed signs of restlessness and dissatisfaction with the new government but few signs of any ability or readiness to fight the Bolsheviks. Yet a new force was arising at the other pole of the Russian sphere—at the extreme left. This was the party of the Russian Anarchists.

They considered the government of Lenin nothing more than a regime of usurpers. They felt it was possible and even necessary to fight the Bolsheviks— with arms, ruthlessly. The Anarchists were not numerous but furious. They held meetings, gathered weapons, seized villas for their headquarters. In brief, they were using the same methods by which the Russian Communists had come to power only a few months before.

But see the interesting transformation of Lenin's Communist party into a "pillar of order"! Just as a few short months earlier the bourgeois had been indignant over the excesses of the Bolsheviks, so now, in the spring of 1918, the Bolsheviks were enraged by the similar action of the Anarchists. The Cheka kept careful tab on the gatherings and plans of the Anarchists. All Bolshevik leaders frowned and decreed that it was "high time to liquidate these Anarchist bands, in one good blood bath." I heard such remarks from them as I discussed routine matters of economics with Larin and other leaders.

The alarm grew throughout Moscow. One evening I was walking home, past the villas recently seized by the Anarchists. I saw Anarchist flags flapping in the spring breeze over these mansions, I saw Anarchist soldiers in clusters in front of these houses and heard their remarks: "Tomorrow all Moscow will be ours!" As I heard them, I was surprised at my own subconscious reaction. I felt that something should be done to stop the Anarchists, to maintain order and prevent chaos, even if the Communists were to become indeed the guardians of our order.

Along the streets marched battalions of Lettish Rifles, the very first armed units of the Red Army then in formation. Their task was to preserve order. Would they prove to be stronger than the Anarchist?

I entered my room, which was a large second-story chamber in a government-owned building, with windows facing a corner of the Arbat Plaza. The streets were full of noise and excitement. For a long time I lay on my bed fully dressed, listening to the incessant sounds of soldier's boots below. At two in the morning I was awakened by a machine gun's chatter. Military commands were shouted. Soon artillery boomed somewhere near by. A shell burst in the plaza below, and the impact of the explosion threw me to the floor. When I tried to rise, I noticed that there was the sky with its stars above me instead of the corner wall and the ceiling—which had been shot off by the shell! I thought: "This must be the Anarchist attack on government buildings."

It was, instead, the Bolshevik artillery in action, shelling the mansions seized by the Anarchists and, accidentally, some of its own. Within a few weeks the Anarchists were completely crushed.

But the Anarchists in themselves alone had not been a danger. The menace was in what they might have become to the masses. The people's strength, awakened by the revolution, might have been thrown to the Anarchists, against the new law and order developing out of the revolution. For the peasants and the soldiers of Russia would not at first obey the new discipline, even though it was demanded in the name of the revolution. They were already showing signs of approving the lawlessness and other alluring promises of the Anarchists. The peasants especially might have turned away from the Bolsheviks, toward the Anarchists. Lenin later appraised the episode in these few words: "This petit-bourgeois counterrevolution was really more dangerous than Denikin, Yudenich, and Kolchak put together, for in our country the proletariat is in a minority." Hence the energetic action of the government of Lenin to suppress the Anarchists early and thoroughly.

Lenin understood this situation and its implications better than anyone else. In him were intertwined all the ingredients necessary to mold a leader: wisdom, will, character. He once said:

"If I, for the greatest good of the greatest possible number of people, subordinate the masses to my will, I am right. For I do not do this for my own selfish interests. I do this for the greatest good of the greatest possible number of people."

And Gorki once said that Lenin had told him: "Do you think I would stay here one minute if I did not think I was doing good?"

This is the key to his political tactics—to his entire party line, set once and forever. Lenin was a monolithic personality in matters concerned with the revolution. He believed that history had chosen him to create a new Russia in accordance with the theories of Marx and Engels. No second thoughts, no doubts, bothered him as he strode forward to this goal. To reach this goal, all means were good. He was convinced that all the healthy elements of his country agreed with him and followed him. That is why, I think, his conscience was clear and his heart unburdened as he filled the jails of Russia with those who dared to criticize the new order.

And in this, perhaps, lies the fundamental difference between Lenin and Stalin. The former persecuted his enemies as critics of the basic principles of the Communist regime; whereas the latter tends to see a traitor in everyone who opposes him personally, who opposes Stalin as Stalin. For to Stalin, Stalin is the very personification of the new regime, and therefore Stalin is no mere man. Here we can see the true explanation of Stalin's curious behavior at public functions when the audience rises to applaud Stalin—and Stalin joins in the applause. For you are to understand (or he wants you to understand) that he applauds not himself as a human being but himself as the supreme symbol of the Soviet state.

Nevertheless, history will also recognize a similarity in the respective attitudes of Lenin and Stalin toward their own roles in the building and running of the Soviet state. This similarity is the belief of each man in his own mission. This belief provided self-justification for both Lenin and Stalin, each in his own time and his own fashion, for changing his tactics constantly—making sharp jumps over political and economic fences hither and yon, confronting the world with sudden surprises, which, however, each always alibied with a proper quotation from Marx.

Much has been said and written about the implacability, fanaticism, and cruelty of the Bolshevik leaders, ruthlessly sweeping all obstructions from their path. But much less attention has been given to the motives underlying their actions and to the real nature of their tactics. Let us consider these for a moment.

Far be it from me to justify the cruelty and the historic injustice committed by the party leaders of today toward some of the old comrades of yesterday—toward the junior eagles of Lenin's nest. Many of the victims of those purges of the 1930's were personal acquaintances of mine. For many years in the past I had been in close touch with them, and I knew them then as sincere revolutionaries devoid of any selfishness. It is true that some of them did not do well by me in 1925, did not stand by me when the O.G.P.U. was after me and I desperately needed their help. Still, even now, I cannot for a single moment believe that they sold themselves to Russia's enemies for those thirty silver pieces or any other price that figured in the purge trials. My explanation of those "confessions" is this: Any revolution has its own laws. One of the most savage among these laws is that the revolution devours its own children.

And yet these Moscow trials were also unfortunate for the Russia of today because they fostered in the minds of many hostile observers the impression that, if one Soviet leader could be bought for 150,000 marks, any one of them might be bought at a certain price, which is just as absurd and unbelievable as the charge which sent those defendants of the Moscow trials to their doom.

Speaking of the tactics of the Bolsheviks, it is imperative to emphasize at all times that from the very beginning of the Soviet state its leaders showed a marked elasticity, an ability to maneuver this way and that. These men of the revolution knew quite a bit about evolution—when evolution was in order. Those who (even if led by sincere beliefs) would not accept this evolution had to be exterminated.

Lenin's main idea was that, although you cannot really create a revolution, you can seize upon a situation fraught with revolution and deepen and expand it. Russia, having in March, 1917, liquidated her autocracy, was in the "bourgeois phase" of her revolution. The Bolsheviks were not content with this. They saw potentialities in this bourgeois revolution. They wanted to let loose these potentialities, transforming the political revolution into a social upheaval. They went to work at it with a will.

Having grabbed power, the Bolsheviks soon realized that this transition from the political to the social phase of the revolution presented enormous difficulties. Their progress toward their social revolution and its aims could not be along a straight line. Zigzags and even retreats were inescapable. But these were always excused and even sanctified by that final aim—the perfect socialist state at the end of the bloody rainbow.

In the economic field, for instance, the Soviet leaders have labored long and strenuously as they progressed from abstract principles to life's reality (although Lenin stated that the revolution itself was a miracle and that his aim was to inflame the sky). They groped; they learned by trial and error. They committed numerous absurdities and lapsed into excesses of the kind Larin perpetrated, to give but one example. But gradually they left their excesses behind and conquered the chaos of the first years of the revolution.

Many observers outside the Soviet Union regard the Bolsheviks even now as theorists and fanatics. These observers forget that a quarter-century's experience in administering a state of 180,000,000–200,000,000 people cannot fail to have its effect. The Bolsheviks used to be utopians, but meeting life head-on transformed many of them into practical, business-like, realistic administrators of the type that run the Soviet republic at present. Those who could not adjust themselves to this process of transformation were cruelly dumped overboard.

From the very onset of their reign, the Bolsheviks made use of a method which recently has been employed in a remarkable way in warfare. Long before Hitler, the Communists of Russia understood that in politics, too, the warfare of positions is a thing of the past, that a political campaign should be conducted along the fluid lines of movement and diversion, and that the task of the attacker is to break through deep into the rear of the foe, there to seize at once the best strategic points possible.

Only Lenin could summon enough daring to abolish the Constituent Assembly, an institution which to Russian intellectuals seemed the essence of the revolution. But Lenin did away with the assembly precisely for the sake of this revolution. Lenin's step was viewed by many as one that opened the gate to the forces of the counterrevolution. But he was not afraid. He believed too strongly in the forces of the revolution to fear a triumph of the reactionary elements through this or any other act of his.

In Lenin's time the Kremlin, with the young Soviet government in it, resembled a besieged fortress, wherein Lenin, the revolutionary strategist, was busily and calmly working out his tactical plans. Lenin taught his followers that at any given historical moment they must learn to distinguish the decisive factor in the march of events. As a tool wherewith to use what he thought was the basic principle of the early Soviet phase, Lenin created the Third International. His main aim was to break through into the deep rear of his foe with the help of the Third International. Lenin also had some such ideas in the back of his mind when in 1922 he initiated the Treaty of Rapallo between the Soviets and Germany, in spite of the general wonder as to what reciprocal good could come out of a pact between a poverty-stricken Russia and a similarly impoverished Reich. For the same reasons—to find a strategic spot in the chain around Russia and effect a break-through of his enemy's positions— Lenin inaugurated his policy of concessions. This he did despite the opposition of the Soviet labor unions which, because they did not understand that these concessions were only a means of sowing disunity in the capitalistic camp, considered them a betrayal of Communism. Characteristically, Lenin sometimes used military terminology when speaking of his political maneuvers on the international stage. Of his plans to give Kamchatka as a concession to Americans, he said: "This is a deep-reaching diversion in the rear of our foes."

The basic aim of a given era always dominated all the compromises and zigzags of the Bolsheviks' foreign policy. Every pact with a bourgeois state; the latter-day participation of the Soviet Union in the League of Nations; the *rapprochement* between the Moscow government and this or that foreign power, whether democratic or dictatorial; every diplomatic step, up to and including the Soviet-Nazi pact of 1939—all were part of a "war of maneuvers," a series of diversions and other tactical movements dictated by "realism," which for many sincere liberals doubtless often bordered on sheer cynicism.

The flexibility and opportunism of this policy can, in the long run, be explained by the ability of the Communists to adapt themselves to changing circumstances; also by their profound conviction that all means are good that reach out toward the set goals—the goals dictated by the interests of the revolution.

The same elasticity distinguished the Soviet regime's domestic policy. Not for long did the Bolsheviks remain in their orthodox positions of 1918. They changed with every year; they traveled away from the purely theoretical, implacable premises of the party doctrine. Yet the Communist leaders doubtless remained true to the main principles of the party. Furthermore, they preserved the old terminology as they justified each zigzag of their so-called "general line" with referencs to Marx and Lenin. But in actual practice they compromised with life and so lived through a tremendous political and socioeconomic evolution of a kind that the Communist revolutionaries of 1917 had not even dreamed of. Still, it would be an error to attribute this evolution to any

207

lack of principles in these Bolsheviks or to a reluctant, humiliating surrender. In reality, the Bolshevik leaders of 1945 are true disciples of Lenin.

Quite often we hear that the evolution of the Communists is a recent phenomenon, which has come about almost entirely through the influence and guidance of Stalin. This is not so. From the very beginning of its existence, the Communist Kremlin made concessions to life. The truth is that the social revolution of Karl Marx's vision was buried by Lenin at the time of the New Economic Policy, in the early 1920's. That is why Lenin attacked so ferociously all those who, in those interesting times, dared to call a spade a spade. But even earlier, in the era of the civil war, the true Marxist theory was violated when the Bolsheviks called for a union of the peasants and the workers against the remainder of the bourgeoisie. Later the Bolsheviks tried to form themselves into a bloc of workers and poor peasants against the richer peasants or the *kulaki*. This phase was followed by the breathing-spell of the New Economic Policy, which to a certain degree gave opportunity to private economic initiative in the countryside as well as in the city. Thus the *seredniak* peasant raised his head boldly—the middle-class muzhik who was neither too rich nor too poor. The Soviet government used him to clamp down on the poor peasant, who had by then became obstreperous and obnoxious. And this, too, went against the genuine Marxist dogma. Yet Lenin openly stated that the Marxist theory was not a dogma for the Communists but a tool for shaping the revolution in accordance with life's exigencies.

The next stage of Soviet development was the fight for collective farming. This was Stalin's attempt to rescue from stagnation the "socialist sector" of the nation's economy—its heavy industries—at the expense of the peasantry. Lenin used to warn against this step, but Stalin, under changed circumstances, took up the challenge as the only way to rescue the "socialist sector." In this policy the Red regime sought its support among the working class, the Red Army, and that part of the peasantry which had accepted the new order in its entirety and sympathized fully with the idea of collectivization as the only way to save the Soviet system.

This period was that of the triumph of the idea of "socialism in one country." The Soviet government no longer banked on a world revolution. In the era of Russia's industrialization, the Soviet government found its most active support among the specialists, the new intellectuals of lower-class and toiling origin, the skilled workers, and the body of Soviet officials and clerks which had been formed in the years 1925–29.

Yet later, Stalin openly declared that his chief hope of support was in the so-called "non-partisan Bolsheviks." Having scattered or annihilated the old Communist guard, having strangled the opposition threatening him from the left as well as from the right of the party, he actually based himself on Russia's youth. And this youth, having never known the old regime, having been reared in the atmosphere of revolutionary times, came from the depths of the working and peasant classes and sincerely considered itself the owner of the young, rich, and fast-developing country.

It is noteworthy, though, that throughout all the changes of its policy the Soviet government strove to widen its base, to find new followers in the great masses of the population. It is here, perhaps, that we see the fundamental paradox of the nature of the Soviet power, the paradox baffling so many observers and the cause of endless arguments. By its nature and methods Bolshevism is, of course, a dictatorship. It cannot be fitted into the framework of a democracy the way democracy is generally understood. On the other hand, this dictatorship is different from other dictatorships. It seeks support in the masses. It bases itself on wide strata of these masses. It acts, not only in the name of the masses, but also for their good.

In other totalitarian states a dictatorship is an aim in itself, the crown of the entire state; it finds its expression in one person—the leader. But according to Lenin's teachings, a dictatorship is a temporary evil marking a period of transition, an evil necessary to safeguard the interests of the toiling masses until such time as the new regime of people's power takes definite forms and becomes strong enough to deal with its foes both at home and abroad.

These days we often regret that one of the most ideally conceived of all democracies—the Weimar Republic of Germany—was not strengthened (even by extraordinary measures) against the onslaught of the reactionaries which finally led to the Nazi catastrophe. Many sincere democrats, as they now face the Weeping Wall, admit that the German people were not ready to accept and defend this democracy. They admit that some special force or other was needed in Germany during that period. And that force perhaps should have been a temporary "dictatorship"—to make the democracy of Germany steadier on its feet than it proved to be, better fitted for the battle against the domestic reactionaries than it was.

Is there anyone who would dare to assert that the Russian people would have been as ready as they were to defend their new life and social conquest if there had not been that temporary dictatorship, busily occupied in improving the economic and cultural situation of the masses and in building up a people's army? And in the absence of this Russian link, where would the world of democracy be now? How confused are certain superficial observers of Russia, who try to compare the economic achievements of this temporary dictatorship with Western standards, forgetting that three-quarters of Russia is Asiatic and that improvements can be gauged only by comparison with the prerevolutionary situation of the mass of the people! Often the judgment of these observers is warped by their point of departure. If they come from the East, Russia's achievements seem great compared to China or India. If they come from the West, they are shocked to find the Soviet people so much worse off than the workers of America.

In so far as the dictatorship, according to the Bolshevik concept, is but a temporary measure, we can afford to be optimistic. We can hope that the toiling masses of the U.S.S.R., having demonstrated during this war their political maturity and their close tie with the Soviet system, will take an ever growing part in their own political life. They will find a parallel in the experience of their ancestors, when the returning veterans of the Napoleonic Wars brought back many progressive and liberal ideas. It is possible that the leaders of the Soviet Union will understand the necessity of such an evolution of the Soviet regime. The first swallows of that spring seem to be appearing on the horizon even now.

The peculiarity of the Soviet system leads to constant confusion when experts try to define it. Whoever considers the bond between the Soviet government and the masses of the people as the most important factor is ready and willing to call this system a democracy. But whoever sees nothing but a dictatorship and the dominance of one political party indignantly denies the existence of any democracy in Russia and brands the Soviet order as the worst possible type of political tyranny.

Each of these two views takes into consideration only one facet of the Soviet reality. The entire reality of the U.S.S.R. is far more complex and many sided than the standard textbooks of civics and sociology make it appear. What we actually see in Soviet Russia is a social democracy within the limits of a political dictatorship.

At all times Moscow has acted in the name of the popular forces. With the help of such popular forces the Kremlin fought those groups or classes which it regarded as the foes of the Soviet order. The leaders in the Kremlin well knew that statesmen should follow the example of the dog, which runs ahead of its master but looks back continually to discover where to go. The men of the Kremlin have always looked back most carefully and thus have always been in touch with their people's needs and desires.

It is a mistake to say, as some observers do, that the masses of the Soviet Union are not allowed to have a will of their own. They had their will and their rights even in the worst, sternest period of the Soviet dictatorship. The very slogan proclaimed by Lenin in 1917—"All power to the Soviets!"— brought forth a new social democracy. It is true that this slogan was implemented in the name of the abstract idea of Communism. But, in fact, it did help to mold a tremendous amorphous mass into units—into cells and other organizations which gradually took as their charge the most elementary needs of the populace.

All these county and provincial committees, all these factory committees or "Committees of the Poor," so characteristic of the initial phase of the revolution, did prove to be forms of social democracy. To belong to a collective or to receive the help of a committee became for individuals the very necessity of life, the thing to do in order to survive. To obtain food, take a train ride, go to a doctor, attend a theater, or send a child to school, the Soviet citizen of that period had to have a certificate testifying to his membership in a collective or

210

a cell. It was natural for all men and women to seek such a membership in an organization recognized by the government. And we must note that in those days the leaders of such committees and cells were not appointed from above (as they were later on) but were elected by the entire membership. Of course, this new democracy often was not a matter of sincere belief. One's membership even in the Communist party was on occasion regarded not from the viewpoint of one's political faith but from the practical standpoint—of what actual good this membership brought a person in those difficult times.

People were hungry. People needed bread above everything else. And the social democracy of those numerous committees and cells revolved mainly around the stark problem of bread. Nevertheless, initiative and co-operation were learned by the people through those committees and cells. No longer did the masses look upon the government as something from God. No longer were they passive. The Kremlin, by hammering in the idea of a "government by workers and peasants," did teach the people that the state emanated from them—from the people. It did constantly demand from the people an active participation in the economic and social life of the country.

A besieged country (as Russia was after the revolution) was obliged for its own survival to accept and demand heavy sacrifices from its people, and particularly from the working classes that were the spearhead of the revolution. As such, it was necessary for them to take the lead in accepting these necessary, but obviously temporary, sacrifices, even if in so doing they drew on Russia the criticism of Western liberals, unaware that Russia then was too poor and ignorant to exploit quickly its own riches. At that point the Soviets could offer no comfort to their people except to remind them that if they were suffering it was in their own interest to pave the way to a better future life. It was the realization by the Russian workers and farmers that they were Russia itself that prompted them to accept even greater sacrifices during this war of survival. Russia's survival was their own.

At first, of course, all this social democracy was quite uncouth and often took ugly or comic forms, as could be expected from the low cultural level of the masses of the time. I have previously spoken of the "inventors," also of the interference of certain ignorant or unduly ambitious local organizations in the complicated business of running the timber industry. Instead of the old tsarist bureaucrats with their exterior polish, crude and shabby men headed the offices of the new state. In the industries, commanding posts were taken over by homespun mechanics and inexperienced youths, who were regarded with scorn by the old-time engineers and other long-established personnel.

In general, the first years of the revolution witnessed a shocking lowering of the cultural level of the governing personnel. Everywhere we saw managers and officials who were almost illiterate, newcomers from the depths of the aroused people. In all branches of life and endeavor, even in the arts, quantity replaced quality. It would take time before we could have a new and higher quality, based on a wider social foundation. And in the meanwhile these newcomers would even try to fight many of the attempts of their own central Soviet government to regulate them and their local organizations. Thus grew and developed this new social democracy, over the years raising the masses to their present high standard of feeling and effort—to their splendid stand against the Nazi invaders.

The civil war of those years threw Russia into a horrible chaos. But, at the same time, it drew hundreds of thousands of Russians into the active struggle for their homeland's survival and better future. The Russian civil war was a stern but valuable school, where parochially minded men learned to think on a nation-wide scale; acquired much military, economic, and administrative experience; and found out how to issue commands, as well as how to obey. The present-day marshals of the Red Army came from that school; so did many remarkable builders of Soviet economics.

One man, a certain Chubar, was a typical example of such a home-grown economist of the revolution. He was a simple Ukrainian worker by origin, elevated by the revolution to the management of all the heavy industries of Russia; then to a high post in the Supreme Council of Economy; and, finally, to the presidency of the Ukrainian Council of People's Commissars. I frankly admired him. I had tremendous respect for him as I watched him in action, issuing his orders. Any old-time high-salaried administrator of a large capitalistic enterprise could learn things from Chubar. He neither flattered the specialists working under him nor "picked" on them. All his remarks and instructions bore the stamp of his profound understanding of the problems he dealt with. He spoke calmly and in a business-like manner; and as you listened to him, you simply forgot the illiterate mixture of Russian and Ukrainian which was his customary lingo.

And how many big and little Chubars came to the fore in the endless expanse of Russia, thanks to the revolution! They displayed a typical peasant-like stubbornness as they mastered their new tasks. They were used to hard work. Also, they had the horse sense and the ingenuity peculiar to a simple but intelligent Russian of the people. Above all, they brought into their new work not only enthusiasm but also a fine understanding of the masses from which they came.

But when I talked to such men about general political problems, they looked at me significantly and said: "This is none of our business. Lenin solves such questions for us." They preferred to talk of the specific needs and cares of their own local offices and organizations and hardly ever of higher politics.

We must not forget that a revolution differs from a coup d'état—from a palace revolution—in that it elevates a new class to power. The Russian revolution meant the coming-to-power of workers and peasants representing 90 per cent of the population. The old was uprooted violently. The new bosses hated the bourgeois. Often they considered a man as belonging to the old regime merely because he wore a necktie or had certain cultured habits or was used to the elementary comforts of life. The revolution brought with it acts of crudeness, madness, and bloody ruthlessness; for the revolution was being made by people just emerging from the darkness of ages, people who were bitterly overflowing with a desire to avenge themselves for the yoke they had worn for centuries. Revenge and destruction were inevitable under such circumstances.

And that was why the status of the specialists was so unfortunate. We were just tolerated by these new bosses. They needed us, but we were a foreign body, and it was hard for us to adjust ourselves to the new life in Russia. This was felt with especial sharpness by those of us who, at the time of the revolution, were past forty. At such an age it is not easy to change. We were part of a generation doomed to die out, and I do not curse and condemn as I recall those harsh years. On the contrary, I am happy that I could give some of my strength to the building of that new Russia, which, despite all the death throes of the old regime, despite the chaos and ruin, was then a-borning.

In this connection I must mention again the part played in the initial phase of the Soviet regime by the moderate socialists and liberal intelligentsia, as well as by the old specialists.

Scan the lists of the Soviet technocracy of 1918 and the following few years, and what do you see? A preponderance of men of moderate socialist parties, occupying responsible economic posts alongside a number of prominent specialists of the old capitalistic world! It was Lenin who had first drawn them in. Doing this deliberately, Lenin had tried to convince his fellow-Communists that no danger threatened the Soviet power from these non-Communists, provided the latter abstained from politics while discharging their duties in Soviet service. Many important posts in the Supreme Council of Economy were filled by Mensheviks. True, within a few years most of them were arrested by the Cheka and its successor, the O.G.P.U. Nevertheless, the new regime did avail itself of the services of the remaining Russian intelligentsia.

At the same time, the Soviet government tackled a whole series of projects that had originally—and in vain—been offered to the tsarist government by wise Russian economists. When today we speak with admiration of certain farsighted and able measures of the Soviet regime—measures which reorganized Russia and prepared her to defend herself against the German invader—we must not forget that the initiative in many of these measures was that of the old specialists—the representatives of the now vanished intelligentsia of old Russia. The redivision of Russia into economic regions instead of the artificial political provinces of tsarist times; the decentralization of heavy industries, accompanied by much shifting of mills and factories away from vulnerable borders; the development of industries among certain nationalities of Russia—these were but a few of such projects. But these sweeping reforms could be carried out by no other power than that of the Soviets, the force that so cardinally altered the social structure of the nation and destroyed the resistance of private interests, which in the past had often stood in the way of these necessary changes.

The coming of a new class into power meant that the road was open to talent, no matter how humble its origin. The men and women of the masses could now reach out and obtain anything they wanted: education, any profession, any job, a part in the government. The masses, awakened by the revolution, evidenced energy, enthusiasm, a will to build on a large scale. It seemed at times as if they had rediscovered Russia, so tumultuous was their desire to create new cities, to bring to life the desolate fringes of the land, and to dig into the bowels of their earth for its natural riches. Their pioneering spirit was as courageous as that of the early builders of the United States of America.

I felt all this most acutely when I observed Soviet youth. The material welfare of a boy's or a girl's parents—or, rather, the lack of such welfare—no longer deprived the youngsters of the education they wanted. One's social origin and one's social behavior were the deciding factors. The local organizations of the new Soviet order, such as factory committees, labor unions, and Communist party cells, designated their candidates for higher schools. The youth of the Soviets knew that their personnel careers were bound up not with their own families, as was the case in tsarist times, but with various collectives. The tie with the family had by then been weakened. The youngster was aware of the fact that collectives were all-important and so, quite naturally, endeavored to keep up a steady contact with this or that collective, to earn and maintain the latter's attention and approval. The new generation also realized that somehow it had to pay for whatever favors and help it received from the state and its collective organizations. The privileges had to be well merited. Thus the feeling of social duty was developed in the young Soviet citizen.

The Soviet youth "gnawed the granite of study," as the Russian saying has it. The Soviet youth struggled onward, overcoming gigantic handicaps. Many of the boys and girls were illiterate peasants when they first resolved, or were picked by the collectives, to become engineers. They had to be taught their *ABC*'s first.

But as they climbed up the steep cliff of their schooling, these children from the dark Russian villages knew that they were advancing socially as well. They studied with a will and a conscience, and achieved remarkable results. I recall often being present at various discussions in factory clubs where purely technical problems were involved—say, the latest methods of sawmill work. Young workers, recent graduates of special courses in the field, would debate these problems with their experienced fathers—and frequently best them!

It was clear that Russia was rearing new cadres of skilled industrial workers in all fields. While Europe was puzzling over this or that zigzag of the Soviet policy, foreign or domestic, the entire land of the Soviets was aflame with the spirit of learning. A new generation of engineers, technicians, foremen, generals, physicians, and savants were being readied—the very same men and women who lived to show their brilliant skills and high moral mettle in the stirring, bloody days of Sevastopol and Stalingrad.

This new Soviet youth argued little or not at all about socialization or nationalization, for there was nothing for them to argue about. To them these doctrines were matters of plain fact. They were so used to socialization and nationalization that the argument was no argument to them. And, mark you, this matter-of-fact attitude of the young ones, this taking of Russia's socialization and nationalization for granted, could not fail to influence their parents, too—those who still survived. The oldsters came to be proud of the achievements of their sons and daughters.

I observed one example of such adaptation right in my own home. We had a maid, Masha, a woman of about forty, of peasant stock and almost illiterate. When our four-room apartment was divided into three dwellings, with two workers' families brought in as our cotenants, Masha was highly indignant and blamed the Communists and the Soviet regime. According to her, all evil stemmed from Lenin and Trotsky. But one day her young daughter came from the village to live in Moscow. In time the girl met a Red Army soldier who soon afterward was tapped for an officers' candidate school. The two got married. The bride learned to read and write, and the groom was soon an officer. Masha was delighted—think of it, she was an officer's mother-in-law! Each Sunday, proudly she went to visit the young pair at the Kremlin. Presently we heard from her that only because of the revolution—because of the Soviet government—could such happiness be possible for poor people like herself, her daughter, and her son-in-law. No more would she blame the Soviet regime for whatever troubles she was still witnessing. Instead, each time she derided the defunct tsarist government which had left to the Russian people various evils as their sad inheritance. She now regarded the Kremlin with the same awe she had formerly felt for her church. And of such Mashas there was, of course, a multitude.

The new generation also had a new attitude toward labor. That was surely its distinguishing feature. Not that all these young people were true Communists to a man; for many, Communism served as a convenient shell only. Each one, nevertheless, felt that he was working for the good of the nation, for the common cause—to build a new society. Out of this feeling came the Soviets' opportunity to demand a maximum effort from everybody. Out of this also came the chance to institute competition and mutual controls.

The Soviet leaders strenuously fostered this attitude toward work as something being done in a common cause. Their propaganda was spread not only by word, printed and oral, but also by personal example. Doubtless the tsarist regime, too, had known statesmen who regarded their jobs as selfless work in behalf of the nation; but such statesmen had been the exception rather than the rule. Under the Soviets, however, this personal sacrifice on the part of the leaders became the rule. No one could say that Lenin, for instance, craved power for reasons of self-enrichment or that Stalin exterminated his opponents so as to give himelf a life of luxury. The Bolshevik leaders had early managed to achieve a strict discipline and stark asceticism in their party. They were always sharply aware of their responsibility before the nation—before the masses of the people—to work hard and live simply.

State and society came first in the field of economics as well. This was something totally new. In tsarist times, although some statesmen had lived modestly because they felt they had to give all to the state, personal and class interests had reigned supreme in the realm of economics, where the principle of personal enrichment had been the basic driving force.

Of course, we find in the Soviet today certain manifestations of personal ambition, of vanity, of honors-chasing, of intrigues and struggles for top places. All such traits are human, and Soviet Russians are human, too. But these manifestations are not typical of the Soviet Union. The main thing to remember is this: Social positions, high salaries, privileges and rewards, and fame can be earned in Soviet Russia only if a person works hard as part of a collective, proving his worth to society, to the people, to the state. This new understanding of labor and its role in man's life permeates the entire psychology of the Soviet masses and exerts a tremendous influence upon their views and habits.

And this concept is closely bound up with the feeling that the Soviet masses have that they are really enjoying equality of opportunity. Anybody can get ahead by working in this common cause. The personal welfare of each citizen is directly dependent on the success or failure of this common work. The quantity of bread, the quality of consumers' goods, the conditions of everyday life, the conveniences and comforts of this life—everything depends on the personal efforts and labor of everyone in this new Soviet society.

This equality of opportunity means also equality of the sexes in Russia. Only those who lived in Russia during the first years of the revolution can truly assess the outstanding role played by women in the acceptance of the new government by the general run of the populace. For the Bolsheviks had early and wisely proclaimed their slogan of "Breaking the Woman's Chains." When Lenin declared that each cook, each simple housewife, should take a direct part in the building of the new state, it was not only an expression of the abstract idea of drawing the lower classes into the business of government but also a tactical maneuver on Lenin's part—a maneuver designed to win over the women of the country and so to widen the base of the new regime.

In giving the female all the rights enjoyed by the male of the species, especially in freeing the women of Asiatic Russia, the Bolsheviks indeed won many a staunch ally. Women were active and enthusiastic followers of the Soviet government almost from the very beginning of the revolution. The woman of Russia felt her new equality tangibly, and she felt it everywhere—in the factory, in the countryside, and, of course, in the bosom of her family. It is interesting to note that during the first years of the revolution it was the woman who ardently supported all sorts of committees and cells—for in these primitive organizations

216

she found ready assertion and advocacy of her newly won rights against man's reluctance or refusal to recognize such rights. When a peasant or a worker tried to use the old method of "teaching" his wife—when he tried to beat her—she protested vehemently saying: "These aren't tsarist times, you know! I'll go to the factory committee [or the village Soviet, or the Communist party cell] with a complaint against you!" In truth, the factory or house committee, the village Soviet, and the party cell did intervene, for it was definitely instructed to do so by Moscow.

The Kremlin's policy in this particular respect proved to be wise and far-sighted. The women of Russia entered the social life of the country as a genuinely creative element. They assumed an exceptional place in the industries, agriculture, cultural work, and even the armed forces.

The new generation also increasingly revealed its cultural hunger. Literature, painting, the theater, all arts as well as sciences, found their way to the masses—at first lowering their erstwhile high quality, losing their subtlety. But, as I have already remarked, in time the quantity did not detract from the quality either. My own glimpse of this was especially vivid in the field of the theater.

The Soviet government never forgot that, for the people, circuses are as important as bread. And though the rations of the period were unavoidably those of starvation, the theater was ample and inexpensive, open for everyone to share. The hungry actors of the time were ready to perform for a bag of flour or even a loaf of bread. House committees and labor unions distributed theater tickets free of charge.

At first, proletarians rather scorned the theater. They frankly said that they would prefer sugar or bread to these free tickets. On returning home from a show, they often laughed as they recalled what they had just seen—they laughed at it, they remembered the surface effects, they hardly understood the meaning of the play. But the influence of the stage grew and deepened by degrees. The Soviet cinema was in those years still embryonic, while foreign films were banned for fear of their counterrevolutionary and demoralizing effect. Thus the theater remained the only source of amusement. The people gradually became accustomed to the Russian theater; they came to accept their national art, and thus the stage proved to be a mighty weapon of culture. This, in turn, helped to improve the actors' status and material welfare. The stage folk organized themselves into special unions of their own, and this aided them in receiving the support, not of the government alone, but of workers' organizations as well.

Once the theater re-entered the life of Russia on this new and widened basis—once it became something of a necessity for the masses of the people and plays were performed not only in central theaters of cities but also in villages and in factory clubs—a bond with the finest traditions of the old stage art was re-established. In studios, both in the capitals and in the provinces, once again work was resumed under the guidance of experienced and outstanding authorities. Thus the theater of the Soviets was brought to great heights. The same phenomenon could also be observed in other fields of cultural life as well.

As illiteracy, by the party's decrees, was reduced throughout the land, the popular interest in literature made itself felt, resulting in the publication of both Soviet books and old Russian classics in editions of millions.

This cultural growth, accompanied as it was by an unprecedented thirst for knowledge and by a reawakening of national consciousness, culminated, in the years immediately preceding the invasion of Russia by the Nazis, a fusion of the old and the new. The younger generation finally felt itself not only the owner of the country but also the inheritor of the country's history and culture. The entire evolution of Moscow led to this new-old "national state." This state was unique; composed of so many nationalities and tribes, it emphasized their cultural autonomy. But all these divergent elements were molded together by the Soviet, "all-Union" patriotism. The new order instinctively sought its support in the very sources of old Russia. The history of the great French Revolution in a way repeated itself in the Soviet Union: the French Revolution, as a certain famous historian put it, tried hard to veer away from old France yet finished by returning to the sources of French history.

A foreigner who does not know Russia is puzzled by this new love of the Communist state for such old-time heroes as St. Alexander Nevsky, Prince Alexander Suvorov, and Count Michael Kutuzov and their remarkable feats of yore. But one who has followed closely the entire development and evolution of the U.S.S.R. is not really surprised. Patriotic tendencies in Soviet Russia were already clearly visible a number of years ago, when Alexis Tolstoy's *Peter the First* was published in Moscow as a novel and then both staged and screened. The tremendous success of this work was proof of the fact that the younger generation of Soviet Russia did indeed count itself as part and parcel of Russian history, of the Russian nationality, as a continuation of Russian national tradition.

Of course, all this was not wholly spontaneous. A deliberate campaign of propaganda emanating from the Kremlin did play its part. For years the leaders were drumming it in—that the nation was being constantly encircled and threatened, first by the world of capitalism, then by fascism. The masses had come to assume that it was imperative to defend themselves against that foreign foe. And what was there to defend? Not only the socioeconomic achievements of the revolution but, logically and naturally, also the land itself —the country, the nation—where these achievements had been won. Nationalism was a logical consequence. Thus Russia's history and national culture became as important as the new winnings of the revolution.

The well-known elasticity of the Bolsheviks, their ability to adapt themselves to the needs of the given moment, made it easy for these former "internationalists" to head the new nationalistic movement in Russia—to be the patriotic leaders of the fatherland in its life-and-death struggle against the invader.

Whoever continues, as I do, to believe in the basic principles of democratic socialism and humanism, will see in these facts a confirmation of his objective appraisal of the Russian revolution. And this appraisal is as follows: Despite the political dictatorship, despite the terror and the sufferings and all the excesses, a new democracy has been born in Russia. It is not a political democracy as that is understood, let us say, in the United States—"by the people, for the people, and of the people." In Russia this formula has never been applied in its entirety, for there the government ruled the people *for* the people but not *of* the people. Yet life marches on, and there are reasons to hope that the future may bring changes in this direction, too.

At this crucial moment of her gigantic struggle for survival, Soviet Russia is displaying both her tremendous physical might and her high moral qualities. The war, summoning such an unheard-of tidal wave of energy and sacrifice, showed—for all the world to see—the inexhaustible reserves of spirit, of bravery, possessed by this Soviet democracy. I have always been confident that at a critical time the "new" Russian nation would display its traditional collective genius, its giant strength. Not too long ago such a view was considered light-minded, to say the least, even by many of my friends. But it proved to be the only true view.

I was thus emboldened to hope that another prediction of mine will yet come true—a prediction based on everything I lived and suffered through in Russia, as well as on my many thoughts about that country since I left it—the prediction of Russia's democratization. The process of democratization had already begun but was interrupted by Hitler's invasion of Russia. It will be resumed now that Hitler is defeated. I do not know what forms the process will assume, or how rapid it will be. But I firmly hold that this process will be a reality, beginning with the integral application of the Constitution of 1936; and that it will lead my first fatherland—which is paying such a horrible price for this victory over fascism—to a morally, materially, and politically juster life for all and to a friendly alliance with all great democracies of the Old World and the New.

Whatever you see in the Soviet regime—whether socialism or state capitalism—you come to recognize that the U.S.S.R. is a singular phenomenon, peculiarly Russian. There is no doubt that the Soviet system is different from anything else to be found in non-Russian Europe or in America.

It was the Marxists of an "internationalist" way of thinking and acting who created this new Russia, yet it is a Russian state above all. The Bolsheviks strove to dig and widen a great chasm between the two Russias—the prerevolutionary one and the postrevolutionary one. They tried to break with the Russian past. But even before June, 1941, it had become quite clear to all that the profoundly national traits of Russian psychology and history—the people's habits and way of life—had survived.

Hardly anyone differentiates now between these two concepts, Soviet and

219

Russian. To take but one example, the Kremlin's foreign policy follows the paths first blazed by the tsars of Moscow and the emperors of St. Petersburg. In its domestic policy, too, certain forms of "service to the state" appear to be an echo of the Muscovite laws and customs of the seventeenth century. This seems rather paradoxical to some observers. Foreign experts see the Soviet Union as a complex, hard-to-understand Janus, one face that of its new Soviet system, the other that of the traditional national Russia. Indeed, how can one explain a country in which Lenin and Peter the Great are revered almost equally?

For the postwar world the most important questions involving the Red republic are three: (1) Will Russia and the rest of the world coexist and even collaborate after the war despite their different socioeconomic and political systems? (2) Will the Russian government plot revolutions outside its borders? (3) In what direction will this Soviet Russia seek an outlet for its great strength, particularly in Europe and Asia?

By insisting on "socialism in one country," Stalin and his men have, for some time, proclaimed that the Soviet Union can live on and develop regardless of whether or not other countries follow its example and try its experiment. But this principle of "socialism in one country" was practiced amid conditions of Russia's voluntary isolation from the rest of the world. And the outside world, by its hostile attitude, helped Russia to remain isolated. This hostile attitude was in part based on the conviction held abroad that the Soviet regime was a temporary one, that it would either degenerate or peter out, if, indeed, it was not demolished either by the Russians themselves or by some foreign foe. But none of these possibilities has come true. The fact remains: The Soviet system is not only very much in existence but has become greatly strengthened in the crucible of this war. The postwar world will have to face the Soviet republic as one of the most decisive factors of the shape of that world to come.

Nor should we forget that a total isolation was impossible for the Soviet Union even before 1941. No state lives in a vacuum. There was Soviet trade with the rest of the world; there was, after September, 1934, the Soviet membership in the League of Nations. Since June, 1941, the Soviet Union has been one of the United Nations, an ally of Great Britain and the United States. The appearance of the Red Army in Europe has brought Russia into the wide arena of history in the making—has broken the spell of Russia's deliberate isolationism of the 1920's and 1930's.

This is where the outside world asks the question: Can Russia and the rest of the world be good neighbors? I believe that the answer is "Yes." The history of the world is full of examples of the peaceful coexistence of widely divergent economic, social, political, and religious systems. In this particular problem of Russia and her system, so different from the way of life in many other great nations, several practical considerations indicate the possibility of collaboration.

On the one hand, Europe is already experiencing an evolution in the direction of planned economy, based on democratic principles and solidarity of nations. In a degree, this will take Europe closer to Russia. Such trends are plainly noticeable in England, France, and the countries of central Europe. On the other hand, as a result of this war, Russia may become more democratic —she may, while preserving her socioeconomic structure, get rid of some of the exaggerations and excesses which have repelled true democrats the world over. Thus we will have favorable conditions for a better understanding and harmonious co-operation between Russia and the other nations.

There will, of course, remain numerous differences between the two systems, politically as well as economically. But such differences will hardly cause sharp conflicts. The Soviet Union, exhausted by this terrible war, will want and sorely need peace and quiet for its own reconstruction. There is scant danger of the Kremlin's trying to communize Europe; the Soviets have emphasized again and again that they do not want to violate the domestic affairs of the countries liberated by the Red Army, provided these countries adopt truly popular democratic governments which can be expected to be friendly to Russia. Russia's main task is the safeguarding of her own security and the improvement of her own welfare. This will for a long time occupy all her attention and claim all her energy. The Kremlin will want to preserve good relations with the United States and Great Britain because it will need the good will of both these Western democracies to help preserve the postwar peace and to aid Russia's reconstruction. Trade between Russia and America, geographically the closest of neighbors, will probably reach unprecedented proportions after the war, and this economic collaboration will be the guaranty of a moderate course in Russia's foreign policy.

Do I hear arguments that there is dynamite in the very essence and existence of the Soviet system—of a state which has abolished private property? That this collectivized state is ever a tempting, magic attraction for, and influence upon, the working classes of the other nations? Well, let there be competition, so dear to the hearts of all true followers of the capitalistic principle. Let these two systems—the Soviet one and the one of private capitalism—compete with each other. Either a combination of the two will result (which I predict), or one or the other will sooner or later prove that it is really the better, that it can give the masses a better livelihood, a better set of conditions for a good life. A peaceful rivalry of ideas and systems cannot and should not be avoided.

The early Russian Communism was a direct product of a situation in which an infinitesimal minority on the top controlled all wealth, while the overwhelming majority of the people lived in abject poverty. It was not unnatural for the wave of hate caused by this condition to engulf and destroy the few privileged ones in order that the great mass of the people might gain a better life. This, however, could not happen in the Western democracies, where the wealth is more evenly distributed, on all kinds of levels, from the really poor to the very rich, without anything like the abrupt chasm that existed in Russia. The vast middle classes, reasonably content and capable of improvement,

221

which form the backbone of the West, had no counterpart in the tsarist domains; but they would be the first to oppose any spread of Communistic ideas in their own countries.

Many of the mental reservations or open antagonisms against the U.S.S.R. in other countries have no other origin but a basic misunderstanding of the difference between prerevolutionary Russia and present-day Western democracies. Some of the apparently more objective criticism of the Soviets is also based on a misunderstanding. People willing to admit that the Russian situation needed redress contend that the revolution caused more hardships and suffering than they had known before to the very people it wanted to save. Outwardly this seems true, but outwardly only. When a very few controlled all the wealth of a country of 180,000,000 souls, these few could squeeze enough wealth to satisfy their greed from the exploitation of the masses. When, however, these masses became their own masters and wanted to improve their condition, they had, first of all, to obtain the tools in order that in the future the needed wealth could be squeezed out of the country's natural riches rather than from its people's labor. Many honest observers were horrified when Russia in the twenties exported grains while the people almost starved. Yet it was this export that made it possible for the Soviets to acquire the technical means, the industrial and farm implements, with which to develop the country's resources, to increase its productivity, and, thereby, to raise the standard of living of the people. Had it not been for those lean years, Russia would not have been able to emerge victorious from the Nazi assault, and not only the Russian people but also their Western Allies would have been the sufferers.

There is yet another factor pointing toward a peaceful collaboration between Soviet Russia and the lands of capitalism in the postwar period. This is the existence of Asia, particularly eastern Asia, as elbow-room for the Soviet republic and as a fruitful meeting-point for Russia and the other great powers. The Five-Year Plans of the Soviet Union, all three of them, were distinguished by the same eastward urge which had marked Russian history throughout the previous four centuries. The central weight of the Russian economy has, for decades if not centuries, been shifting toward the Urals and farther east—to the Altai Mountains, the Yenisei River, and so on. Between the Volga in the west and the Yenisei in the east lies one of this planet's richest areas of raw materials. Farther east, between Lake Baikal and the Lena River, on the one side, and the Bering and the Okhotsk seas, on the other, stretches an almost equally promising region of raw materials, which so far has hardly been touched. There are other areas of raw materials in Asiatic Russia, too, where coal, steel, and oil are concentrated. The ravages of this war have not impaired these bases in the least. On the contrary, the war has caused a tremendous development of new industrial centers behind the Urals.

Near as it is to China, this region will prove the Soviet road to that great nation. Russia, after building a bridge of good fellowship and co-operation with her Western neighbors, will play an important role in the industrialization of China, which is sure to begin in the postwar period. This is not to say that Russia will assume a monopolistic position with regard to China's economic development but merely that she is bound to have an important advantage. In their age-old eastward push the Russians have revealed an amazing ability to assimilate or rule the people and tribes of eastern Russia. Free of racial prejudices, not keeping aloof from men of other color than their own, the Russians have won significant successes in Asia, both as colonizers and as merchants. This will make it easy for them to expand and improve their relations with China, Korea, Iran, Afghanistan, and India.

It is true that Russia will not be ready to export immense quantities of manufactured goods or machine equipment to China. She will need these herself in the years following this war—to reconstruct what has been destroyed during the hostilities and to raise the standard of living among her own people. And whatever Soviet Russia finds it possible to share with China and other Asiatic nations will be, in both quantity and quality, far below the goods and machinery offered to those markets by the highly developed industries of the United States. But a collaboration of American capital and Russian colonizing initiative and ability will be possible in Asia after the war—in co-operation with Britain, a nation vitally dependent on her foreign trade.

For the sake of future security, collaboration will also be the order in the Near East. The example of Iran shows that Russia's interests in the Near and Middle East cannot be ignored—that they can, and should be, recognized in an amicable manner. Again in the case of Iran, we see that Russia is insisting on her interests not because of her desire to bring in Communism but because she is taking up the old traditional thread of her economic relations in the East. Giant nation of land expanses that she is, Russia is striving toward sea outlets, whether in the east of Asia or the northwest or southeast of Europe. This is a natural, logical drive that can be peacefully satisfied within certain limits.

The future Soviet policy in eastern Europe is a legitimate object of speculation for the Western democracies, but it should cause no worry. Russia's neighbors have an economy which is primarily agrarian and, except in Poland, the land is pretty well distributed among small and medium-sized holdings. Communism and farm collectivization would not only have no appeal for those populations but may indeed arouse their antagonism. Thus, while it is as reasonable for Russia to demand friendly, popular governments on her borders as for the United States to want them in the Western Hemisphere, one may well expect the Kremlin to seek a solution along truly democratic lines, patterned after Czechoslovakia, with whom the U.S.S.R. never had any quarrel. The friction with Poland is, in spite of an ugly tradition, basically a squabble among cousins, and it is not unreasonable to suppose that a genuinely democratic Poland, once launched on the road of an overdue land reform and secure in her new borders, will form around Russia, with other Slavic nations, a friendly constellation with whom Rumania, in her own interest, will want to live in peace and harmony.

The knowledge and experience gained by Russia from the sufferings of this war and the newly acquired friendship of the industrialized Western World will also give the country a chance to put its own soil to better use. Thus the revolution, far from squeezing more out of its people, will squeeze more and more out of the national riches, providing an ever growing standard of living for its workers and peasants. Furthermore, a rising standard of living in Russia will shorten the distance and increase the understanding between the workers of Russia and those of the Western democracies, contributing to better harmony among men everywhere. *Will soon jump*

Once these basic trends of Russia's policy are taken into consideration, there is no need to fear any future conflicts between her and the other great powers. The United States especially can well understand Russia's position. In the century and a half of Russian-American relations there have never been any serious clashes. In the future, too, we can hope for and confidently expect a coinciding of the respective interests of Russia and America on the international stage. To strengthen the traditional friendship of the two great nations, meanwhile, we must do our best to dispel the poisonous atmosphere of mutual suspicion and distrust that still obstructs the possibility of peaceful, calm collaboration in the years to come. Suspicions and distrust vanish if nations can mutually understand and correctly appraise each other's historic problems.

March 14, 1945

INDEX

225

New Economic Policy, 69, 94-95; old problems like labor and capital, workers wage rate, revived, 103; its effect on diplomatic relations with Russia's neighbors, 123-26; government drifts away from it after Lenin's death, 183; gave opportunity to private initiative, 208

Nobility, political power lost with nationalization of land, 199

Noghin, Victor, member of delegation to England, 112

Non-Communist officials in Soviet regime, 27, 60; regarded with distrust, 183-84; see also Specialists

North Timber Trust; see Soviet North Timber Trust

O.G.P.U.: questions Liberman about his activities in London, 142; persecutes Liberman, 155; see also Cheka

Oldenburg, Prince, 53

Opposition to trade with France: by conservatives, 130; overcome by various influences, 130

Peace treaty between Latvia and Russia, 123-24; includes concession of large tracts of woodland, 123-24

Peasants: preferable to soldiers for forest work, 75; after delivery of produce as tax, free to dispose of remaining property, 94; danger of being won over by Anarchists, 204

People's Commissariat of Government Control, 39

Perm, plan to move government to, 36

Peters, Jacob, 38

Piatakov, George, 73

Pine cones (fuel), 29, 31

Polish-Russian negotiations leading to Treaty of Riga (1921), 124

Politbureau, influence of subordinate organs on, 192

Political education, 200

Provincial factories under local authority, 91

Public opinion, lack of, 192

Purges, 205

Rakovsky, Christian, appointed Soviet representative in London, 168

Rapallo, Treaty of, 207

Rasputin, Gregory, assassination of, 54

Ravikovich, proposes pine cones as fuel, 29-30

Rebellion of 1905, 52

Red Army, 69, 73, 75, 92

Reikunov, vice-chairman of Central Timber Committee, 35

Revolution of March, 1917, 56

Revolutionary dictatorship, 192

Russia; see Soviet Russia

Russian-American relations, 224

Russo-Polish war, 120-21

Ryckov, Alexis: Liberman's chief in Supreme Council of Economy, 8; objects to making Stalin member of Timber Committee, 12; demands Larin's resignation, 22; approached by Liberman concerning German infiltration in Russian industry, 25; antagonism against Dzerzhinsky, 29; Liberman's impossible situation revealed to him, 39; characteristics and personality, official activities, 64-70

Sawmill machinery: bought in Stockholm, 114; model sawmill being built with latest equipment, 114-15

Secret police; see Cheka; O.G.P.U.

Shchasny, Admiral, arrested and executed by Trotsky's orders, 16

Smuggling, 63

Social revolution of Marx abandoned by Lenin, 208

"Socialism in one country": to replace slogan of world revolution, 208; insisted on by Stalin, 220

Socialist party of France, 134

Soviet government: prepares to evacuate Moscow during civil war, 36-37; domestic policy of, 207

Soviet North Timber Trust, 127; auxiliary companies, 141; buys mines in Spitzbergen belonging to Anglo-Norwegian company, 156

Soviet Russia: economic collapse in 1918, 14; provisional government of 1917, 4; administrative councils, 13; policy in Poland, 120-21; political and economic status, 183; regarded as a democracy, 201; Soviet government one of peasants, 202

Soviet system, 210-11, 219-20

Soviet workers in employ of foreigners, 154

Specialists: regarded with distrust, 183-84; just tolerated, 213; see also non-Communist officials

Spitzbergen mines, bought by Soviet North Timber Trust, 156

Stalin, Josef: first encounter with Liberman, 12; to play decisive role in history of Russian revolution, 80; biographical outline, 80-87; characteristics and personality, 82-87; nationalities question his earliest interest, 82-84; appointed secretary-general of Communist party, 85; in contrast to Lenin, 205; sets hopes on Russian youth, 208

Stinnes, Hugo: discussions with Liberman about government systems of Russia and Germany, 127-29; handled reparation deliveries in kind for Germany, 131

Supreme Council of Economy, 68; all committees brought together in it, 90; puzzled about Meshchersky and his plans, 176; divided into